Cultural Production in and Beyond the Recording Studio

Recording studios are the most insulated, intimate and privileged sites of music production and creativity. Yet in a world of intensified globalisation, they are also sites which are highly connected into wider networks of music production that are increasingly spanning the globe. This book is the first comprehensive account of the new spatialities of cultural production in the recording studio sector of the musical economy, spatialities that illuminate the complexities of global cultural production.

This unique text adopts a social-geographical perspective to capture the multiple spatial scales of music production: from opening the "black-box" of the insulated space of the recording studio; through the wider contexts in which music production is situated; to the far-flung global production networks of which recording studios are part. Drawing on original research, recent writing on cultural production across a variety of academic disciplines, secondary sources such as popular music biographies, and including a wide range of case studies, this lively and accessible text covers a range of issues including the role of technology in musical creativity; creative collaboration and emotional labour; networking and reputation; and contemporary economic challenges to studios.

As a contribution to contemporary debates on creativity, cultural production and creative labour, *Cultural Production in and Beyond the Recording Studio* will appeal to academic students and researchers working across the social sciences, including human geography, cultural studies, media and communication studies, sociology, as well as those studying music production courses.

Allan Watson is a Senior Lecturer in Human Geography at Staffordshire University, U.K. An economic geographer with research interests in the creative industries, Allan has been researching the music industry for 15 years. He has published articles in leading journals including *Environment and Planning A, Area,* and *Global Networks.*

Routledge Studies in Human Geography

For a full list of titles in this series, please visit www.routledge.com

This series provides a forum for innovative, vibrant and critical debate within Human Geography. Titles will reflect the wealth of research which is taking place in this diverse and ever-expanding field. Contributions will be drawn from the main sub-disciplines and from innovative areas of work which have no particular sub-disciplinary allegiances.

Published

25 International Migration and Knowledge
Allan Williams and Vladimir Baláž

26 The Spatial Turn
Interdisciplinary perspectives
Edited by Barney Warf and Santa Arias

27 Whose Urban Renaissance?
An international comparison of urban regeneration policies
Edited by Libby Porter and Katie Shaw

28 Rethinking Maps
Edited by Martin Dodge, Rob Kitchin and Chris Perkins

29 Rural–Urban Dynamics
Livelihoods, mobility and markets in African and Asian frontiers
Edited by Jytte Agergaard, Niels Fold and Katherine V. Gough

30 Spaces of Vernacular Creativity
Rethinking the cultural economy
Edited by Tim Edensor, Deborah Leslie, Steve Millington and Norma Rantisi

31 Critical Reflections on Regional Competitiveness
Gillian Bristow

32 Governance and Planning of Mega-City Regions
An international comparative perspective
Edited by Jiang Xu and Anthony G.O. Yeh

33 Design Economies and the Changing World Economy
Innovation, production and competitiveness
John Bryson and Grete Rustin

34 Globalization of Advertising
Agencies, cities and spaces of creativity
James R. Faulconbridge, Peter J. Taylor, Jonathan V. Beaverstock and Corinne Nativel

35 Cities and Low Carbon Transitions
Edited by Harriet Bulkeley, Vanesa Castán Broto, Mike Hodson and Simon Marvin

36 **Globalization, Modernity and the City**
John Rennie Short

37 **Climate Change and the Crisis of Capitalism**
A chance to reclaim self, society and nature
Edited by Mark Pelling, David Manual Navarette and Michael Redclift

38 **New Economic Spaces in Asian Cities**
From industrial restructuring to the cultural turn
Edited by Peter W. Daniels, Kong Chong Ho and Thomas A. Hutton

39 **Landscape and the Ideology of Nature in Exurbia**
Green sprawl
Edited by Kirsten Valentine Cadieux and Laura Taylor

40 **Cities, Regions and Flows**
Edited by Peter V. Hall and Markus Hesse

41 **The Politics of Urban Cultural Policy**
Global perspectives
Edited by Carl Grodach and Daniel Silver

42 **Ecologies and Politics of Health**
Edited by Brian King and Kelley Crews

43 **Producer Services in China**
Economic and urban development
Edited by Anthony G.O. Yeh and Fiona F. Yang

44 **Locating Right to the City in the Global South**
Tony Roshan Samara, Shenjing Ile and Guo Chen

45 **Spatial-Economic Metamorphosis of a Nebula City**
Schiphol and the Schiphol region during the 20th century
Abderrahman El Makhloufi

46 **Learning Transnational Learning**
Edited by Åge Mariussen and Seija Virkkala

47 **Cultural Production in and Beyond the Recording Studio**
Allan Watson

48 **Gender, Development and Transnational Feminism**
Edited by Ann M. Oberhauser and Ibipo Johnston-Anumonwo

49 **Fieldwork in the Global South**
Ethical challenges and dilemmas
Edited by Jenny Lunn

50 **Intergenerational Space**
Edited by Robert Vanderbeck and Nancy Worth

51 **Performativity, Politics, and the Production of Social Space**
Edited by Michael R. Glass and Reuben Rose-Redwood

Forthcoming

52 **Knowledge and the City**
Concepts, applications and trends of knowledge-based urban development
Francisco Javier Carrillo, Tan Yigitcanlar, Blanca Garcia and Antti Lönnqvist

53 **Migration, Risk and Uncertainty**
Allan M. Williams and Vladimír Baláž

Cultural Production in and Beyond the Recording Studio

Allan Watson

NEW YORK AND LONDON

First published 2015
by Routledge
711 Third Avenue, New York, NY 10017

and by Routledge
2 Park Square, Milton Park, Abingdon, Oxon OX14 4RN

*Routledge is an imprint of the Taylor & Francis Group,
an informa business*

© 2015 Taylor & Francis

The right of Allan Watson to be identified as author of this work has been asserted in accordance with sections 77 and 78 of the Copyright, Designs and Patents Act 1988.

All rights reserved. No part of this book may be reprinted or reproduced or utilized in any form or by any electronic, mechanical, or other means, now known or hereafter invented, including photocopying and recording, or in any information storage or retrieval system, without permission in writing from the publishers.

Trademark Notice: Product or corporate names may be trademarks or registered trademarks, and are used only for identification and explanation without intent to infringe.

Library of Congress Cataloging-in-Publication Data

Watson, Allan, 1978–
    Cultural production in and beyond the recording studio / by Allan Watson.
        pages cm. — (Routledge studies in human geography ; 47)
    Includes bibliographical references and index.
    1. Popular music—Production and direction.   2. Music and globalization.   3. Music—Social aspects.   4. Technology—Social aspects.   5. Sound studios.   I. Title.
    ML3470.W387 2014
    306.4'842—dc23
    2014019260

ISBN: 978-0-415-85606-5 (hbk)
ISBN: 978-0-203-72826-0 (ebk)

Typeset in Sabon
by Apex CoVantage, LLC

Printed and bound in the United States of America by Publishers Graphics, LLC on sustainably sourced paper.

Contents

Figures	ix
Tables	xi
Preface	xiii
Acknowledgments	xvii
Introduction	1

PART I
Inside the Studio

1	Studio Technologies: Changing Concepts and Practices	13
2	Technology, Collaboration and Creativity	32
3	Emotional Labour and Musical Performance	47
4	The Studio Sound-Space	62

PART II
Beyond the Studio

5	Recording Studios in Urban Music Scenes	85
6	Recording Studios in Project Networks (1): The Networked Studio	104
7	Recording Studios in Project Networks (2): A Global Urban Geography of Music Production	119
8	MP3s and Home Recording: The Problems of Software	135

viii *Contents*

PART III
Working and Networking in the Recording Studio Sector

9   Changing Employment Relations and Experiences of Work   157

10   Networking, Reputation Building and Getting Work   171

Conclusion   184

Glossary   193
References   197
Index   211

Figures

1.1	Close-up of Neve VR60 Legend 60-channel recording console with labeling showing separate tracks of audio	15
1.2	24-track 2-inch tape machine	15
1.3	Recording to multiple channels of audio on a Neve VR60 Legend 60-channel console	16
1.4	Close-up of Neve VR60 Legend console showing moving fader automation system	17
1.5	Multi-track recording through a console integrated to a DAW	23
2.1	Modes of collaboration in pop music production	33
4.1	Recording drums with ambience, Parr Street Studios, Liverpool	64
4.2	Lyndhurst Hall, AIR Recording Studios, London	66
4.3	Baffles around a bass guitar amplifier to prevent sound leakage	68
4.4	Recording "live," Ocean Sound Recordings, Norway	71
4.5	A studio engineer adjusting the input level on a microphone preamplifier during a recording session	74
4.6	Rack of outboard equipment including preamplifiers and effects units	75
4.7	Microphoning for recording of a solo performance— guitar and vocals	77
4.8	Setting up microphones to record drums	78
4.9	Mastering room, Master+ mastering studio, Rennes, France	81
6.1	Example album project network: Franz Ferdinand *Tonight*	107
6.2	Geographic mobility of a sample of London-based recording engineers	117

x *Figures*

7.1 Global urban networks of recording, U.K. digital
music market   128
7.2 Global urban networks of recording, U.S. digital
music market   129
7.3 Global urban networks of recording, Australian digital
music market   130
8.1 The issue of recording for the MP3 music format   142
8.2 A range of high-quality headphones on display
in a supermarket   144

Tables

5.1	Urban recording studios and "sounds" of the city	96
7.1	Top five cities ranked by output of albums; U.K. digital music market	123
7.2	Top five cities ranked by output of albums; U.S. digital music market	124
7.3	Top five cities ranked by output of albums; Australian digital music market	125
7.4	Top five mastering studios in networks of musical production, U.K. digital music market	125
7.5	Top five mastering studios in networks of musical production, U.S. digital music market	126
7.6	Top five mastering studios in networks of musical production, Australian digital music market	126
7.7	Top cities ranked by total number of connections, U.K. digital music market	127
7.8	Top cities ranked by total number of connections; U.S. digital music market	129
7.9	Top cities ranked by total number of connections; Australian digital music market	130
7.10	Centrality measure rankings for London, New York and Los Angeles	131

Preface

> In the popular imagination the recording studio is, somewhat unfortunately, regarded as a mysterious place—a fiercely guarded environment full of expensive, complex technology, arcane processes and riddled with jargon.
>
> (Warner 2003, 35)

> Even now, after a century of sound recording, the process of making records remains at least a partial mystery to the majority of those who listen to them.
>
> (Zak 2001, 26)

Recording studios are spaces that run deep in the popular musical imagination. Particular recording studios have become "iconic" through their link with particular music scenes and particular recording artists, even to the extent they have become a site of pilgrimage; one only has to think of the connection between the Beatles and Abbey Road, or between Sun Studios and Elvis Presley, for example. Yet, despite their central place in the development of rock 'n' roll folklore, there is very little understanding of what actually takes place in these spaces as music is created and recorded, outside of those involved in the production of music. Partly, this is due to the fact that recording studios are associated with complex technologies, although as home recording is becoming increasingly common, many of these technologies are becoming much more widely understood and used. But it is also in large part due to the fact that very few people have ever seen the inside of a recording studio, let alone witnessed a recording in progress. It is, as a space, figuratively (and sometimes literally) a "black box." Yet, there is an interest and intrigue about the way in which music is recorded. Why? Well, amongst other reasons, the music that comes from within these studios excites, moves and touches people. Our connection with music is both personal and intimate. Often, music is recorded in such a way as to allow fans to feel a direct connection to an artist through an intimate moment of musical performance, as if they were *in* the space with the artist. In this

xiv *Preface*

way, the way music is produced directly relates to notions of originality, authenticity and genre.

The aim of this text is to open up the "black box" and to reveal and examine the technological and creative processes that take place when music is created and recorded. It is certainly not the first academic text that attempts to do this; there are a number of comprehensive accounts of recording studio technologies and their relation to changing concepts and practices of recording. Here I point readers to Virgil Moorefield's *The Producer as Composer* (2010); Albin Zak's *The Poetics of Rock* (2001); and Paul Théberge's *Any Sound You Can Imagine* (1997) in particular. This book draws significantly on these and other texts. But it also looks to go beyond them, by employing a *geographical* and *relational* framework for analysing music production. Key to such an approach is considering the many and various relations involved in the production of music, and the various spatial scales at which they occur. The book is concerned with the various interrelationships that occur between people, technology and space, not only within the insulated space of the studio, but also beyond the walls of the studio, from the urban centres in which recording studios are (typically) located, to the global urban and digital networks of music production. The idea of viewing studios as *relational spaces of creativity* in this way is one that was inspired by Chris Gibson's (2005) paper on that very theme, and is therefore one for which I cannot take credit. However, the size of this volume provides an opportunity to fully extend this line of thinking and, I hope, to provide a discussion which goes some way to doing justice to the technological, emotional and spatial complexity of music production in the digital age.

The process of research that has informed this book was both long and challenging, and hugely rewarding. It would not have been possible without the love and support of my wife, Kate, and my three boys, Harry, Jack and Charlie. I thank them all for their patience and support through the great many hours of writing. There are many others who I must also thank for playing their own valuable parts in the production of this book. First and foremost, my thanks go to Steve Williams, who was involved from the very conception of this text, helping me to form the proposal and subsequently commenting on the chapters as they took shape. The book is both stronger and more coherent for his input. I also want to thank Phil Hubbard and Michael Hoyler, who have supported this research from its origins in a PhD scholarship in the Department of Geography at Loughborough University. My thanks also go to Fiona Tweed for her support. I owe much to Jenna Ward, whose valuable help in shaping ideas around emotional labour in a recording studio setting has much improved this work; and to Christoph Mager for his involvement in shaping ideas around networks of musical production in the city. Some aspects of this work have been published in journals and have benefited greatly from insightful comments from reviewers. At Routledge,

Preface xv

Max Novick and Jennifer Morrow have carefully and patiently guided me through the production of this text, making it as painless as possible. I must also give my thanks to the three reviewers of the original proposal for this text, whose comments helped broaden the book's scope. Finally, I must thank all of the record producers and studio engineers who gave up their time to be part of this research, and whose involvement was central to the research which this book reports.

Acknowledgments

The author and publisher would like to thank the following:

Tony Draper for permission to reproduce the photographs in Figures 1.3, Figure 4.1 and Figure 4.4.

Katie Tavini for permission to reproduce the photographs in Figures 1.5, Figure 4.7 and Figure 4.8.

Jamie Tate for permission to reproduce the drawing used in Figure 8.1.

Sound on Sound magazine for permission to use an extract from an article by Hugh Robjohns published in April 1999, in Box 8.2.

Jan Schubert and Pion Ltd. for permission to reproduce material from the article "Creating the Right 'Vibe': Emotional Labour and Musical Performance in the Recording Studio" by Allan Watson and Jenna Ward, published in *Environment and Planning A* 45(12): 2904 – 2918, in Chapter 3.

Figure 6.1, Figures 7.1 to 7.3, and Tables 7.1 to 7.10 are reproduced from the article Watson, A. 2012. "The World According to iTunes: Mapping Urban Networks of Music Production." *Global Networks* 12 (4): 446–466. © 2012 The Author(s) Journal compilation © 2012 Blackwell Publishing Ltd. & Global Networks Partnership, under licence from John Wiley & Sons.

Chapter 5 of this book reproduces and re-works some text adapted from: Watson, A., M. Hoyler, and C. Mager. 2009. "Spaces and Networks of Musical Creativity in the City." *Geography Compass* 3 (2): 856–878. © 2009 The Authors. Journal Compilation © 2009 Blackwell Publishing Ltd., under licence from John Wiley & Sons.

Chapter 9 of this book reproduces and re-works some text adapted from: Watson, A. 2013. "Running a Studio's a Silly Business: Work and Employment in the Contemporary Recording Studio Sector." *Area* 45 (3): 330–336. © 2013 The Author. Area © 2013 Royal Geographical Society (with the Institute of British Geographers), under licence from John Wiley & Sons.

Introduction

Largely acting as an independent service within the contemporary recorded music industry, recording studios form the direct link between the record companies and artists and the creation of a final recorded musical product. As such, they form a key component in the networks of creativity and reproduction (see Leyshon 2001) of what is now a highly globalised music industry, and an economically important one. In 2012, global recorded music sales totaled US$16.5 billion (http://www.ifpi.org/facts-and-stats.php; accessed 21/02/14). Whilst only estimates exist for the economic value of the recording studio sector, it is the case that, compared to record companies and publishing companies, the value and level of profitability of the recording studio sector in itself is relatively low (Leyshon 2009). However, the sector does act as a "crucial part of the overall value chain of the musical economy, producing commodities upon which large parts of the industry depend" (ibid. 2009, 1315). However, it is not the case that the importance of recording studios lies only in the production of music as an *economic* commodity. Recording studios also play a central role in the creating the "sound" of particular music scenes, and act as a focal point for networks of musicians and musical creativity. As such, recording studios and the skilled engineers and producers who work within them have played a central role in shaping the production of music as both an economic and *cultural* commodity, and as such, in shaping both local cultural production and global popular culture.

Despite the evident importance of recording studios to musical production, there is relatively little academic literature focusing on recording studios and the recording studio sector more widely. This is particularly the case in geography, with just two notable exceptions: Andrew Leyshon's (2009) work on the decline of the recording studio sector, and the work of Chris Gibson (2005) on recording studios as relational spaces of creativity. Outside geography, a limited body of work on recording studios has emerged from the fields of musicology, sociology, cultural studies and science studies. One might pick out in particular the work of Paul Théberge (1989, 1997, 2004, 2012); Antoine Hennion (1989); Susan Schmidt Horning (2004, 2012); Albin Zak (2001); Virgil Moorefield (2010); and

2 *Introduction*

Timothy Warner (2003). The relative dearth in literature is perhaps due in part to a view that recording studios lie on the "periphery" of the recorded music industry (see Théberge 2004) when compared to record companies, on which the majority of the academic literature on the music industry has focused.

This book aims to take a significant step toward filling this gap in the geographical literature, by placing recording studios at the centre of an analysis of the spatialities of cultural production. More specifically, the text employs a geographical and relational framework for analysing music production. Key to such an approach is considering the many and various *relations* involved in the production of music, and the various spatial scales at which these relations are manifest. The book is concerned with the various inter-relationships that occur between people, technology and space, not only within the insulated space of the studio, but also beyond the walls of the studio, from the urban centres in which recording studios are (typically) located, to the global urban and digital networks of music production. In short, it aims to undertake a comprehensive exploration of the technological, emotional and spatial complexity of music production in the digital age. In doing so, the text covers a range of themes that have relevance to academic work on cultural production and the creative economy more widely. Four themes are particularly prominent in this respect. First, the impacts of technology upon cultural production and consumption, including debates around creativity and the democratisation of production and consumption. Second, the increasingly networked and globalised nature of cultural production. Third, issues around employment and precarity, and related to this, experiences of work, of obtaining work and social networking practices. Finally, issues around emotion, collaboration, performance and authenticity.

THE RECORDING STUDIO SECTOR: A VERY BRIEF HISTORY

Paralleling the wider global music industry, the recent history of the recording studio sector is also one defined by technological change. In the 1940s and 1950s, most recording studios were extremely modest facilities with very basic recording equipment. In America, many recording studios were little more than converted radiator shops (for example Sun Studio in Memphis) or fruit and vegetable refrigerators (for example J&M Studio in New Orleans). Throughout the 1950s and 1960s, however, recording would become increasingly professionalised, and a smaller number of large professional studios would come to dominate commercial recording. While many were run by major record companies, such as EMI Studios in London (better known as Abbey Road) and Capitol Studios in Hollywood, California, there were also many large independent recording facilities, such as AIR

Studios in London and A&R Studios in New York. Large financial investment in such studios, fuelled by booming sales of recorded music and large recording budgets, resulted in highly acoustically engineered spaces containing advanced digital recording consoles with multiple channels for recording, operated by highly skilled sound engineers. Certain cities would become key centres for recording as their musical economies developed "institutional thickness," (Leyshon 2009) especially London, New York and Los Angeles. In 1960s New York, for example, there were at least 16 major studios clustered together in a small area between Fifth Avenue and Broadway in Manhattan (see Simons 2004).

As Leyshon (2009) describes, these large studios, with large acoustic spaces for orchestral recording, sit at the top of a hierarchy of studios, below which are a set of smaller studios that cater to the recording of rock and pop music, and then a long tail of budget recording studios. The dominance of the large studios has, however, been open to constant challenge, in particular due to developments in recording technologies. The increasing availability and affordability of recording technologies through the 1980s and 1990s would, for example, allow entrepreneurial producers to open their own "project" studios; while more recently developments in recording software have allowed for the production of music in home studios. Perhaps even more significant was the development of the MP3 software format and associated file-sharing technologies through the 1990s and 2000s which facilitated the illegal distribution of digital music, resulting in a crisis of funding in the music economy. This crisis resulted in severe economic pressures for studios, and especially for the larger recording studios that have traditionally relied on recording projects commissioned and funded by record companies. The result has been a spate of high-profile studio closures, for example the closure of Olympic Studios in London in February 2009, and depletion in the institutional thickness of key recording centres (Leyshon 2009). Between 2000 and 2003, for example, the musical economy of the San Francisco Bay area was impacted heavily by a wave of studio closures (Johnson 2006). Studio closures would also be in part about the high value of property in the key recording centres, and many recording studios have been sold for redevelopment. In New York, for example, Pythian Temple on 70th Street and Columbia's 30th Street Studio would become apartment buildings, while Mediasound Studio on 57th Street and Webster Hall on 11th Street would become nightclubs (Simons 2004).

For those studios that do survive into the 2010s, they do so in a recording industry that has substantially changed, financially and technologically. Due to the development of technologies for home recording, for example, the recording studio sector is now one in which the threat of closure for many large studios goes hand-in-hand with increased opportunities for individual producers to run their own smaller project studios. Théberge (2012), for example, reports data from the U.S. census that shows an increase both in

4 *Introduction*

the number of commercial studios and people involved in sound recording between 1997 and 2002. Yet such data hides the changing nature of the studios themselves.

Yet another example of the way technological developments are impacting upon the sector, most recording studios now incorporate technologies that allow for their networking with other studios in geographically distant locations, giving rise to the concept of the "networked studio" (Théberge 2004). Such technologies link studios in complex ways to other studios in geographically distant locations, and enable musical recording projects to be coordinated on a global scale. In 1995 for the first time a single was recorded and mixed simultaneously between two geographically distant recording studios. Japanese guitarist Hotei, playing in Singapore's Form Studios, was linked to Jesus Jones at Real World studios near Bath, U.K., a distance of over 7,000 miles and covering two different time zones, via Solid State Logic's WorldNet system (Cunningham 1998).

RECORDING STUDIOS AS RELATIONAL SITES OF CULTURAL PRODUCTION

Recording studios are sites that are privileged to the most intimate moments of musical creativity and emotive performance; insulated spaces that give musicians the required conditions in which to experiment and create music. These creative moments are produced not by the musician alone, but through relations between musicians, producers, engineers and recording technologies. Small's (1998) account of "musicking" is helpful here, in which he argues that there is no such thing as music, but rather practices of musicking. Central to the concept of musicking is understanding music as practice and performance—a "doing" of music. As Wood et al. assert, "Music making is a material practice: it is embodied and technologised; it is staged; it takes place" (2007, 869). Furthermore, for Small, the act of musicking establishes in the place where it is happening a set of relationships between the people who are taking part in the performance. Musical performance is therefore understood as "an encounter between human beings that place through the medium of sounds organised in specific ways" (1998, 10). Therefore, while musicians are recognised as the creators of music, some commentators have termed studio producers and engineers as "cultural intermediaries" (see, for example, Hennion 1989) or as "gatekeepers" (Pinch and Bijsterveld 2004). These skilled studio workers mediate music through various stages of production and usage of technologies (Negus 1999), and the ability of musicians to make music in the studio is dependent upon them (Pinch and Bijsterveld 2004; Shuker 1994). Thus, for Gibson (2005), recording studios can be considered as *relational spaces of creativity*, that is to say that they constitute sites of relational creative practice:

Introduction 5

What we hear when we listen to recorded music is not just a product of musician's creativity, but an emotive performance produced in particular spaces and through affective relations between musicians, producers, engineers and technologies.

(Gibson 2005, 192)

Relational creative practice is not however contained to the space of the studio alone; as Rogers argues, "even when creative practices are situated, they operate through networks and flows that link locations together" (2011, 663). Recording studios are at once insulated spaces of creativity, isolated from the city outside, and spaces that influence, and that are, influenced by, the wider urban contexts in which the studios operate and the urban music scenes in which they are situated. Furthermore, the tools and techniques that continue to be developed for networking studios in geographically distant locations, in complex ways (see Théberge 2004), that allow the coordination of recording projects on a global scale. Thus, studios might be considered as relational spaces of creativity that operate across a *multitude of spatial scales*.

CULTURAL PRODUCTION IN AND BEYOND THE RECORDING STUDIO: A RELATIONAL PERSPECTIVE

In undertaking a study of recording studios as relational sites of production, this book takes as its conceptual starting point the "relational turn" that has occurred within geography. This turn has seen relational approaches becoming ever more influential, not only in terms of what geographers study, but also how they study it (Storper 1997; Boggs and Rantisi 2003; Murdoch 2006; cf. Bathelt 2006; Bathelt and Glückler 2011). Such a turn has been particularly evident within economic geography (see Sunley 2008), but also more widely across its sub-disciplines, and has in part been brought about through the engagement of economic geographers with literature from economic sociology. Particularly influential have been Granovetter's (1985) work on embeddedness (see Grabher 2006) and Coleman's (1988) work on social capital. Within this "turn," three inter-related shifts can be identified, as follows.

Agents and Their Inter-Relations

First, and perhaps most significantly, there has been an ontological and methodological shift (Boggs and Rantisi 2003) from the macro-level of firms and economic structures to the micro-level of *agents* and their inter-relations. As such, there has been a broad shift in emphasis from structure to agency. In economic geography, the firm has generally been considered to be the elementary unit of collective commercial agency, largely unproblematised as

6 Introduction

unitary and coherent actors (Yeung 2003; Maskell 2001; Taylor and Asheim 2001). However, more recently the relational turn has seen the centrality and reification of the firm being challenged. Grabher (2002a), for example, has argued that the integrity of the firm as a basic analytical unit is being undercut by organisational practices that are built around projects involving a multiplicity of organisational and personal networks (such as those occurring in the music industry). This results in a pressing need for new relational conceptions of economic activity that are centred on the individual agency of workers.

Furthermore, there has been an increased recognition of the importance of non-human intermediaries. Here the relational turn in geography has gained further impetus from the influence of Actor Network Theory and its emphasis on the construction of diverse, heterogeneous networks involving both human and non-human actants (Sunley 2008). Non-human actors, such as technological artefacts, are not considered as simply resources or passive actors, but rather can "intervene actively to push action in unexpected directions" (Callon and Law 1997, 178). Unintended impacts can occur when non-human actors are used and employed by different actors in different ways and in different contexts (Dicken et al. 2001). Thus, within heterogeneous networks, it is argued that "non-humans play a critical role in embodying and shaping action" (Law 1994, 383).

In this regard, rather than the focus of this text being on the economics and economic geography of the recording sector *per se* (which has previously been outlined by Leyshon 2009), its focus is on the work of record producers and recording engineers as the key social and economic actors in the recording studio sector, along with recording technologies as key non-human actors. These are the actors involved in the "daily practices of work" (Ettlinger 2003) in the sector. The relational perspective developed in this text is in particular concerned with the embodied *agency* of studios workers. In order to examine this agency, the text undertakes a micro-scale study of music production, concerned with the technological, social, emotional and economic relations involved in the production of music.

Part One of the book is entitled "Inside the Studio" and is concerned with these relations as they occur within the space of the recording studio as music is being made. Chapter 1 begins by providing an introduction to the recording technologies commonly found in modern recording studios, as well as those technologies which are increasingly found in home studios, before describing how developments in these technologies have gone hand in hand with changing concepts and practices in recording. This provides important context for the discussion presented in Chapter 2, which considers the role of technology in the collaboration and creativity occurring between artists, record producers and/or recording engineers. Chapter 3 considers the relationships between people in the recording studio, and in particular the role of the emotional labour performed by producers and engineers in developing trust with clients and fostering an environment conducive to musical creativity and performance. Chapter 4 is concerned with the physical space of the studio, and the relations between this physical space, technology and people. It considers how the studio is used an "instrument" that shapes the sound of the music produced, and the creation of "live" music soundscapes through creative interaction within the space of the studio.

Relations Across Spatial Scales

Second, and related to the above, within economic geography there is now a broad concern with how the social network relations of economic agents at different *spatial scales* shape the geographies of economic performance. This challenges models of scales based on top-down vertical imaginaries, and instead emphasises an ontology composed of more complex, emergent spatial relations. Marston et al. (2005), for example, argue for the discarding of vertical ontologies and, in their place, propose a "flat ontology" that requires "sustained attention to the intimate and divergent relations between bodies, objects, orders and spaces" (2005, 424). They contend that these relations occur within "social sites" (for example, a recording studio), with each site an emergent property of its interacting human and non-human inhabitants, and "materially emergent within its unfolding event relations" with other sites (Marston et al. 2005, 426).

Leitner and Miller (2007) argue however that a flat ontology does not account for power hierarchies and the production of inequalities. Whilst also recognising that spaces exist in nested relationships to other spaces, they argue that these relationships create differential opportunities and constraints for practices of individual and collective agents. Actants, they suggest, are not only implicated in spatialities, they are also enabled and constrained by them. Thus, while in the relational turn there has been a broad shift from structure to agency, structure still matters, albeit it is viewed as the outcome of multiple actions and actants.

As Dicken et al. (2001) assert networks are neither purely organisational forms nor structures; rather they are "relational processes . . . realised empirically within distinct time- and space-specific contexts" (Dicken et al. 2001, 91). Thus, a relational perspective on economic geography explicitly draws attention to the importance of economic actors and how, when and where they act and interact in space (see also Bathelt and Glückler 2003). Viewing networks as relational processes also requires us to recognise that while networks are manifested at a multiplicity of geographical scales, they do not consist of unbounded flows and connections; rather they are at the same time embedded within particular territories (for more on the debate regarding relationality and territoriality, see Amin 2002, 2007; Jones 2009). Dicken et al. (2001) argue therefore that an understanding of the global economy must incorporate multiple scales of economic (along with political, cultural and social) relations, and that too often a particular (for example local) or bifurcated (for example global-local) geographical scale is used

8 Introduction

in ways that "obscure the subtle variations within, and interconnections between, different scales" (2001, 90). In network formation and networking processes, there is a complex intermingling of geographical scales. A relational view of social actors and their networks, they therefore argue, must always be sensitive to the geographical scales at which they operate. As Jessop et al. (2008) argue territories, places, scales and networks must be viewed as mutually constitutive and relationally intertwined dimensions of socio-spatial relations.

In the case of music production, key to a relational perspective then is the examination of relations of production across multiple spatial scales; from those occurring within the insulated space of the recording studio as examined in Part One of this text, through the urban centres in which recording studios are (typically) located, to the global urban networks of production in which recording studios are embedded; and more recently, across digital networks of music production. Often subtle variations in technical practices of recording and social and emotional practices exist within, and between, these different scales; as Yeung argues, if relationality is constituted through interactions and tensions, then there is "clearly a great deal of *heterogeneity* and *unevenness* in these relational processes" (Yeung 2005b, 44; emphasis in original). Thus to develop a relational approach for researching and understanding music production, research must aim to develop an "understanding of intentions and strategies of economic actors and ensembles of actors and the patterns of how they behave" (Bathelt and Glückler 2003, 125).

Thus, from Part One to Part Two, the book moves from a micro-level or "micro-space" (Ettlinger 2003) examination of work within the recording studio, to a macro-level examination of recording networks, in order to capture the full range of practices of record producers and studio engineers working in the contemporary recording industry. Part Two of the book is entitled "Beyond the Studio" and is concerned with the stretching of relations outside and beyond the insulated space of the recording studio. Chapter 5 considers the relationship between recording studios and the urban centres in which they are (typically) located, and specifically their role in urban music scenes. More generally, it is concerned with musical creativity and production at the scale of the city, and the ways in which urban geography is a crucial mediating factor in the production and consumption of music.

The subsequent two chapters are concerned with the wider project networks in which recording studios are embedded, and which often stretch out into inter-urban networks at a global scale. Chapter 6 sets the economic context behind the networking of studios, and examines the Internet-based technologies which are enabling new forms and intensities and networking between studios. As Dicken et al. suggest, such non-human actors enable social actors to "develop and maintain modern social relations; relations that span out across space at all scales via networks" (2001, 102; emphasis in original). Further then, the chapter considers the nature of creative relations that occur at-distance, and the working and networking practices and communication strategies adopted by producers and engineers to build and maintain creative relationships at-distance. Building on this discussion, Chapter 7 undertakes an empirical examination of these networks, based upon data on the social connections occurring through project work. Specifically, the chapter examines the working flows that occur between recording studios, based in cities across the globe, when they are part of temporary creative projects that are brought together to produce recorded music albums. The end result is a mapping of global urban networks of music production, and specifically the power and centrality of particular cities within these networks. For Dicken et al. (2001) and Yeung (2005a) a central component of a relational analysis is recognition of the existence of differential power relations within actor-networks, with power defined as a relational and emergent concept manifested through practice (Allen 1997).

Finally, Chapter 8 considers two key technological developments which have impacted directly both the way recording studios operate and their future viability as formal, professional spaces of recording: the development of the MP3 software format, and the increased availability of software for home recording. The chapter describes the unforeseen negative impacts of these developments, explores the shifting out of music production beyond recording studios into home spaces and considers the likely future outcomes for recording studios.

Economic Relations

Finally, as part of the relational turn there has been a growing concern with how the interests of particular individuals may diverge from the material interests of the firm, and the implications this has for economic practices (Boggs and Rantisi 2003). Empirical work has demonstrated that individuals may form networks within and outside firms that can either advance the interests of their employers (see, for example, Amin and Cohendet 1999) or prioritise personal interests over those of their employers (see for example Christopherson 2002). There are then a set of economic relations between employer and employee that shape individual work practices, experiences and interests. These in turn are influenced and often determined by wider economic circumstances. In the recording studio sector for instance, as with the creative industries more widely, there has been the relatively recent development of flexible and freelance models of employment, and accordingly, the development of relationships between employer (the recording studio) and employee (producer or engineer) that is transactional, contractual and short-term.

The final part of the book, Part Three, is entitled "Working and Networking in the Recording Studio Sector," and is concerned with these changing employment relations within the contemporary recording studio sector. In particular, it is concerned with the pervasive effects of the neoliberalisation

10 Introduction

of work in the sector, and its impact on the work of producers and engineers. Following the discussion of the negative impacts of new technologies presented in Chapter 8, Chapter 9 considers how this neoliberalisation of work is reducing employment security and eroding working conditions in the sector, including the exacerbation of exhaustive work regimes and an undermining of the viability of long-term careers in recording.

However, as Granovetter (1985) argues, individuals do not act atomistically without context. Rather, their identities and resource capabilities are co-constituted by their relations with other actors (Boggs and Rantisi 2003) and their decisions are always shaped by the structure of social relations with other actors and shared institutional conditions (Bathelt and Glückler 2005). These relational resource capabilities include social capital (see Coleman 1988; Bourdieu 1986), which Bathelt and Glückler suggest cannot be attributed to individual actors or firms; rather it refers to "the opportunities that actors draw from the quality and structure of their relations with other actors in order to pursue individual objectives" (2005, 1555; see also Bathelt and Glückler 2003). Social capital, they argue, is a result of ongoing social practices; it cannot be possessed or built without the active involvement of others—it is built collectively. Chapter 10 builds on the preceding chapter through an examination of the strategies adopted by producers and engineers to cope with this increasing precarity. In particular, the chapter considers the importance of networking in developing social capital and networked reputation, both of which it is suggested are crucial assets in obtaining work in a sector increasingly marked by structured job insecurity.

The discussion presented in this book draws upon a wide range of secondary sources, including academic texts and papers, record producer and musician interviews and biographies, popular texts on the recording industry, "how-to" guides for recording, newspapers and magazines, and a range of websites and online forums. This secondary data is supplemented by primary data from 20 semi-structured interviews with record producers and recording engineers working in recording studios in the U.K. (primarily in London), between June 2010 and May 2013. All of the interviewees were male (reflecting the fact that music production and recording engineering remain almost exclusively male forms of employment), were from a range of employment categories (freelance, contracted to a recording studio, or owner-operator of a studio) and worked in studios that ranged from very small project studios to large, internationally renowned recording facilities. Interviews lasted between 30 minutes and two hours, resulting in a total of almost 19 hours of recorded data. All interviews were recorded and transcribed, and transcripts were subsequently analysed using systematic coding and recoding based around key themes and common categories emerging from the data, considered in relation to the overall theoretical framework.

Part I
Inside the Studio

1 Studio Technologies
Changing Concepts and Practices

As a basic definition, recording studios can be considered as sites in which "appropriate and available technologies are assembled and hired to musicians and producers for periods of time, for the purpose of sound recording" (Gibson 2005, 196). These technologies include recording/mixing desks, often linked to music recording software on computers, as well as a wide range of effects processors and digital music-making machines, a range of microphones, and storage devices for capturing the recorded sound such as digital hard drives and tape machines. The history and evolution of recording studios is one that has been shaped by technological developments; from the post-war introduction of tape recording, that for the first time allowed the editing of recordings through cutting and splicing; through the introduction of multi-track recordings consoles and tape machines in the 1960s and 1970s; to the arrival of digital samplers and drum machines in the early 1980s and subsequently the computer software-based digital audio workstations (DAWs) of the 1990s and 2000s.

However, as Théberge (2012) argues, it is important to recognise that the modern history of the recording studio is not only one of technological and economic contexts and changing studio configurations, but is also one of changing *concepts* and *practices* in sound recording. For example, multi-track recording concepts and practices, he argues, differed in fundamental ways from those associated with earlier forms of record production; thinking of music as a series of individual "tracks," rather than a single performed "event" enabled producers and engineers to develop a more compositional approach to the recording process (see also Moorefield 2010).

The purpose of this first chapter is twofold. First, it traces technological development in the contemporary recording studio, from the beginning of the age of multi-tracking in the 1960s, through the development of digital music-making machines in the 1980s, to the development of software and computer technologies for digital multi-tracking in the late 1990s/2000s. Second, the chapter considers the impact of these technologies on the roles that the record producer and recording engineer play in the recording studio, in particular how technology has acted to position producers and engineers as key intermediaries in the creative process of music production.

14   *Inside the Studio*

1.1   STUDIO TECHNOLOGIES: A RECENT HISTORY OF DEVELOPMENT

The Rise of Multi-Track Recording and Mixing

The multi-track recording studio is the basis for our contemporary notions of what a recording studio is, how it operates, and how music is made (see Théberge 2012). Now the most common technological method of recording popular music, multi-tracking is a method of sound recording that allows for the separate recording of multiple sound sources to create a cohesive whole. Musical instruments and vocals can be recorded, either one at a time or simultaneously, onto multiple tracks of audio that can be individually processed and manipulated, either during or post-recording, to produce the desired results. As Warner describes:

> Artistically, whether using digital or analogue systems, the rewards of multitrack overdub recording are enormous; first, recording each track separately enables the user to attain a much higher level of musical accuracy, specifically timing and tuning; second, each track can be recorded in minute sections, bit by bit, and as a consequence, levels of performance are achieved which would be impossible "live"; third, the complete separation of each track offers control of volume, timbre, and spatial positioning of the signal on the track *in relation to the other tracks*; and finally, decisions as to suitability of virtually all the separate sounds need only be made at the mixdown stage—that is, when the multitrack tape is "mixed down" to the stereo format that will be the final product.
>
> (2003, 23; emphasis in original)

Multi-track recording machines became available as early as the late 1950s and early 1960s following the pioneering work of Les Paul. In the U.S. eight-track Ampex recorders existed as early as the late 1950s, with Atlantic Studios in New York the first studio to operate one (Simons 2004), while in the U.K. Abbey Road Studios would see the arrival of one-inch, four-track recorders late in 1963 (Moorefield 2010). However, it would be through the development of in-line digital recording consoles in the late 1960s, led by the U.K. technology companies Solid State Logic (SSL) and Neve (Box 1.1), that would really define the beginning of the era of multi-tracking. As Théberge (2004) notes, the entire development of multi-tracking, along with the practices associated with it, is inseparable from a simultaneous evolution in the design of recording and mixing consoles. These consoles not only had the facility to record multiple tracks of audio (Figure 1.1), but also to mix these multiple tracks together into a single stereo recording, allowing the producer and engineer to adjust elements of the source recordings and add effects in order to finalise the balance of sound within recordings, before storing these to tape via multi-track tape machines (Figure 1.2). Sixteen-track recording became widespread in professional studios by 1971, and by

Figure 1.1 Close-up of Neve VR60 Legend 60-channel recording console with labeling showing separate tracks of audio

Source: Author

Figure 1.2 24-track 2-inch tape machine

Source: Author

Box 1.1 The development of multi-track recording consoles: SSL and Neve

In the late 1960s and early 1970s, the U.K. technology companies Solid State Logic (SSL) and Neve (AMS-Neve since 1992) pioneered the development of multi-track in-line digital recording consoles. With each microphone and effect having its own set of faders and controls, these consoles gave producers and engineers a new level of control over the various sounds and components that were recorded in recording studios (Figure 1.3).

Figure 1.3 Recording to multiple channels of audio on a Neve VR60 Legend 60-channel console

Source: Photograph courtesy of Tony Draper

Console development would take a further leap forward in the late 1970s as SSL and then Neve integrated computer software and memory into recording consoles, allowing producers and engineers to save settings across as many as 32-tracks and easily reestablish the settings between recording sessions, ensuring these were exactly the same from session to session—"Total Recall." The Total Recall system incorporated a sensor on each and every fader, button and knob on the console and saves a "snapshot" of the desk's status. This means that at the end of a project the entirety of the desk's settings can be saved onto disk and recalled at a later date for recalls, remasters, remixes and overdubs etc.

In 1977, SSL introduced the SL 4000 B console which integrated a studio computer system with an in-line audio console. In the same year, Neve installed the world's first moving fader automation system, Necam (Neve Computer Assisted Mixdown) at London's AIR Studios, which would later be followed by SSL's automated fader system, launched in 1991. Automated faders (Figure 1.4) allowed the recording of fader moves made during a mix, which will then play back automatically. So if, for example, an engineer wanted to ride guitars up in the chorus, they would drop the guitar faders into record on the automated faders system, play the track, and physically push the faders up for the chorus. That move is recorded, and will then be played back by the motors inside the faders when the mix is played back.

Figure 1.4 Close-up of Neve VR60 Legend console showing moving fader automation system

Source: Author

The digitalisation of consoles progressed into the 1980s and 1990s; in 1980, Neve produced the world's first digital audio console, the DSP, and in 1988 AMS released the world's first fully dynamically automated digital console. In 2001 Neve released the 88R, which they termed the "ultimate analogue recording console." Both companies continue to produce recording consoles and associated digital recording technologies today, with many of the new developments aimed at the post-production and film industries as well as the music industry.

Sources: Leyshon (2009); http://ams-neve.com/about-us/ams-neve-history/70s (accessed 08/03/2013); http://www.solid-state-logic.com/about/history.asp (accessed 08/03/2013)

18 *Inside the Studio*

1973 24-track recording had been introduced (Moorefield 2010). Subsequently consoles would be developed which allowed for up to 96 tracks to be recorded and mixed.

As Leyshon (2009) discusses, the innovations made by SSL and Neve in developing these recording consoles made them the control desks of choice for leading freelance engineers and producers, and as such "consoles integrated with software and with the capacity for memory became obligatory passage points for studios wishing to attract producers" (2009, 1323–1324). Thus particular recording desks, combined with particular palates of technologies in particular studios, would become key assets in attracting client bases for recording studios. Most major studios therefore invested in one or both of these types of control desks. For example, the control room of Studio One at London's Abbey Road has a 72-channel Neve recording console, while Studio Three has a 96-channel SSL recording console. The control room of Lyndhurst Hall, the orchestral recording space at AIR Studios, London, has the world's largest Neve 88R console, with a total of 96 channels (costing approximately £600,000), and Studio One has a 72-channel AIR-custom vintage Neve desk, while Studio Two has a 80-channel SSL desk. Studio One at Capitol Studio, Los Angeles—the studio's orchestral recording space—has a Neve 88RS console, while Studios Two and Three also have Neve consoles.

Even today, the major studios continue to invest in expensive Neve and SSL desks. The control room of Studio Two at Abbey Road was newly refurbished in January 2011 to accept a new 60-channel Neve mixing console; while in 2010, the Engine Room, located in Bermondsey in London (part of the large Miloco Studios group) became home to an SSL 4056G 56-channel console that had been obtained and refurbished following the closure of the renowned Olympic Studios in London, at the cost of tens of thousands of pounds. However, the high costs of these consoles are prohibitive for most small studios working on very small budgets. For these studios, investment in one of the wider range of budget mixing consoles available on the market is the only option; however, these desks can be given some of the functionality found on the larger software-integrated SSL and Neve consoles, if they are integrated to a computer via an analogue to digital converter.

Digital Music-Making

The late 1980s saw a new range of automated digital music-making music machines become available on the market. Drum machines, for example, enabled musicians to programme rhythmic patterns without actually hitting any drums (Goodwin 1988); the first drum machine which employed sampled sounds, the Linn LM-1, was released in 1979; the Linn Drum, popular with producers of 80s disco and pop music, would follow in 1982 (Moorefield 2010). Around the same time a number of digital sound-processing and recording technologies became available, including the first personal computers, sequencers, sampling computers and synthesizers. The first commercially available sampler, the Fairlight CMI, came onto the market in 1979 (ibid.). The introduction of the Musical Instrument Digital Interface (MIDI) protocol would be of particular importance (Box 1.2), as it provided a system that enabled the connection of, and communication between, multiple digital devices (Bennett 2009). As these technologies began to dramatically fall in price, they became accessible to a much wider range of producers and studios; the first sampler at a price affordable to a broad market, for example—the Ensoniq Mirage priced at less than US$2,000 (roughly one-quarter the price of other samplers on the market)—was introduced in 1984 (Rogers 2003). Such developments were in no small part the reason for the emergence of "project studios"—smaller studio installations that began to take on commercial work (Théberge 2004).

Box 1.2 Musical Instrument Digital Interface (MIDI)

The Musical Instrument Digital Interface (MIDI) code was developed in 1982 by American engineer and musician Dave Smith. Before the development of MIDI, it had been all but impossible to control multiple digital synthesizers, samplers, signal processors and mixing desks. This was due to the incompatibility of the various systems being developed by manufacturers, meaning that one manufacturer's systems could not synchronize with those of another. MIDI provided a single interface and code through which multiple digital music-making machines could operate together, and as it was adopted by many of the leading manufacturers including Yamaha, Roland, Casio, Akai, Korg and Kawai, it meant that compatibility issues between various systems were resolved.

MIDI allows one musical instrument/device to control another device: for example, when a note is played on a MIDI instrument, it generates a digital signal that passes along a MIDI cable and triggers a note on another instrument. A numerical value is assigned to each aspect of a note, including its pitch, its duration and loudness. These signals can be stored and manipulated using a MIDI "sequencer" (which can be a dedicated device or a program on a computer) and then can be combined with other MIDI channels. This allows musicians to combine instruments to achieve a fuller sound, or to create combinations of different sounds. Using a MIDI-based sequencer controlling synthesizers and samplers, a record could be constructed in an improvisatory manner using a multi-track overdub technique, mixed over a variety of audio systems and using an array of signal processing devices. Thus the enormous control over sound provided by MIDI enabled a flexibility to working with sound that had previously not been possible.

Sources: Warner (2003); Théberge (1997)

20 *Inside the Studio*

The reduction in the cost of these technologies also resulted in the emergence of a much wider consumer music production market, with access to recording studio technologies greatly increased beyond specialist, highly skilled technical workers in the formal recording studio sector (Knowles and Hewitt 2012). Théberge (1997) argues that this was encouraged by new recording technology magazines which acted as part of a "double-production industry" in which the growth of digital technologies occurred simultaneously with the press producing consumers for these technologies:

> New technology has been reified as the tie that binds a community of musicians together, while, at the same time, it is the object of consumption whose success in the marketplace is essential to the survival of the electronic instrument industry. In the final analysis, there is a double production going on: One industry produces technology and the other producers consumers.
>
> (Théberge 1997, 130)

As Bennett (2012a) notes, the emergence of audio industry and music technology periodicals happened almost simultaneously with the release of new technologies. Such publications from the mid-1980s onwards contained "page upon page of equipment advertising" (2012a, 121) as well as equipment reviews that largely emphasised the positives of new products coming onto the market. In this way, Bennett argues, the music technology press acted "not as independent or impartial advisors to consumers, but as business partners with technology manufacturers" (2012a, 123).

Importantly, such magazines also contained "how-to" guides for setting up MIDI systems. Subsequently, the ability to use, and to program, the latest machinery became a more widespread skill, moving out beyond the formal recording studio sector, resulting in the breakdown of the amateur/professional status in the production process (Warner 2003). Furthermore, as music has increasingly become more of a programmer's medium, recording studios and producers will often employ engineers and programmers who specialise in particular kinds of equipment (Goodwin 1998).

The increasing popularity of digital music-making technologies would give rise to new forms of music in the mid-late 1980s which would come to define the "pop" music genre as we understand it today. As Warner (2003) argues, the transition to digital technologies not only brought about a revolution in working practices, but also played an important role in how pop music as an art form has evolved over the past 25 years—the use of sequencers to control synthesisers and samplers removed much of the emphasis that rock places on individual instrumental dexterity, and they now supply many, and in some cases all, of the sounds heard on pop recordings. The synthesiser-based pop music of U.S. artists such as Michael Jackson and Madonna would become huge sellers globally, whilst in the U.K. the

Studio Technologies 21

synth-pop music of bands such as the Pet Shop Boys and Erasure would come to define the decade of the 1980s (Bennett 2009).

The digital revolution not only came to define pop music, however. Drum machines, which were originally created to replace the drummer as realistically as possible, would subsequently be used to create new types of music which were built around the mechanical rhythms it produced (Moorefield 2010), and the 1980s would see the emergence of new electronic dance music genres. During this period, for example, German electronic music group and technological innovators Kraftwerk would create a distinctive sound around electronically created repetitive rhythms and catchy melodies, a sound which has had a lasting effect across many genres of modern music. The 1980s would also see the mainstream debut of hip-hop with artists such as Run DMC and Public Enemy (ibid.). In the case of hip-hop, samplers and synthesisers enabled the development of a collage of sounds that often included non-music elements such as voices, street noises, gun shots and sirens, connecting the music to the urban environments to which it was emerging (Danielsen 2005) and lending the music a particular form of "authenticity." However, as Bennett (2009) describes, to some, especially musicians and fans in rock genres, with their emphasis on performance, musicianship and "authenticity" (see Warner 2003), these new forms of electronic music were seen as inauthentic compared to the "live" performances and instrumental dexterity of rock bands. The renaissance of these forms of music in the 1990s would reemphasise the importance of the studio as a "live" space of recording rather than purely a tool for digital composition (see Chapter 4).

During the late 1980s and early 1990s a new generation of computer software emerged that combined recording capability and MIDI sequencing. This new generation of software was enabled primarily by the increased level of processing power and storage capacity found in personal computers from the 1990s onwards (Théberge 2004). Writing in 2000, Berk suggested that:

> . . . the future of music technology is likely to be centred on the desktop. Advances in desktop processor speeds and hard disk capacity have made it possible to run all the elements of a virtual electronic studio—multitrack recorder, signal processors, and sound sources—on a single machine.
>
> (Berk 2000, 201)

In what are commonly now referred to as computer-based or software Digital Audio Workstations (DAW), a computer both acts as a host for an audio interface and software and provides processing power for audio editing. The software controls all related hardware components and provides a user interface to allow for recording, editing and playback. Most computer-based DAWs have extensive MIDI recording, editing and playback

22 *Inside the Studio*

capabilities. Prominent examples of software include Avid Technology's Pro-Tools, Apple's Logic Pro and Steinberg's Cubase (see Box 1.3).

This enabled multi-track recording and mixing on a level only previously afforded by large, expensive recording consoles. In some respects, the capabilities of DAWs even exceed the capabilities of these consoles, for example by allowing the automation of every parameter within them, such as fader rides, EQ cuts and boosts, compression settings and FX sends. Further, they also incorporate inbuilt effects processors that were previously only available as expensive "outboard" units separate to the consoles. Given their flexibility, today recording is largely done into these digital audio workstations, and even where studios have recording consoles they are today integrated to software DAWs for recording and mixing (Figure 1.5).

Box 1.3 The development of software Digital Audio Workstations: Steinberg's Cubase

On the back of developments in digital music-making machines and the MIDI code in the 1980s, a number of engineers began focusing on the development of computer-based stereo audio editing software. It is from this period that the origins of today's best-selling software DAWs can be traced, including Steinberg's Cubase software. In 1984, using a Commodore 64 computer and a self-built MIDI interface, Charlie Steinberg developed a multi-track sequencer, and in the same year co-founded Steinberg Research GmbH. Pro-16, the first software product to carry the Steinberg name, was released.

In 1986, the Atari ST home computer became available, and offered both a graphical user interface and a built-in MIDI interface. This proved to be an important development—Steinberg would use this computer as a basis for Pro-24, which offered 24 MIDI tracks and a variety of music editing facilities, while Gerhard Lengeling and Chris Adam developed a MIDI sequencer program for the Atari ST that would later become Apple's Logic Pro. Cubase 1.0 was released in 1989 with a new graphical representation of the composition using a vertical list of tracks and a horizontal timeline, which has since been copied by other software DAWs. By 1991, it had become possible to record audio data directly into a computer, and by 1996 Cubase incorporated a real-time studio environment including EQs, effects, mixing and automation of the type only previously achievable through the use of expensive recording/mixing consoles and outboard equipment.

By the late 1990s, affordable personal computers had become powerful enough to run advanced audio-production software such as Cubase, and in 1999 Cubase became available to the consumer market. The availability of digital DAWs to amateur musicians and engineers working in home recording studios (they have previously been too expensive—the first version of Avid's Pro Tools, launched in 1991, cost US$6,000) would have a significant and lasting impact on the spaces and practices of music production.

Sources: http://www.steinberg.net/en/company/aboutsteinberg.html

Figure 1.5 Multi-track recording through a console integrated to a DAW
Source: Photograph courtesy of Katie Tavini

The development of software DAWs have had a significant beneficial impact for smaller project and home studios, in particular as laptop computers became powerful enough to run audio-production software and affordable enough to become part of a musician's home studio (Knowles and Hewitt 2012). Today, the importance of commercial recording studios as the primary sites for musical recording is being challenged by new these new developments in digital equipment (see Chapter 8).

Alongside these developments in computer software has been the development of technologies for sharing digital music files between recording studios in geographically distant locations, such as File Transfer Protocol (FTP). More recently the emergence of the Integrated Services Digital Network (ISDN) has enabled the development of technologies for simultaneous recording that allow musicians, producers and engineers to collaborate in real-time and at distance. Théberge (2004) argues that these technologies have given rise to "network studios'," which in their attempt to service a highly mobile clientele (recording artists, producers and engineers) have "... increasingly adopted recording technologies and practices that enable them to expand and co-ordinate their activities on a global scale" (Théberge 2004, 761) (see Chapters 6 and 7).

24　*Inside the Studio*

Mastering

The final stage in the production of recorded music is the post-production process of *mastering*. Mastering is "the stage of post-production where the overall final product is adjusted in terms of dynamics processing, levelling, equalization and noise reduction so that it is intelligible, in audio terms, across all playback systems" (McIntyre 2012, 159). When prepared, the final mix is transferred to a master copy on a data storage device, from which all subsequent copies are produced (Leyshon 2009). Mastering has its origins in the "cutting" of records, the term used to describe the transfer of a recording onto vinyl records. Vinyl as a medium for storing recordings has particular limitations, most notably that fidelity declines as playback progresses due to there being more vinyl per second available for fine reproduction of high frequencies at the large-diameter beginning of the groove than exist at the smaller diameters close to the end of the side. Therefore a key role of the mastering engineer was to master the ability to transfer recordings to vinyl, adjusting the sound of the recording accordingly to deal with this limitation so as not to effect playback. More recently, the introduction of the compact disc supplied a storage medium without any technical limitations. This resulted in a change in the role of mastering engineer, from "transfer engineer" to "sound engineer," with the focus on obtaining the optimum sound from a song rather than limiting its sound.

Whereas a recording or mixing engineer can engineer sound by adjusting faders on multiple tracks, a mastering engineer usually only receives a completed two-channel mix. To engineer sound, a mastering engineer uses a specialised mastering console and sound processing equipment to tune in on frequencies and edit particular sounds and areas of the sound spectrum, without it interfering with other sounds in the song. The type of edits and adjustments typically made include adjusting volume; editing minor flaws; applying noise reduction to eliminate clicks, dropouts, hum and hiss; adjusting stereo width; adding ambience; and equalizing audio across the tracks on an album.

More recently, the role of the mastering engineer has once again begun to change, with the introduction of "stem-mastering'." This is a technique derived from stem-mixing, a method of mixing audio material based on creating groups of audio tracks and processing them separately prior to combining them into a final master mix. With mastering engineers now beginning to receive recordings as a series of stems in the place of a completed two-channel mix, the potential for mastering engineers to be creative with audio are increasing (see Chapter 2) and the line between mixing engineer and mastering engineer has begun to blur. Moreover, the introduction of the MP3 digital music format (see Chapter 8) has resulted in the need to provide digital masters; however, while digital storage of masters is now pervasive throughout the industry, much of the mastering process is still undertaken using analogue processing equipment attached to very expensive high-quality monitoring speakers due to issues of sound quality with digital equipment.

1.2 TECHNOLOGY AND THE CHANGING ROLES OF PRODUCERS AND ENGINEERS

The "Producer as Composer"

The role of the record producer has evolved greatly with the technological developments outlined in the previous section of this chapter. The high level of control over the recording and manipulation of sounds enabled by multi-tracking, followed subsequently by developments in digital technologies (in the form of digital musical instruments and samplers in the 1980s and recording software in the 1990s) acted to enhance the role of composition in recording music:

> Over the last fifty years, the philosophy and technique of music production have undergone a major transformation. As the activity of recording has widened in scope from a primarily technical matter to a conceptual and artistic one as well, it has assumed a central role in areas such as instrumental arrangement and the sculpting and placement of audio samples. The concept of sound in the sense of a stylistic choice, and the ability to capture and mould it, have grown in importance as recording technology has become increasingly complex.
>
> (Moorefield 2010, xii)

Prior to the invention of multi-track recording in the 1950s, the relationships between sounds were controlled at the time of recording (Tankel 1990). For Horning (2004) the ability to record in such a way that the instruments and voices were properly balanced was the subtlest form of "engineering the performance'." However, multi-track recording and mixing technologies would make the studio a tool for musical composition; as Moorefield (2010) describes, the recording studio became a "meta-instrument" used to shape entire compositions. The concern for capturing music as realistically as possible was replaced with a new aesthetic of composition—one in which "individual performances became less important than the manipulation of individual strands of recorded sound material" (Théberge 1997, 216). In this new aesthetic of composition, the quest for the ability to present the illusion of physical reality was replaced with a desire to create the appearance of a reality which could not actually exist—"a pseudo-reality, created in synthetic space" (Moorefield 2010, xv). As Tankel notes:

> A "studio" recording is a distinct entity not bound by the strict limitations of performance—the compilation of discrete performances or

26   *Inside the Studio*

activities mixed to create a unique whole. A "live augmented" recording utilizes studio technologies to create the illusion of a performance by recording and mixing performances that *seem* to be performed as a unit.

(1990, 38; emphasis in original)

Parallels began to be drawn between this new form of music production and film-making, in which the director shoots multiple takes (more than they actually use) and edits together the final cut from the available material. Even vocals can be composed; computer technology enables various sections of a number of vocal performances to be edited together and auto-tuned in order to get the best audio recording in perfect pitch. This often requires a vocalist to do multiple vocal takes, which are then edited after the performance, and which do not have to be perfect in pitch; Zak (2001) for example notes that the vocal on Peter Gabriel's "Love to be Loved" was recorded some 40 times with bits from each performance used to construct the one that appears on the final track. In certain genres such as pop, in which the emphasis is on technology and the "artificial" (Warner 2003), a "perfect" or "clean" vocal is often desired, and as such the practice of "composing" a vocal track has become almost the norm.

Théberge (1989, 1997) argues that as this new aesthetic was established, the recording of group performance and social/music exchange between musicians became "rationalized" and "fragmented'," with control over the overall texture increasingly being given to the sound engineer and producer. Music production has become increasingly programmed and controlled, he argues, from the desire on the part of producers for technical control of the recording process, resulting in a "disincarnation" of musical production and a subjection of recorded music to rational process. Goodwin describes how the issue of authorship manifests itself in terms of music-making in the studio:

> . . . consider this scenario, which is now common at the beginning of a pop recording session: before a note is committed to tape, a producer or engineer will use a sampling computer to digitally record each sound used by the group. At this point, it is sometimes possible for everyone but the producer to go home, leaving the computerised manipulation of these sounds to do the work of performance and recording.

(1998, 39)

Furthermore, as their control over the process became more total, concern for perfection crept in to the record-making process (Simmons 2004), resulting in "finely wrought music arrangements painstakingly assembled over many hours of work" (Warner 2003, 25). This aesthetic of composition, then, acted to give a greater importance to the role of the record producer, making them an indispensable interpreter between the technical and artistic aspects of making records (Moorefield 2010). It is from these developments which stem current understandings of the technical-engineering and aesthetic-artistry skills associated with "mixing" tracks and composing a recording, what Moorefield (2010) terms *the producer as composer.* As McIntyre (2012) notes, record producers have developed an important role as cultural intermediary in the studio where their decisions contribute significantly to the final creative product. As Longhurst (1995) argues, by the early 1960s many producers had become artists in their own right and were known for their own distinctive "sound." Furthermore, as Théberge (1997) notes, at a level beyond the recording studio itself, producers became increasingly responsible for musical production within the overall economic organisation of the record industry.

But for some producers, their involvement in the production of music goes beyond the composition of music through recording and mixing. The emergence of digital automated music-making machines and samplers in the 1980s allowed producers for the first time to produce and compose music without the presence of musicians; as Goodwin notes, perhaps the most significant result of innovations in pop music production lies in the "progressive removal of any immanent criteria for distinguishing between human and automated performance" (1988, 39). Therefore, while it had become increasingly common through the 1960s and 1970s for musicians to produce their own music, digital technologies would result in the increased blurring between the roles of artist and producer, particularly in electronic music genres. Moorefield (2010) argues that contemporary music (for example, hip-hop) is conflating the role of the producer and that of the auteur, with producers often creating the instrumental parts; increasingly, he argues, "writing" has come to mean the deft combination of samples from various sources, and the skilled manipulation of technology such as samplers, synthesizers, mixing boards, and computers" (2010, 92). The development of digital audio workstations and audio-editing and sampling software has acted to further enable music-making without musicians. This can be seen in the creation 'of "mash-up" music (see Shiga 2007) in which audio-editing software is used to splice and combine samples from existing music to produce hybrid recordings (see Chapter 8).

Recording Engineering: Between Technology and Aesthetics

However, to focus on the producer alone is to miss the central role played by studio recording engineers not only in the technical process of recording but also in the creative process. Horning (2004) argues that, in allowing a greater control over engineering, the advent of multi-tracking not only increased the dependency on the technical knowledge of the studio engineer working in the control room (see also Théberge 2004), but also rendered the recording engineer a member of the creative team, becoming more involved in the musical decisions made during recording.

28   *Inside the Studio*

With the know-how to operate the highly technological equipment in studios, recording engineers are most often seen as "technologists" (Horning 2004). Kealy (1990) describes the complex set of technical abilities and tacit knowledges that engineers and producers are required to have: these include knowing the characteristics of hundreds of microphones and a variety of acoustic environments, and how to employ them to best record a musical instrument; the capabilities and applications of a large array of sound-processing devices; the physical capacities of recording media (such as tapes and discs) for accepting and reproducing sounds; the operation of various recording machines; and how to balance or "mix" the analogue or digital signals coming from a variety of live and pre-recorded sound sources, to produce a recording that is "a recognizable and effective musical experience" (Kealy 1990, 208). One interviewee described the role of the engineer as being to:

> . . . ensure that the sound is correctly produced and the microphones are set properly and the desk is working, run the equipment and basically be like a conduit to make sure that all the creative process from the musicians comes through and is recorded without them really feeling like they're intruded upon.
>
> (Interview 15, male engineer, thirties)

While a producer is controlling the creative process and having the overall responsibility for the collective endeavour of recording music and creating the sound of the end product, he will ask the engineer to deliver particular styles of sound on the recording. It is then the engineer's role to use the equipment available to create the required sound on the recording. An experienced engineer should fairly instinctively "know what to do to get those sounds . . . when you're recording a band, you're very rarely using your conscious brain" (Interview 11, male engineer, twenties). One interviewee saw his role as ". . . a translator from what they are trying to do into recorded [sound]" because he spoke the "language with all the buttons" (Interview 13, male engineer-producer, forties).

Noting that record production is a mode of creative expression, Zak (2007) argues that "turning musical utterance into electrical current requires, by the project's very nature, an intervening aesthetic sensibility which may, in turn, impinge on the final result" (2001; no pagination). Therefore, while engineers have largely been considered to perform a technical role, arguably their role has never been purely technical. As Kealy argues, the aesthetic decision-making skills of engineers blur the boundary between "technology" and "art'," and that ". . . sound mixers commonly hold an occupational self-image that includes such elements of craftsmanship as technical mastery and artistry" (1990, 208). This was highlighted in an interview with engineer Geoff Emerick who states that "I was never that technically minded, but I had sounds in my head. I've always described the job as painting a picture with

Studio Technologies 29

sounds; I think of microphone as lenses. Engineering is such a wrong term for music mixing, really" (quoted in Massey 2000, 84).

As Shuker notes, a movement towards greater importance can be traced for some recording engineers, who "have converted a craft into an art, with consequent higher status and reward" (2001, 53). More generally, recording engineers are increasingly assisting musicians with the production of their music (Longhurst 1995), and making aesthetic judgments that are usually perceived to be the performer's domain (Tankel 1990). Interview responses suggested that this situation has become increasingly common due to the falling budgets of the record companies and an increase in the number of self-funding artists:

> . . . the business is changing; we're not dependent on record companies as much. A lot of the projects we do are self-funded, people finding their own investment. So you'll find a lot of projects here is all private money or part-partnerships with sponsors and backers, and that in a way is a good thing but also brings its own challenges because you're dealing with people who are not necessarily used to working in a studio. So you've got to help them through that . . .
> (Interview 12, male engineer-producer, forties)

These self-funding artists with more modest budgets often cannot afford the cost of a producer, and so when recording in the studio they rely on the studio engineer for creative input. One interviewee describes how:

> The major labels make much less investment in new bands and new artists. The indie labels don't have as much money, so you're working a lot with bands that are coming and financing their own records, and often they don't have a producer or they don't really know what they're talking about technically. So you have to, you do a lot more producing, even though you don't get paid for it.
> (Interview 11, male engineer, twenties)

For these engineers, competently performing their technical role whilst also making aesthetic judgements and giving creative direction to the recording process is often a very difficult balancing act. While the role of a record producer means that their intuitive capacity for making music can "exercise itself spontaneously and in a non-cerebral fashion" and a producer can "allow himself to give into his feelings, to react to what he perceives as purely physical sensations" (Hennion 1990, 201), an engineer is expected to find the balance between artistic expression and engineering possibilities. Beer terms this the "precarious double life" of the recording engineer:

> This precarious double life might be understood to exist as a result of the tension that is created as the recording engineer balances their

30   *Inside the Studio*

practice at the lines between artistic sensibility and logistical or technical know-how. . . . The recording engineer, it would seem, is valued for their technical skill—their ability to place a microphone, to manage effects, to wire up studios, to place sound dampening sheets, to capture sounds, to handle software plug-ins, to get sound levels consistent, and so on—but is also expected to be artistically sensitive and orientated to the realisation of artistic vision.

(Beer 2013, 1–2)

Although this might be identified as a general shift in the role of the engineer, as Beer suggests, it is perhaps more representative of a set of changes that are negotiated on an individual level. As one interviewee noted:

. . . often on some of the projects that I do that are smaller projects you're producing and engineering at the same time, which is really hard because you have to split your head into two different worlds at the same time, so one side is doing a very technical job and thinking about cables and computer editing and the other side is going oh hang on a minute is this the right tempo or is the song in the right key or how can I make that section work better . . . so that's quite difficult.

(Interview 15, male engineer, thirties)

The difficulties presented by the blurring of production and engineering roles appear to be exacerbated by the fact that the skills required by a producer are rather different from the often more tangible technical knowledge needed by a studio engineer. Music competence in production can be defined as a form of "structured listening" (Théberge 1997) and as a set of "listening skills" which are mediated by the vast array of sound equipment found in recording studios (Pinch and Bijsterveld 2004): it is not musical "skill," in the traditional sense of the term, that defines the role of producers; rather, it is their ability to listen, to feel what is "right" for the given musical context that is their focus in the studio (Théberge 1997, 219). One interviewee noted that "your ears and your taste are probably more important than the equipment" (Interview 13, male engineer-producer, forties); another interviewee, a former studio engineer who has gone on to become a commercially successful record producer, noted of his transition from engineer to producer:

. . . I didn't actually know what I was doing to be honest looking back. . . . I didn't know *how to listen.* You can learn how to use all this stuff but it took me years to actually get to a point where I could actually listen and get the sort of technology out of my brain . . . to stop thinking about pressing buttons and just think about it as a piece of music.

(Interview 19, male producer, forties;' emphasis added)

1.3 CONCLUSIONS

As noted at the very beginning of this chapter, the history and evolution of recording studios is one that has been shaped by technological developments. There has only been space in this chapter to give a relatively cursory coverage of this lineage of development[1]. The problem of providing a comprehensive account of technological development is further exacerbated by the fact that, in the age of computer software, technological developments in recording continue apace, meaning that by the time many readers come to this chapter, it will already to be to a lesser or greater degree out-of-date. As Warner (2003) suggests, the technologies used in recording are in a state of almost continuous development and refinement. However, despite these limitations, providing such an overview of the technological development of recording studios is important due to the way in which it sets the context for much of the discussion presented in this book. The following chapter, Chapter 2, for example, considers the types of creativity and collaboration that have both driven, and been enabled by, the technological developments described in this chapter.

NOTE

1. For comprehensive accounts of recording studio technologies and their relation to changing concepts and practices of recording, readers should refer to Moorefield's *The Producer as Composer* (2010); Zak's *The Poetics of Rock* (2001); and Théberge's *Any Sound You Can Imagine* (1997).

2 Technology, Collaboration and Creativity

In the previous chapter, a discussion was presented detailing recent developments in recording technologies and the way they have developed hand-in-hand with changing concepts and practices in sound recording. As we have seen, technological developments have not only altered the ways in which music is produced and recorded, but also have impacted fundamentally on the roles played by those working in recording studio, putting producers and engineers at the very centre of the creative process as artistic collaborators with musicians. Technology plays a crucial role in this respect; not only does it enable new forms of musical creativity, but it also facilitates and enables particular modes of creative collaboration. In the recording studio, technology has an intimate relationship with creativity.

The purpose of this chapter is to examine the role of technology in enabling the creative process of music recording. In particular, the issues of creative collaboration and of musical creativity and experimentation are considered in relation to the technologically laden environment of the modern recording studio. The first section of the chapter considers collaborative work in the studio, drawing on Edward Kealy's three "modes" of music production. Specifically, it considers the relationship between different recording technologies and recording aesthetics; and particular dynamics of collaboration between producers, engineers and artists as they play out in the studio. The second part of the chapter then moves on to consider in various ways musical creativity in the studio, including how technology can be used creatively through experimentation; the issue of "learning" how to employ technologies in a creative way; and the impact of time constraints on creativity. In the final section, the chapter discusses mastering as a creative part of the music production process.

2.1 CREATIVE COLLABORATION

> ... given the array of aesthetic sensibilities engaged in the making of a single recording, the creative activity of the recording studio is very much a collective one.
>
> (McIntyre 2012, 150)

Technology, Collaboration and Creativity 33

As Negus and Pickering (2004) assert, creativity is never realised as a creative act until it is achieved within some social encounter. The key social encounter in this respect in the recording studio is the creative collaboration that occurs between a producer and/or engineer and musicians. With this in mind, when considering the impact of recording technologies on creativity in the studio, it is important to consider the ways in which recording technologies affect the social organisation of creative musical processes. Figure 2.1. displays a number of modes of pop music production. The first three of these—"craft-union," "entrepreneurial" and "art," are drawn from Kealy (1990). Each is associated with a particular technology of recording and each has different collaborative dimensions. Kealy argued that while the "craft-union" and "entrepreneurial" modes of collaboration are associated with older recording technologies, a new "art" mode of collaboration has developed since the 1960s and the introduction

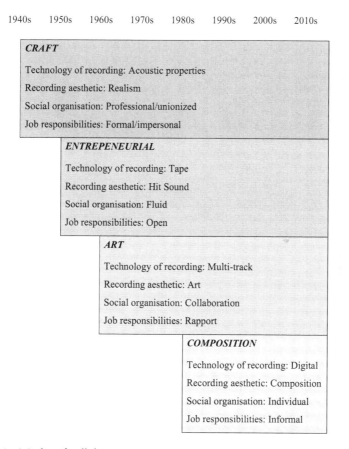

Figure 2.1 Modes of collaboration in pop music production
Adapted from Longhurst 1995, following Kealy 1990

34 *Inside the Studio*

of multi-track recording. This saw the engineer moving into a more collaborative relationship with the artist working in the studio. The desire was to establish a rapport between them that would enable them to express themselves in the resulting music (Longhurst 1995). As noted in the previous chapter, the goal was to produce an artistic statement, often an "experiment in sound," rather than the drive to capture realism or produce a hit record as associated with earlier modes of collaboration. This most collaborative mode of production, in which rapport between producer/engineer is important, represents the way of working in most professional recording studios today.

Zagorski-Thomas notes that, in defining these modes, Kealy was referring primarily to the North American industry, and differences existed in the development of these modes between the U.S. and U.K. He suggests that "the entrepreneurial mode associated with smaller studios developed more quickly and more extensively in the US than the UK where the craft/union mode associated with the large institutional studios held sway for longer" (2012, 66). However, as Longhurst (1995) suggests, while these modes can be seen as developing in a chronological fashion (as is indicated in Figure 2.1), it is important to recognise that one does not necessarily replace another. For example, Longhurst suggests that large studios may still operate in accord with the craft mode of production. Furthermore, the "art" mode of production, which emerged as large recording studios adopted multi-track recording technologies in the 1960s, is now a less common mode of production in large studios, because as recording budgets have fallen, budget-associated time pressures increasingly impact on the ability to be creative (see next section). Some smaller recording studios, which as noted in the previous section tend to have more flexibility regarding recording time, may continue to operate in accord with the art mode of production, although the entrepreneurial mode may be more representative of the way most small studios operate.

It is important to note however that these are idealised modes of production and in reality there is some overlap between them, in particular with regards to the technologies used in production. Depending on the work setting, a producer or engineer may adopt a particular "mode" and approach the collaborative elements of recording in a different way. The creative process can be thought of as operating a sliding-scale of collaboration between the producer/engineer and the musician/recording artist recording in the studio, where true collaboration exists between two extremes. At one end of this scale, the producer or engineer may take a strong directing role over the recording process. One interviewee noted that "some producers and engineers are quite dictatorial in their approach" (Interview 13, male engineer-producer, forties). This, he speculated, was because such producers were getting paid by a record company and so felt a responsibility and pressure to finish the recording project on-time and to deliver a product which met the expectations of the record company:

Technology, Collaboration and Creativity   35

... maybe more successful producers are like that ... they have different pressures because they are paid by the record company to produce this artist, so the record company goes "we want you to do this" and then they are going to have to be more dictatorial possibly.

(Interview 13, male engineer-producer, forties)

As such, often producers are not particularly responsive to the creative input being offered by musicians or recording artists. A second interviewee, a commercially successful record producer, noted the importance of ensuring the quality of the final product above everything else, asserting that he is "just thinking about the final thing. The final two track mix that's all I'm worried about. I don't care what anything else is happening and sometimes you've got to be brutal ... and sometimes people are upset" (Interview 19, male producer, forties). This is demonstrative of the way in which producers (and increasingly engineers) are caught in a tension between the creative inspirations of artists and the commercial aspirations of record companies. But it is also demonstrative of the fact that each person working on a record has a set of creative concerns that are tied to their own reputation and competence (McIntyre 2012); in this case producers are looking to ensure their own success by demonstrating their competence to the record company paying them.

However, another interviewee, also a successful producer, carefully noted that there is little point in being "belligerent" when it comes to a producer attempting to shape and put a stamp on a music product. Rather, he suggests that it is very important for a producer and engineer to understand what a client wants to get from the recording project and "adapt their ears" accordingly. This is the other end of the scale, where a producer or engineer will take a back seat and let the musicians and artists direct the creative process and have the final say in the style and sound of the recorded product. As Leyshon (2009) outlines, this type of "service ethic" in the studio sector, wherein the client's needs are valorised above all others, became apparent as early as the 1970s and corresponded with the rise of independent studios. However, for the most part, the creative process relies on a level of collaboration somewhere between these two ends of a scale, in which both the producer/engineer and the musicians/recording artists work together towards achieving the best outcome. These collaborative experiences involve the open sharing of ideas, from which "the good idea prevails from whoever came up with it" (Interview 13, male engineer-producer, forties) and where neither producer/engineer nor musician/recording artists are offended if their ideas are rejected by the other party.

The importance of this collaboration not only with clients but also between various studio workers in the recording studio was highlighted in an interview with one of the U.K.'s leading record producers in the pop and R&B genres, based in West London. Beginning his career as a session keyboard player, he would go on to produce 14 top-10 U.K. hits. He explained how his ability to produce these styles of music was very much dependent

36   *Inside the Studio*

on working with other skilled people in the studio, describing how "no producer is independent. I am dependent on engineers and DJs and vocal producers." He also went on to explain how his decision to produce using young, talented black DJs gave him an "edge" in terms of music production, especially given that "I do black music and I'm white. It's important that I have a black DJ in the room while I'm doing it." His emphasis on the importance of the relationship between himself and DJs in his production is demonstrative of the fact that, in the recording studio, record producers, sound engineers and other skilled musical professionals are as important in the production of recorded output as are the musicians or recording artists themselves (Pinch and Bijsterveld 2004). The creative input that they offer is central to the continued value of recording studios in a digital age.

To Kealy's original three modes of collaboration, we might add a more recent mode of production, termed here as "composition" (Figure 2.1). This mode is one emerging due to the software-based digital recording and music-based technologies emerging in the 1980s and 1990s, and is based around the individual producer-artist working in a home or project studio. Thus it is a mode of "non-collaboration" rather than collaboration. Whereas in a professional studio, music production has always been a collective project between recording artists, musicians, producers and recording engineers, in small digital home studios, there multiple roles are performed by a single person (see Chapter 8). That a single person could perform all of these roles would have been unthinkable without the enabling power of technology—in particular digital synthesizers, sequencers and drum machines; as Théberge notes, "only with the aid of these technologies was it possible for an individual to perform all the roles necessary to make a successful recording" (1997, 222).

2.2   CREATIVITY AND EXPERIMENTATION THROUGH TECHNOLOGY

In the previous chapter, we saw how in a period of 50 or so years, technologies have changed concepts and practices in recording in dramatic ways. One significant change is the way in which a concern for capturing live music performance as realistically as possible was replaced with a new aesthetic of in-studio *composition*. Perhaps somewhat inevitably, this has given rise to a number of technologically deterministic accounts of the effects of technology on musical practice and performance, which express anxieties over the dissolution of boundaries between human-generated and automated musical expression (Rogers 2003). One such account is Attali's *Noise: The Political Economy of Music* (1985), in which he suggests that the technical process of recording had wrung the passion from performance due to the ability to record multiple tracks and to edit performances after the event. Théberge's (1989, 1997) accounts of the "rationalisation" of recording, as described in the previous chapter, is similarly pessimistic regarding the role of technology in recording, as is Goodwin's (1988) account of sampling. Such accounts are typical of

Technology, Collaboration and Creativity 37

arguments that technologies will "inevitably have negative effects, leading to the decline of musicianship, the end of true musical creativity and the development of a kind of 'programmed' music" (Longhurst 1995, 84).

However, such accounts are partial and limited in their understanding of the role of technology in the recording studio. First, they fail to recognise how technologies can have different effects in different social situations; for example their role in enabling particular forms of creative collaboration between artists, producers and engineers, as is evident in the "art" mode of production identified by Kealy (1990). Second, as Tankel (1990) argues, they fail to appreciate the aesthetic potential of the recording technology itself. Third, they fail to consider the *musicianship* and instrument skills of digital music producers, failing to recognise the many parallels with the musical skills associated with more traditional instruments (see Box 2.1), the loss of which they bemoan.

Box 2.1 Sampling as musicianship

In the face of pessimistic accounts of musical production concerned with the difficulty in distinguishing human from machine-generated music, Rodgers (2003) provides a passionate and informed defence of sampling as a creative process. Sampling is a process that involves the recording and/or selection of sound pieces or "aural fragments," and their editing and processing, to be incorporated into a larger musical work. Using a MIDI sequencer, samples can be arranged with other audio components to complete a track.

Countering technologically deterministic accounts of digital music production that bemoan the loss of musicianship and skills with traditional instrument, Rodgers argues that there is a need for a greater understanding of the musical attributes samplers and other digital instruments, which can be considered as a new "family" of instruments with a particular set of musical possibilities to be learned and explored. Thus, Rodgers uses the terms "electronic musician," "producer" and "samplist" interchangeably. Rogers is critical of Sanjek's (2001) account of sampling, which suggests that digital music machines are "tools" and that if one can use a computer one can compose music. Rather, Rodgers asserts digital music machines as *instruments* that are learned, played and which involve performance gestures as with any other instrument:

> Like the practice of learning and playing almost any musical instrument, sampling is a laborious, and eventually habitual, embodied physical routine . . . performance gestures on digital instruments (pressing a button or turning a knob) are not a prescribed, fixed routine, but are instead a site of continual negotiation among users, and ultimately, a measure of one's connoisseurship of and intimacy with the instrument.
>
> (2003, 315)

Sampling is then, for Rodgers, a creative musical endeavour and as such is a process that resonates with various forms of non-digital music-making.

Source: Rodgers (2003)

38   *Inside the Studio*

As Warner argues, the availability of new technologies mediates creative actions and offers the potential for high levels of innovation and creativity[1], meaning that "since so much is possible with digital editing systems, it is the creative imagination of the pop musician that becomes the determining factor in pop music production, rather than any physical limitations" (2003, 21). When asked about using technologies creatively in the studio, interviewees spoke about the importance of not working to "narrow formulas" and instead *experimenting* whilst in the studio; as Zak notes, "there are standard practices, to be sure, but there are also innumerable techniques developed through creative experimentation or out of the need to meet the demands of a specific situation" (2001, 119). Such experimentation may range from quite subtle changes in microphoning technique (an aesthetic decision in itself) to changes to parameters of the sound being recorded, to more technically complex forms of experimentation. Digital recording technologies in particular play a crucial enabling role with regards to experimentation, due to the way in which engineers now work with flexible recording platforms that enable them to move sounds backwards and forwards, change the EQ and tempo, and alter the intensity of the performance.

Given its concern with non-human actors, Actor Network Theory provides a useful framework for thinking about the enabling role played by technologies in the process of creating and recording music in the recording studio. In simple terms, one can think of musical creativity as a process involving relations between human actors (producers, engineers, musicians) and non-human actors (instruments, recording technologies), with these non-human actors playing a crucial role in enabling role in human action. As Tjora (2009) notes, a human composer's work with a technical artefact produces results, with different users producing different results with the same pieces of equipment. Thus with different "palates" of technologies found in different recording studios (Leyshon 2009), the various pieces of recording equipment are used and employed by individual engineers and producers in specific ways and in different contexts, resulting in a very wide variety of different sounds. Following Felix Guattari, we can think of the artistic practices performed by engineers and producers through the use of technologies as "machinic performances" with technologies "shifting-out" functions from the bodily to the mechanical domain (Latour 1992). Technology mediates ideas and enables particular forms of musical production. However, it is not just the intended outcomes of these interactions that are important; very often human-technology interactions result in unintended outcomes that in themselves are an important part of musical creativity and production. As such, rather than being simply technological resources, these technologies and their various capabilities "intervene actively to push action in unexpected directions" (Callon and Law 1997, 178). The other key non-human element in this respect is the acoustic space of the studio, which will be discussed in more detail in Chapter 4.

The above discussion withstanding, a high degree of experimentation during recording sessions is not always considered to be beneficial to the final product. The expectation of an outcome that will satisfy commercial aspirations, for example, puts a pressure on producers that can affect creative decisions in the studio and their attitude towards experimentation. As Zak notes, "producers must strike a balance between unpredictability, which may yield something extraordinary, and control, which keeps the project focused and on budget" (2001, 134). Furthermore, a discussion with one particular interviewee was revealing of the "technological fetishism" that is being driven by the use of computer and digital effects (Gibson 2005), with the interviewee noting with regards to experimentation with new recording techniques and equipment that "guys get totally bogged down about that type of thing, but at the end of the day they can't produce a good sounding track" (Interview 9, male producer-engineer, thirties). He goes on to say that his "theory has just been 'know what you have, know how to use it, make sure it sounds good.'"

"Learning" to be Creative with Technology

The seemingly simple matter of "knowing how to use it" raised in the above quote is revealed as being actually very complex if one thinks about the issue of *learning* about technologies and how to employ them. Since the work of recording engineers involves both technological and aesthetic decision-making, their knowledge, skills and learning must go beyond technological know-how. It must go beyond crucial skills that can be codified into certificates—to a level of understanding of technologies that enables them to employ them in very creative ways. It involves skills that, rather than being objectivised in formal degrees, are linked to experience in the workplace (see Grabher 2001a, 2001b). Engineers are not only required to know how to operate technically complex equipment, but also to have the tacit knowledge and craft skills, that is to say an "experiential and intimate understanding" of how technologies implicate the final product (Beer 2013, 7). Their learning then, necessarily involves not only the development of the type of technical knowledge that can be codified into manuals; it also involves the development of tacit knowledge. Zak describes this as "experienced technique'," noting that "recording does not simply capture sound, it transforms it and in the transformation lies an array of decisions informed by artistic intuition as well as experienced technique" (2001; no pagination). This is the type of knowledge that can only be gained through observation, demonstration, practice and experience and which "can only be produced in practice" (Maskell and Malmberg 1999, 172). Such skills are indispensable to artistic creativity within the studio. As Horning notes:

> Although the recording engineer's dilemma has changed over time, from limited control over the behaviour of sound to perhaps too many options for manipulating it, the need for tacit knowledge has not

40 *Inside the Studio*

diminished, even in the technologically sophisticated recording studio. Despite the ever changing technological landscape of the recording studio, the growth of formal training in engineering, and continued evolution of technology individual skill and artistry in recording engineering continue to be valued as the technology and practice of recording continually shapes, and is shaped by, the musical landscape.

(2004, 725–726)

Perhaps the most obvious example is the selection and placement of microphones in the recording studio based on the instrument or voice to be recorded, which is a skill that can only be acquired through practice and trial and error (a discussion of which is provided in Chapter 4). Thus the way in which engineers practice their technical skills involves elements of aesthetic decision-making (Kealy 1990). However, Gibson argues that the digitisation of studios and the ability to manipulate digitally sound waves changed the kinds of skills required from engineers so that "long years of experience in certain acoustic spaces, and with different kinds of microphones, became less important to being able to tweak a sound recording within a software programme" (2005, 198). This is certainly true to a degree, but the development of tacit knowledge also extends to a range of other technologies beyond microphones, including digital technologies and software. As Beer argues, having an experiential and intimate understanding of technologies means that the full possibilities of using the technologies can be explored. Going beyond textbook knowledge to develop an "under the bonnet" knowledge of various technologies means that they can not only be used but also misused. Such a "creative appreciation of the technology being used" (Beer 2013, 8) adds another level of creativity to the work of engineers through experimentation and stretching the capacities and boundaries of the technologies.

Given the above, and the constant development of new technologies and associated techniques, for recording, editing and mastering music, continuous learning becomes a crucial part of developing the "craft" of production and engineering:

> Every time the software gets updated there are new sets of stuff to work. It gets more and more advanced and has more different features and different things you can do, so there's all those sort of things to learn. And then when it comes to mixing and things like that there's all sorts of techniques to learn as well as you're going along really. It's just developing your own craft I suppose.
>
> (Interview 14, male engineer, thirties)

Self-learning is an important part of this continuous learning process. One way this is achieved is through the reading of "how to" books, websites, trade journals and magazines targeted at recording and mastering engineers. One interviewee for example described how "I get magazines like this mastering magazine, which a lot of people around here have scoffed at, but I think you can see what's going on out there in the world of computers and plug-ins and what people are up to. I think that's very important" (Interview 6, male mastering engineer, fifties). Another described how learning through self-learning can lead to new technical skills:

> What you've got to do is you've got to want to keep learning and you've got to assume that you don't know everything. And you can read through a book or something and come away and go "yeah, yeah I pretty much know that." But then you could also read something and go "do you know what I never thought of doing it like that." And then you come in and you give it a go. . . . And then at some point a job will come in and you go [clicks fingers] "I'll try that" . . .
> (Interview 3, male mastering engineer, fifties)

Furthermore, recent years have also seen the rise in popularity of internet forums that allow for an exchange of information between engineers that is not limited by geographical space. The internet forum "Gearslutz" (http//www.gearslutz.com, accessed 24/06/11), for example, has over 133,000 registered users who have made over five million posts relating to new technical equipment and recording and editing techniques. The site also has question and answer forums with "expert" engineers, as well as a producer and engineer "self-help" forum for non-technical issues. Virtual networks such as this provide participants with electronic anonymity and a discussion forum where people can connect, share information, discuss experiences and express grievances (see Saundry et al. 2007; Antcliff et al. 2007).

In addition to the above, the availability of music recording and editing software that runs on home computers has enabled studio engineers to learn and experiment with recording and editing sounds outside of the studio environment, without the need for expensive equipment and not subject to the time constraints of a the formal studio environment (see Chapter 8). For Gibson these methods of self-learning have "democratized technology and made sound engineering a hobby" and allowed engineers to "experiment with various effects, piles of instruments, samplers, pedals and mixing equipment, whether in a home or commercial studio" (2005, 199). A number of more established engineers and producers noted that young highly skilled freelance engineers coming into studios brought with them new ideas, skills and techniques. One producer noted how for his recording projects he used "these young programmers and they blow me away," going on to say that because of what he is able to learn from them "I haven't picked up a manual and learnt how something new works for years" (Interview 4, male producer, forties). Another interviewee noted that young engineers experimenting in their own home set-ups were able

42 *Inside the Studio*

to bring some of the techniques they had learned in the studio environment to the benefit of recording projects.

However, despite the importance of self-learning, it has clear limits in terms of the type of knowledge that can be gained. While self-learning from magazines, books, websites and experimentation offers codified knowledge that can lead to the development of new technical skills, it enables engineers and producers to learn little about other more tacit skills that they are required to have. It became clear in the discussions with the interviewees that learning that is gained through experience whilst working on recording projects is the most valuable form of learning, and, in particular, collaborative work in the studio is seen to be particularly valuable due to the way in which it enables engineers to pick up a much wider set of skills and knowledge than technical skills alone:

> . . . you learn a lot from other engineers and other musicians. You don't even realise you're learning and it's hard to define what you learn exactly. It's just the experience of working with musicians and experience of the process really . . . and how things can go wrong, how things can go right, the mood changes, the vibe . . . things that are very difficult to define really.
>
> (Interview 1, male engineer-producer, thirties)

A number of interviewees spoke about the importance of collaborative learning in developing their own skill set. One interviewee noted that there is "always something to be learned from other people, you can always incorporate other people's influences into what you do and, even musically or technically, and it just enhances you and adds to your skills" (Interview 1, male engineer-producer, thirties), while another also described the importance of collaborative learning to personal development:

> . . . it's massively important because otherwise you become really boring and stale and you do the same things all the time . . . lots of producers over the years, they've obviously recorded in hundreds of different studios and they've used loads of different engineers, and they tend to take little engineering ideas that these guys come up with they've used for years and years and years. . . . So you pick and choose the best bits and you kind of add it to your little arsenal of tools . . .
>
> (Interview 15, male engineer, thirties)

Creativity and the Issue of Time Constraints

One of the major constraints on the ability of musicians, recording artists, producers and engineers to be creative and experiment in the studio are the time constraints associated with limited budgets and the high cost of time in the studio. As Gunderson argues, experimentation in the studio is only

Technology, Collaboration and Creativity   43

an option for those artists who can afford to pay for the associated studio time, and as a result most artists treat the recording environment "more as a mimetic recording instrument, as a means of capturing a live musical performance or at least the semblance of a live musical performance, than as a musical instrument in its own right" (2004; no pagination). A number of interviewees suggested that there was very often a need to work expediently and that this was often frustrating in the sense that they could often not be as creative as they would like and deliver the standard of product that they would wish to. More specifically it limits the ability of producers, engineers and their clients to experiment with sounds, performances and new items of studio equipment. One interviewee noted how time constraints make recording:

> . . . challenging in the sense that I very rarely work on projects where I've got enough time to sit there and say let's try it this way and if it doesn't work let's try it another way. It is really a case of going minimal risk unfortunately . . . So I think that it is challenging in the sense that you've got to make the right decision pretty much straight away and it's unrewarding in the sense that you don't often get to experiment as much as you would like to.
>
> (Interview 10, male engineer, thirties)

Another interviewee noted how "we don't really have time for trying stuff out really. So what you end up doing is using stuff you know works and you're in control of" (Interview 12, male engineer-producer, forties). This particular interviewee, an engineer-producer working at one of London's leading recording studios, also noted that the premium rate charged for time in the studio worked against them in this respect and time constraints resulted in the need to work very expediently. This particular engineer speculated that he may be able to do a better job in a smaller studio with lower costs and less constraints in terms of time. This was supported by another interviewee who noted that the big budgets spent on large studio facilities do not "necessarily guarantee a great result because people are working under pressure . . . in many situations I thought the result was not as good as it could have been . . . sometimes the creativity can suffer when you work under those sorts of conditions" (Interview 13, male engineer-producer, forties).

While in many studios, studio time is strictly controlled and determined by a particular budget, a number of interviewees who operated their own studio noted that they could often be more flexible with regards to the studio time for particular recording projects. Here the creative experience and the quality of the final recorded product were often prioritised above financial issues, with some studio owners often reducing rates and even working on non-charged time when projects over-run but budgets are exhausted.

44 *Inside the Studio*

2.3 MASTERING—A CREATIVE PROCESS

The process of mastering is a part of the process of music production that is in some ways removed from the creative process which precedes it, usually being undertaken in different studios, or at least in a different room within a studio, to the recording and mixing stages, and by a mastering engineer who is removed from the stage at which the music was created, performed and recorded. This slightly removed position was considered by one interviewee crucial to performing the mastering process:

> . . . why can't the recording studio make it sound mastered? Why is there a need for mastering? I think most mastering engineers' answers revolved around equipment, the room and all that, which of course is very important, but I think more important is that you give the music to someone who hasn't heard it before, hasn't had to obsess over a snare drum for three days. I'm not involved in any of that. And I think to me that's the most valuable thing about mastering. And you do need a great room and great monitoring and all that, as a kind of foundation for it, but to me a lot more of it is more the kind of psychological, human aspect of having someone who's not connected with the recording to come at it as a fresh project without the baggage, and make it sound exciting and coherent in that way.
>
> (Interview 7, male mastering engineer, thirties)

Originally, mastering engineers were essentially transfer engineers, transferring recordings from tape to vinyl. Although this was a particular skill given the characteristics and limitations of vinyl as a physical format for music, mastering engineering was seen as a technical exercise and not as a part of the creative process. Subsequent developments in CDs, followed by other digital music formats, have removed some of the specialised and more tacit skills involved in transferring music between formats; however, along with technological developments in mastering equipment, they have led to an increase in the level of artistic input that a mastering engineer can bring to a recording project. In particular, modern signal processing techniques such as equalisation and dynamic range expansion and compression allow the mastering engineer to alter the dynamic range of a recording through, for example, making certain parts of a recording louder or quieter or emphasising the natural dynamics of particular instruments in the mix. As one mastering engineer noted, "you've got the scope to be really quite creative with the sound" (Interview 7, mastering engineer, forties). Moreover, as noted in the previous chapter, the introduction of "stem-mastering" is blurring the line between the mix engineer and mastering engineer. Thus now, particular mastering engineers are sought after because of their creative abilities. Mirroring the increased importance of the role of many studio engineers in the creative process of music production, the role of the

Technology, Collaboration and Creativity   45

mastering engineer has evolved to involve a higher level of creative input and importance:

> . . . they are relying on you, because of your skill set, to draw those extra little bits out of what is, really, a finished recording. But yeah, you can be quite artistic, you can come up with ideas, and small changes in mastering can make a big difference to the final product, and final listening experience . . .
>
> (Interview 18, male mastering engineer, fifties)

The "big difference" that mastering engineers can make to the final listening experience is perhaps best demonstrated through the recent "loudness war"—a term given to the apparent competition to master and release recordings with increasing loudness that gained pace through the 1990s and 2000s. The modern signal processing techniques previously mentioned such as compression and equalisation have allowed mastering engineers to increase the loudness of music beyond the defined maximum peak amplitude of a physical or digital format so that the sound more frequently peaks at the maximum amplitude. When the music is listened to, it sounds louder than music that is not processed in this way, and as record companies became of aware of this, pressure was placed on mastering engineers to make recordings as loud as possible. However, this signal processing sacrifices sound quality for increased loudness, often resulting in distortion of the sound, creates music with a small dynamic range (little difference between loud and quiet sections) and can reduce the natural dynamics of other instruments within the recording. There is an irony here then that a set of techniques that have made the mastering engineering a key part of the music production change are also techniques which limit the ability of the mastering engineer to be "creative" in their role.

2.4   CONCLUSION

This chapter has considered creativity and collaboration in the recording studio. In particular, it has considered the relationship between technology and creativity in two key dimensions. First, it has considered how the impact of technology in terms of changing recording practices has fostered and enabled particular "modes" of music production and, associated with this, particular forms of collaboration (or non-collaboration). Second, it has considered technology, and in particular digital music-making technologies, as a key enabler of music creativity. As part of this discussion, attention has been given to the musicianship and learning involved in this creativity. As is suggested through this discussion, the technologies found in any given studio are key determinants that can at any one time allow and/or constrain creativity. However, the technological limitations of the studio are of course

46 *Inside the Studio*

not the only determinants or conditions that impact on creativity. The time constraints associated with limited studio budgets, for example, have been briefly discussed. As we have also seen, the various (and sometimes conflicting) imperatives of those involved in the recording studio—especially the record company, the producer and the recording artists—will impact on the dynamics and outcomes of creative collaboration.

The importance of collaboration to musical creativity has been recognised in this chapter, and some of its characteristics sketched out. However, the interpersonal dynamics of creative collaboration in the recording studio, and how these are managed by the producer or engineer, warrant a more detailed examination. As McIntyre notes, the skills they require in this regard include "degrees of tact and diplomacy so that they can establish a firm rapport with all the people involved, maintain some empathy with the performers and help to interpret and realize the creative vision of the project" (2012, 154). The following chapter considers these "people skills" through an examination of the *emotional labour* performed by producers and recording engineers. In particular it considers the role of emotional labour in the active development of personal relationships of trust with their clients; in obviating interpersonal problems and dealing with client behaviours; and in eliciting emotional performances in the recording studio.

NOTE

1. Such technologies offer the potential for high levels of creativity; however, it is important to note that creativity can also occur when only very limited technology is available, where creativity involves coming up with new solutions or overcoming technical barriers.

3 Emotional Labour and Musical Performance

The discussion presented in the previous chapter highlighted the ways in which the technical and creative talent of producers and engineers is crucial to the performance of the recording studios. However, to focus purely on the production and engineering roles as technologically based risks marginalising a key aspect of studio work, namely the *emotional support and encouragement* required to facilitate the creative process (Leyshon 2009). This chapter examines the emotional labour performed by producers and engineers. In doing so, it shifts the focus of the discussion from the ways in which engineers and producers engineer performances "technically" to the ways in which they engineer performances in a "performative" sense; or to put this another way, the ability to elicit a performance from a musician that is full of "authentic" emotion (Meier 2011). Spaces of musical performance, such as recording studios, are particularly revealing for research into emotions given that they are spaces in which emotions are "routinely heightened" (Anderson and Smith 2001) and where "the emotional content of human relations is deliberately laid bare" (Wood and Smith 2004, 535).

The chapter begins by outlining the emergence of the concept of emotional labour in the early 1980s and its subsequent development in the academic literature. It then outlines the various aspects of emotional labour performed in the studio. First, it sets emotional labour within the context of the recording studio as a space of performance and the role of the producer in feeding energy to the performance. Second, it considers how producers and engineers perform emotional labour as part of "performative engineering" involving the elicitation of emotional musical performances. Third, the chapter considers the way in which producers and engineers actively look to develop personal relationships of trust with musicians recording in the studio. Finally, it examines the role of emotional labour in obviating interpersonal problems and dealing with extreme behaviours.

3.1 EMOTIONAL LABOUR

The Managed Heart (Hochschild 1983) first introduced the concept of emotional labour. Hochschild argued that the development of the service sector had made a new kind of labour prominent in Western society. The flight

48   *Inside the Studio*

attendants and bill collectors that she interviewed were exchanging what was once a private part of their selves for a wage. Their emotions and feelings had become organisational commodities. Emotional labour is defined by Hochschild as:

> . . . the management of feeling to create a publicly observable facial and bodily display; emotional labour is sold for a wage and therefore has *exchange-value*. . . . This labour requires one to induce or suppress feeling in order to sustain the outward countenance that produces the proper state of mind in others.
>
> (1983, 7; emphasis in original)

Hochschild's conceptualisation of emotional labour recognises the importance of regulating emotions in accordance with "situational dictates" (Kruml and Geddes 2000,11) or what she termed "feeling rules" (Hochschild 1979), an extension of Ekman's (1973) display rules. Most of us know which emotions are appropriate at a given time due to social norms. We learn this complex system or "rule book" of emotion regulation from a young age and through parental guidance. In a Durkeheimian sense, the ability to regulate our emotions facilitates social cohesion (Thoits 1985). Emotional labour, then, requires an implicit knowledge of social norms, but in an organisational context these must be further combined with display (Ekman 1973) and feeling rules (Hochschild 1979). However, emotional labour is not only about the inducement or suppression of one's own emotions but also the ability to "produce the proper state of mind in others" (Hochschild 1983, 7). In other words, the ability to elicit appropriate emotional responses from others requires a performance in which your own emotions are managed. Ashforth and Humphrey (1993) argue that emotional labour is particularly relevant to service encounters, as, given the uncertainty created by customer participation in the service, such encounters often have a dynamic and emergent effect.

Korczynski's (2003, 2009) distinction between empathetic and antipathetic emotion management (often emotional labour where performed for a wage) appreciates the complexity of these performances. Korczynski classifies empathetic emotional labour as that which is intended to produce a positive emotional state in others, such as the sense of happiness, safety or care that may be associated with the work of nurses or cabin crew. By contrast, antipathetic emotional labour, which is considerably less well understood arguably due to a lack of empirical focus (Ward and McMurray 2011), is intended to produce a negative emotional state in others, as in the fear and insecurity potentially employed by debt collectors, or prison guards. However, emotional neutrality, Ward and McMurray (2011) suggest, disrupts the empathetic-antipathetic, or positive-negative dichotomy. Defined as a "technique used to suppress emotions felt whilst displaying unemotional behaviour, wherein the suppression of the emotion is the performance itself" (ibid., 1585), emotional neutrality speaks of the unspoken, and often unheard, relational-based elements of what are commonly seen as task-based (Hewitt 2006) or "technical" (Horning 2004) job roles.

Since its introduction emotional labour has been the focus of much empirical work in a number of academic disciplines including psychology, sociology, social-psychology, geography, organisational behaviour and nursing. In particular, literature has revealed the centrality of emotional labour to particular service occupations, including, for example flight attendants (Taylor and Tyler 2000; Williams 2003); nurses (James 1989; Bolton 2000, 2005; Dyer et al. 2008; Major 2008; Batnitzky and McDowell 2011); beauty therapists (Sharma and Black 2001); paralegals (Lively 2002); call-centre operators (Taylor 1998; Shuler and Sypher 2000); adventure guides (Sharpe 2005); Disneyland employees (Van Maanen 1991); domestic workers (Huang and Yeoh 2007); bill collectors (Sutton 1991); and restaurant workers (Crang 1994). However, little has been written about the emotional labour of those working in the music industry or the creative industries more widely. One major exception to this is an emerging literature on the emotional and bodily performances of musicians and audiences (see for example Holman Jones [1999] on women's music; Morton [2005] on Irish traditional music; and Duffy et al. [2011] on festival spaces). Given the emotional nature of musical production and performance, as emphasised in this literature, it is perhaps surprising that the lens of emotional labour has not be turned onto those working in recording studios.

3.2 CREATING AN ATMOSPHERE AND FEEDING ENERGY TO THE PERFORMANCE

In order to fully understand the kinds of emotional labour that occur in recording studios, it is necessary to understand recording studios as *performative* spaces. Music performance in the recording studio clearly takes place in a very particular physical setting; as described in Chapter 4, as a physical acoustic and technological space, the materiality of the studio is a central element in the "sound" of the music being produced. This materiality is also central to performance, because as Wood et al. argue, "what can be worked through, practised, performed is shaped in important ways by the materiality of musical spaces" (2007, 870). However, it is also important to recognise the studio as a relational space. It is not only a physical setting, but also a social setting which determines the meanings being generated by the performance. The recording studio is a space of *musicking* (Small 1998) in which the intimate, emotional quality of human relations is laid bare (see Wood and Smith 2004). In this sense, the atmosphere and ambience that producers and engineers work to create is important, because performing under certain circumstances generates different emotions and different meanings from performing them under others (Small 1998). One example of how the atmosphere and ambience in the studio influences the emotions of individuals and the "mood" of the music can be found in the case of the Talk Talk album *Laughing Stock* (Box 3.1).

50 *Inside the Studio*

Box 3.1   Studio atmosphere: Recording Talk Talk's *Laughing Stock*

The recording of Talk Talk's fifth studio album *Laughing Stock* has acquired an almost legendary status in popular music folklore. The recording sessions, which took place over the space of an entire year, were marked by high levels of musical experimentation and perfectionism, resulting in very demanding recording sessions and a series of personal tensions between musicians. Efforts were made to create an atmosphere in the studio sympathetic with the feel of the album: windows were blacked out, clocks removed and light sources limited to oil projectors and strobe lights. These dark, uneasy and technically testing sessions would not only have emotional impacts on the musicians and their performances, but also on studio engineer Phill Brown:

> Tim and Mark now required a calm, uninterrupted atmosphere conducive to intense concentration . . . although the daily work was not difficult to handle the combination of sitting in the dark in front of a desk full of red LEDs with the oil projector turning round at half a revolution per minute began to affect my state of mind. Added to this, there were many days when we took a section of a song that lasted for just a few seconds and played it repeatedly for many hours. I find it very difficult to describe the "space" that we all travelled to during the making of this album. The combination of continuous darkness, the oil projector (which made everything I looked at appear to move) and the process of listening to the same six songs over and over again, put me in a very dark emotional state. I think Tim and Mark were there too, but each to a different degree. The result was less and less communication, and the three of us often went for hours without talking or looking each other in the eye.

Source: Brown (2010, 296–298)

Nervousness, tension and a lack of confidence in musicians and recording artists when faced with recording in a formal studio space can often be prohibitive to artists producing a desired performance or a "good take." Getting a performance from a musician is often not about "forcing" a performance by putting people under pressure; rather, it is about creating a relaxed atmosphere and teasing out a performance, often by being relaxed and easy-going and putting tense and nervous musicians at ease:

> A lot of people go "oh fucking hell, I'm in a studio" and so . . . as a producer you have got to be supportive, you have got to see them through it. Just kind of hold their hand through it sometimes really and just be there for them. And they appreciate that. At the end of the day they come away feeling good about the session.
>
> (Interview 13, male engineer-producer, forties)

Emotional Labour and Musical Performance 51

Sometimes once that red light goes on people do tend to tense up a bit so getting the best performance isn't about going out there and throwing tea cups at the wall like Alex Ferguson. . . . You've really got to the get the atmosphere right and get everybody relaxed . . . sometimes it happens and sometimes it doesn't.

(Interview 19, male producer, forties)

An open, relaxed atmosphere which encourages emotional expression through performance will come from projecting a relaxed and friendly disposition, which might often contradict the personal feelings of a producer or engineer. Emotional performance is then a key part in creating a particular atmosphere in the recording studio

Performing in a recording studio is very different from performing in other settings, for example in front of a live audience, and this generates different meanings from a performance. In a live setting, the audience are active participants in the musical performance, feeding energy (or failing to feed energy) back to the performers as the performance takes place (Small 1998). Often, live performance involves spontaneous and experimental elements which the audience respond to; see for example Gibson (1999) on rave music; Cooper (2004) on Jamaican dancehall culture; and Fraser and Ettlinger (2008) on drum and bass music. Performances in the studio are also of course to an extent "live," in the sense that they involve spontaneity and speculation, improvisation and mistakes that that only happen as they are being played in the "now" of the performance (Morton 2005). Producers and engineers look to capture a "definitive" version of these performances "on record."

However, unlike in truly live performance settings, studio performances occur without an audience present. Because there is no audience to feed energy to the performer, while they may produce a proficient and "clean" performance in the studio, their dynamic stage presence is not reproduced on studio recordings. In the studio, the producer or engineer becomes the audience. The emotional labour performed by producers and engineers is important in this respect. In giving feedback on a performance, as Hennion (1990) describes, the producer will not only draw upon a set technical criteria, but also more importantly upon their feelings about the music and the physical sensations they experience because of it (Box 3.2). They must also feed energy to performers in the absence of an audience, in an attempt to reproduce the dynamic and emotional nature of live performance within the studio.

Box 3.2   The producer as audience

I have always thought the main role of the producer would be the first audience. An audience is a group of people who reacts in a kind of pure way. You go there, you are sitting, and you are waiting. Whatever happens is going to affect you in one way or the other. You know yourself, when you get to

52　*Inside the Studio*

hear the music, you can feel satisfied, or you can feel excited, or you can feel sleepy, or you can feel pissed off, or whatever. The music is going to have an effect on you. . . . Then the question is, "Why?" The audience listener may not have the answer to that question, may not give a shit. I don't know why this went wrong, it just wasn't right. The producer has to not only have that initial feeling—a very open sort of receptiveness. In the midst of all this political mayhem and chaos in a recording studio, it's not easy. After you hear it and feel it, you have got to be able to express it and, then, take it even further: How do we now change it? How do we make it better? Or that was perfect. Identifying first takes that are right is an acquired ability. I am with producers a lot who are not that experienced. They hear something great, and they think they can get it greater. One of the things you have to learn is when it is right you leave it alone.

Source: Producer John Snyder quoted in Jarrett (2012, 139)

3.3　"PERFORMATIVE ENGINEERING": THE ELICITATION OF EMOTIONS IN PERFORMANCE

Being able to capture the dynamic and emotional nature of a "live" performance on record is crucial as listeners who will buy a recording will not be part of a "live" performance; rather because they will use the recordings to create their own event, it becomes necessary for musicians and producers/ engineers to create performances on record that will serve the purposes of these contexts (Small 1998). As producer Frank Filipetti describes:

In the end the performance is the thing. There are very few people who will buy a record because of the sound of it. . . . Ninety-nine percent of the public buys a record because it does something to them, it moves them, there's an emotional impact, it moves their mind, it moves their body, it does something to them.

(quoted in Massey 2000, 198)

Such accounts challenge Attali's (1985) assertion that the process of recording has wrung the passion from performance. For Jarrett, producers work hard to enable and to record sounds that, when listeners hear them, convey the impression of having "escaped the clutches of production and the constraints of recording technologies" (2012, 129). This, he suggests is a "metaphysics of presence," founded on romantic notions of musicianship. Eliciting emotions in performance, and capturing these emotions on record, is then a key aspect of the emotional labour of producers and engineers.

Producers and engineers are privileged to the most intimate moments of emotive performance. For many producers and engineers, despite the technical aspect to their jobs, getting a good performance, in terms of its emotional content, is more important that getting a great "sound" in a technical sense. As Wood et al. (2007) note, musical performances are about intimate encounters with, and the sharing of an emotional experience with, other people involved in the performance. In many instances, songs, and in particular, lyrics, will be loaded with feeling and emotion drawn from particular emotional experiences of musicians and recording artists. For producers and engineers, displaying sensitivity and empathy towards these emotional performances is imperative. This empathetic emotional labour (Korczynski 2003) involves efforts "to understand others, to have empathy with their situation, to feel their feelings as part of one's own" (England and Farkas 1986, 91):

> ... it is a very exposing experience for a lot of artists to come into the studio and say here's a song I've written because they trust you to not turn around and say it's crap, your voice sounds terrible, your lyrics are awful and you've just told me the whole story about your failed love life and I'm going to rip the piss out of you about it.
>
> (Interview 10, engineer-producer male, thirties)

On the other hand, often studio producers and engineers must attempt to elicit strong emotions from the musician or recording artists to capture an emotive performance. Particularly with regards to vocal performances, it is often necessary to get a recording artist into a particular emotional state in order to achieve a "believable" performance (Box 3.3). Getting this performance may involve creating the type of relaxed atmosphere described in the previous section; however at times it might also require a producer or engineer to make a musician uncomfortable, or even to upset them. Parallels can be drawn here with Grindstaff's (2002) and Hesmondhalgh and Baker's (2008) accounts of television workers being required to elicit the strongest possible version of the emotions felt by contestants on confessional talk shows and talent shows respectively. The management of emotional responses is a key part of the work that takes place within these creative industries.

Box 3.3   Eliciting emotions in performance

If I close my eyes, I'm trying to see in my mind if the singer is telling me the same story as he's written down. If you can do that, that's the biggest hurdle to overcome. A vocal can't just lay there in a linear manner; it's got to take you up and down, depending on what the lyrics are trying to say. If it's sad, you want it to bring tears to your eyes, to make you a little misty. If it's "Fuck you," you want to hear the energy and emotion. If you can do that—if you can look at your lyrics and listen to your vocals and say "It's telling the story, and it's taking me on a journey"—then you've accomplished a great performance. If I'm not feeling it from a vocalist, I'll tell them so. I'll get them to draw from within, to tell that story. There has to be emotion behind the words, no matter what you're saying—I think that's the key.

Source: Producer Mike Clint quoted in Massey (2000, 221)

54 *Inside the Studio*

Through such emotive performances, producers and engineers are exposed to the personal emotions of the recording artist, and often brought into their personal lives. Recording producers/engineers are, then, evokers of and witnesses to emotional displays that in most other work-based contexts, and even social contexts, would be considered inappropriate. Telling the confessional tale of a relationship that ended badly to someone whom you have only met that morning, and recounting it in such a way as to evoke their empathy (or in other words to move them) would not be congruent with social norms outside of the recording studio. In this sense, producers and engineers attempt to redefine the display rules (Ekman 1973) and feeling rules (Hochschild 1979) within the studio in a bid to facilitate powerful, emotional performances.

3.4 BUILDING RELATIONSHIPS

In the performance of emotional labour, then, there are interactive effects between the work context and content, and the emotional state of the individual (Ashforth and Humphrey 1993). In the case of studio work, work content refers to the particular music recording project and the genre of music being recorded, while the work context refers to the studio space and the relationships between studio workers and musicians. Following this line of argument, we would expect that the manner in which a studio worker displays feelings to musicians recording in the studio will have a strong impact on the attractiveness of the interpersonal climate within the studio. This type of relational work, involving the management of emotions in order to facilitate the building and maintenance of relationships, and termed as "emotional labour" in academic literature, was to the producers and engineers interviewed understood to involve "people skills." This highlights a particular form of creative labour that emphasises the relational nature of working rather than the task-based aspect of work *per se* (see Steinberg and Figart 1999; Hewitt 2006; Ward and McMurray 2011). Thus, while in defining the term "emotional labour" Hochschild (1983) was considering service work in its widest context, the concept of emotional labour is particularly applicable to work in the recording studio.

In many instances, these people skills were considered to be even more important than the ability to perform competently a technical role and operate complex studio equipment. As one producer-engineer from a major London recording studio described:

> . . . the art of it is really people-based. So getting a good sound and all that stuff, in the end, ends up being five per cent of your job. Ninety five per cent is people. . . . It's probably more people based than it is

Emotional Labour and Musical Performance 55

technical . . . you've obviously got to deliver on the technical but it's not really the essence of the job.
(Interview 12, male producer-engineer, forties)

An essential part of building relationships that allow for creative collaboration in the recording studio is the development of trust. Trust can be understood as an "interpersonal phenomenon" (Ettlinger 2003, 146) and "a sociospatial process enacted by agents through relations" (Murphy 2006, 429), shaped by, amongst other things, knowledge, emotions, reputation and appearance. As Banks et al. (2000) assert new ties of trust, whether they be strong or weak, are an important part of the creative process, leading to collaboration and new cultural products. It is important from the offset that trust is very quickly developed in the relationship between the producer/engineer and the musician or recording artist. More specifically, following Ettlinger (2003, 146) we can identify two types of trust; firstly *emotive trust* "based on one's personal feelings about others," and *capacity trust* "based on one's judgements about another's capacity for competent performance in a workplace." For Ettlinger (2003), capacity trust is often predicated on emotive trust. A critical part of developing emotive trust inside the recording studio is that studio workers very quickly "locate" their musicians in terms of a range of cultural categories (see Crang 1994) and adjust their own performance to suit each situation. This is a process that begins from the moment the producer or engineer meets the musician:

"The moment I meet [a musician] . . . I've got to try and work out, understand them, read all their body signals, read what they're up to, what they're thinking about. . . . From the moment I meet them I'm always having to . . . I'm having to get their trust straight away"
(Interview 2, male studio engineer-producer, thirties)

How engineers and producers communicate a specific social identity can foster feelings that facilitate the emergence of trusting sentiments (Murphy 2006). Given that trust is rooted in experience with an individual (Christopherson 2002), and that the development of trust involves a range of cognitive, emotive and communicative factors (Murphy 2006), engineers and producers have to work actively and energetically to develop and sustain relationships of trust with musicians. This is something Giddens (1994) terms "active trust." As recording projects progress, which may last from a few hours—for example recording a single vocal take, or guitar or drum track—to a number of months in the case of full studio albums being recorded in a single studio, studio engineers and producers look to build productive working relationships with musicians. Where projects are of weeks or months in duration, and in particular where repeat work is involved, it is very typical that producers and engineers will build quite close relationships with particular musicians or recording artists (Box 3.4).

56   Inside the Studio

> ### Box 3.4   The bond between artist and producer
>
> While it's professional, the bond between an artist and their producer is personal and complex, too. A producer can be closer to the artists than anyone else in his life during the weeks or months they spend together making a record. The intimacy they share is largely unspoken; it touches raw nerves, and if the producer is especially good at what he does, helps peel back the anxiety and fear that dwells within every performer. An artist's anxiety and fears are, by the way, very real. They're normal too. Although the best performers make it seems effortless, putting oneself in front of an audience, TV or motion picture camera, or recording studio microphone requires extraordinary confidence. The normal insecurities that most of us experience from time to time are magnified a hundredfold for an artist who is making a record or rehearsing a show, and I've spent countless hours reassuring artists during late-night telephone conversations. . . . But the investment of such intense, heart-to-heart time usually results in a handsome creative payoff.
>
> *Source*: Extract from Ramone and Granata (2007, 16)

3.5   DEALING WITH EMOTIONS AND BEHAVIOURS

Despite the work that producers and engineers do to build close working relationships with musicians, it is inevitable in an enclosed environment such as the recording studio, in which a number of people come together for a very intense period of work, that tensions will at times rise and egos will clash, and occasionally this may result in disputes. Therefore, besides relationship building and the "engineering" of performance, the other major aspect of emotional labour provided by producers and engineers is the management of the different personalities in the studio and often finding solutions to problems or disputes. As producer Walter Afanasieff describes:

> They're very insecure, very gentle creatures these singers. You pretty much have to be their doctor, their spiritual advisor, their psychologist, their bartender. You have to be all of these personalities, and you have to stroke their egos just enough for their security, and you have to be able to solve problems that they're coming up with—even problems that may not truly exist.
>
> (Quoted in Massey 2000, 270)

A potential point of conflict in the studio is when a producer or engineer makes a mistake in performing their technical role. As producer Phil Ramone describes: "Moments like this are terrifying. There's nothing more humbling than having to tell a musician that they've got to do a retake because you (or someone in your crew) were careless" (Ramone and Granata 2007, 26).

Emotional Labour and Musical Performance   57

It is inevitable that mistakes will be made, and that at times this will result in negative reactions from musicians in the studio. Here, emotional labour is important in regulating interaction and obviating interpersonal problems (Ashforth and Humphrey 1993). For producers and engineers this element of emotional labour often involves the regulation of their own emotions in order to deal with other people's feelings (see James 1989). Whatever the emotions felt by the studio worker, they must maintain the correct outward countenance towards the musicians recording in the studio. An important emotional implication of studio work is then the suppression of anger and frustration on the part of the studio worker in the name of good working relations. It is important that the producer or engineer attempts to placate the musician or recording artists and set the mistake within the context of what they are attempting to achieve on the recording project. As one interviewee noted:

> . . . if you're an engineer in a studio and you erase over the wrong performance, you'll know about it very, very quickly. And I'm quite often trying to say to clients, "Actually, we're making music. We're not solving the Middle East peace crisis. We're just trying to make music here."
>
> (Interview 17, male producer-engineer, forties)

The non-reaction to this kind of abuse is a performance of "emotional neutrality," a type of emotional labour often associated with professionalism (Smith and Kleinman 1989). Outside of the space of the recording studio, in which the social norms have been redefined, this kind of behaviour would not be met with calm professionalism. As Grindstaff (2002,132) so eloquently describes, emotional labour involves "either pretending to care . . . or trying not to care too much," even when someone is being abusive towards you as an individual:

> . . . if someone's being a dick you have to let them, if there's time pressures and you've got to get them to do their performance. You've got to get over the fact that they're calling you an arse hole or they're being a pain . . . you still have to do your job in that fixed timescale so you do it.
>
> (Interview 2, male engineer, thirties)

Another potential point of tension and conflict is when a musician or vocalist believes that they are producing a good performance, but the producer believes the performance is not of the required standard. There is an inherent difficultly around critiquing a performance whilst at the same time maintaining the confidence of the performer and avoiding upset:

> We don't test people out before they come in to record so if they're coming in and they're really not able to perform, not able to sing in tune

58   *Inside the Studio*

> . . . probably the most difficult thing is when you've got to get them to perform better.
>
> (Interview 14, male engineer-producer, thirties)

Critiquing performances is particularly difficult for young producers and engineers working with more experienced musicians. As Ashforth and Humphrey (1993) assert, the less status power the service agent has relative to the customer, the greater the conformity will be to certain emotional "display rules," that is to say in these instances a display of pleasure at the performance of the more experienced musician or recording artist, even it is considered not to be a "good" performance. One interviewee, using the example of the former Beatle Paul McCartney, suggested that a failure on behalf of the producer or engineer to offer constructive criticism to such artists can be to the detriment of the final product, saying that "Paul McCartney's very hard to produce . . . he's said it himself that no one tells him that's a shit song because he wrote Hey Jude . . ." (Interview 8, male engineer, twenties). The management of performance may instead at times involve taking a back seat and letting the musicians and artists experiment, until a point that the producer or engineer feels they need to intervene. This is often considered the best strategy to avoid the creation of tension and to let the session progress unhindered.

Often, keeping musicians happy also requires studio workers to have a liberal attitude towards, or at least a tolerance of, the consumption of alcohol and use of illegal drugs inside the space of the studio. The music industry has a reputation for the high level availability and use of illegal drugs, taken to enhance the creativity of talented musical performers (see for example Shapiro 2003; Raeburn et al. 2003; and Miller and Quigley 2011 on substance use among musicians across a range of musical genres; and also Singer and Mirhej 2006, on the role played by illicit drugs in the evolution of jazz music in the U.S.). This popular image is often borne out within the space of the studio; as one producer explained, as he pointed to a table sitting next to a couch on one side of the studio, "I've seen that table covered in coke, do you know what I mean? And . . . there has been so much" (Interview 4, male producer, forties). This prolific link between the music industry and drug and alcohol (ab)use is one that raises some interesting questions for the emotional nature of the work that takes place within the creative space of the recording studio. Tolerance of alcohol and drug use is seen by many producers and engineers to be a necessary part of studio work, and as a way of creating a relaxed atmosphere in the studio.

Yet there are also associated limits to which their use is helpful to the creative process. A recent case in point that of British rock band Kasabian, who in two high profile interviews with British press admitted to high levels of drug use whilst recording, but stated that in future they would ban drugs from the recording studio because of their negative effects on the quality of their music (Box 3.5). One interviewee recalled his experience of working with a famous guitar band in the early 1990s who had spent the majority of the recording

Box 3.5 Kasabian ban drugs in the recording studio

August 2011: British rock group Kasabian, in high profile interviews with Britain's *News of the World* newspaper and *Q Magazine*, stated that the band would be banning drugs from all of their future studio sessions. As recording and mixing of the band's fourth album *Velociraptor!* (at a home studio in Leicester, U.K. and The Glue Factory, San Francisco, respectively) was finishing, the band suggested that there was a notable difference in the quality of the music on *Velociraptor!* when compared with the band's first two albums, *Kasabian* and *Empire*. The recording sessions for these two earlier albums were marked by partying and heavy drugs use. The group associated the psychedelic and electronic sound of these albums with this drug use, but also suggested that the quality of the work had suffered as a consequence. The stance on drugs use taken by the band contrasts strongly with an interview with *Clash Magazine* in September 2006, as the album *Empire* was being released. In this interview, lead singer Tom Meighan proclaimed that "A rock 'n' roll star should have a drug habit at least once in their career, they should have a Rolls Royce, should smash the fucker up, should have a big house, should get off his head and THAT is a rock 'n' roll legacy," a statement that drew heavily on the link in popular imagination between rock music and drugs use.

Sources:
http://www.nme.com/news/kasabian/58894 (accessed 08/02/13)

http://www.contactmusic.com/news/kasabian-ban-drugs-in-the-recording-studio_1225199 (accessed 08/02/13)

http://www.clashmusic.com/feature/kasabian (accessed 12/02/13)

project "getting off their faces . . . taking a lot of drugs where there's serious work to be done" (Interview 16, male engineer-producer, fifties). Another noted from his own experience that "it's just amazing that you can do that many drugs and actually come out with something at the end of it" (Interview 4, male producer, forties). The acceptance of the use of drugs within the space of the recording studio is demonstrative of the way in which the recording studio has its own social rules that are distinct from the world outside it.

As a consequence producers and engineers have become adept at tolerating behaviours and emotions (either positive or negative) of artists when they are under the influence of drugs and alcohol by managing their own emotions. However, there are consequences that can extend beyond managing the performances and behaviour of musicians to have more direct impacts on studio workers; having been in the presence of people using drugs in the studio for a number of years, one interviewee explained how "I didn't participate for most of the time, and then I succumbed for about seven years" (Interview 4, male producer, forties). The experiences of this particular producer are revealing of the potential physical, mental and emotional effects of such an environment on the people that work in them.

60 *Inside the Studio*

3.6 CONCLUSION

As has been demonstrated in this chapter, the recording studio, as with any other space of musical performance, is constituted by a wide range of different emotional relations. As Wood and Smith describe:

> There are, of course, many types of performance event inhabiting, indeed defining, many kinds of performance spaces. The emotional relations which constitute these also come in all shapes and sizes. They include fear, anger, frustration, yearning, hate and hurt; they embrace well-being, contentment, hope and happiness.
>
> (2004, 535)

Musical performance is a setting in which the emotional is routinely heightened (Anderson and Smith 2001), that is to say the emotions associated with performance are often felt very intensely. Recording studios are unique spaces of music performance, in the sense that the emotions of performances and relations are experienced in a very insulated space, often under conditions of intense collaboration. Thus recording studios are more than simply physical and technological spaces for music-making; they are relational and emotional spaces which determine the meanings generated by musical performance.

This chapter has described the emotional and relational work that take place within the space of the recording studio. Testimonies of this private, enclosed and often "secret" world have identified at least some of the approaches and techniques used to evoke powerful, emotional and creative performances. Producers and engineers actively induce or suppress their own emotions in order to manage the emotions of the artists and musicians, using emotional neutrality and empathy to develop trust, tolerate drug and alcohol use, and redefine social norms, feeling and display rules in a way that liberates artists from that which is socially acceptable. The recording studio thus becomes an emotional space, characterised by trust and tolerance, and free of the social and feeling rules that otherwise shape our emotional landscape, which allows musicians to produce a desired emotional musical performance. This space is actively created by producers and engineers, through their performance of emotional labour. The absence of a "live" audience to feed energy to the often spontaneous and speculative musical performances that take place in the studio lends the emotional labour of producers and engineers an added importance in feeding energy to, and providing feedback on, musical performance in the studio.

The various aspects of emotional labour highlighted in this chapter are demonstrative of how technical expertise must increasingly be combined with the skills and musical ambitions of musicians, as well as emotional support and encouragement for the creative process (Leyshon 2009). Engineers and producers "engineer the performance" of musicians in two ways; first,

Emotional Labour and Musical Performance   61

in a *technical* sense as they are required to use their in-depth knowledge of technical equipment to capture sounds, and edit these captured sounds to create a musical recording; second, in the *performative* sense as they encouraging them to expose their emotional selves in intimate moments of musical creativity and to enable them to express themselves in the resulting music. Producers and engineers are then not just "technologists" (Horning 2004) technically recording the performance—they are also "*performatively*" engineering musical performances, providing the emotional support and encouragement required to facilitate the creative process (Leyshon 2009). As such, studio work cannot be conceptualised as solely an economic or technical performance.

4 The Studio Sound-Space

> Next to the artist and the music, the studio is the most prominent star in
> the recording process. It's the engineer's and producer's tool: a powerful
> instrument used to manipulate air, vibrations, and sound.
>
> (Producer Phil Ramone, in Ramone and Granata 2007, 113)

Music performance in the recording studio takes place in a very particular
physical setting. As the above quote highlights, as a physical acoustic and
technological space, the materiality of the studio is clearly very important to
both the ability of the musicians, producers and engineers to make a record
music, and to the "sound" of the music being produced (see also Leyshon
2009). Wood et al. argue that "what can be worked through, practised, performed is shaped in important ways by the materiality of musical spaces"
(2007, 870). For Horning (2012), as the notion of fidelity in live performances gave way to ideas of "studio creations" in the mid-1960s (enabled
by the technologies outlined in the previous chapter) there was a shift in
emphasis from the acoustic space of the recording studio to the control
room. This led to the concept of "studio as instrument" through composition that was introduced in Chapter 1. However, Horning argues that this
was not an entirely new concept, as in studios in the 1940s and 1950s the
acoustic space of the studio was considered to be an important instrument
in its own right.

Thus in thinking through the concept of recording studio as instrument
as it applies to contemporary recording studios, it is important not to focus
simply on the compositional music technologies of the control room, as
highlighted in Chapter 2, but also to consider the physical sound-space of
the studio. It is to this task which this chapter attends. It begins by intro-
ducing some basic principles of the acoustic design of recording studios, in
particular the materiality and size of recording spaces. It then moves on to
consider how the sound-space of the recording studio can on the one hand be
a set of fragmented, isolated audioscapes, and on the other a shared, exciting
and creative soundscape, depending on the approach that is taken to recording. The chapter then considers how the studio sound-space is "coded" by

The Studio Sound-Space   63

producers and engineers to create particular sounds and, in particular, the importance of microphone selection and placement for recording. Finally, the chapter moves beyond spaces of recording to consider the distinctive sound-space of the mastering studio.

4.1 ACOUSTICS OF THE RECORDING STUDIO: SOME BASIC PRINCIPLES

The acoustic design of recording studios is a highly complex matter that involves an intimate knowledge of the physics of sound, how sound behaves in an enclosed space and how various technologies transmit and shape sound. As Moorefield (2010, 23) suggests, "room acoustics are highly complex, as are the many distortions and realignments undergone by the electrical signal that a microphone sends out to a tape machine before it reaches the listener's ear from a loud speaker." At a simple level, a well-designed room produces a balanced blend of high (treble), middle (midrange) and low (bass) frequencies. If there is too much of any one of these frequencies, the resulting recording will be affected: if there is too much high frequency, the recording will sound shrill; too much midrange lends stridency (a nasal sound, like a voice coming through a telephone) to the recording; too much bass makes the lower frequencies sound muddy and undefined (Ramone and Granata 2007). There are two main ways in which the design of the studio can be modified in order to create a set of spaces with the required acoustical properties.

First, the physical dimensions and shape of the room itself can be designed or modified in order to make the room respond to sound in a desired manner, altering the resonances of particular frequencies. Second, the rooms can be "treated" through the use of absorption and diffusion materials on the surfaces of the room, with the surfaces used being key to the balance of frequencies. Acoustical treatments included reflective surfaces and (to give reflection of high and midrange frequencies) absorbent soft surfaces (to absorb low frequencies), moveable panels, drapes and polycyndrical surfaces (Horning 2012). As the physical "space" in each recording studio is different, "the acoustic environment in each studio often develops incrementally and organically in relation to the nature of the materials used in its construction or to subsequent experiments with baffling and other materials introduced to the studio fabric" (Leyshon 2009, 1320). The specific recording configuration of a particular studio will often have been determined based on experimentation, trial and error and innovative thinking (Horning 2004). Furthermore, the studio can be further "tuned" for particular recording sessions, with acoustical treatments adjusted to obtain particular acoustical results (Horning 2012).

It is often the case that in exercising tight control over particular frequencies through room dimensions/shape and through acoustic treatments,

64 *Inside the Studio*

recording studios become a "dead" acoustic space, meaning one in which sound dies out quickly. To address this issue, beginning in the 1950s and 60s, recording studios would begin constructing echo chambers (Simons 2004) which would be one of the more identifiable qualities of a studio (Horning 2012). An echo chamber is an isolated room specifically designed to give a "live" sound to recording, i.e., a concert hall ambience, to a recording. This is achieved by using materials such as concrete, tile or hard plaster to create surface that reflect sound and create reverb.

The size of echo chambers is not particularly important, as the chamber does not need to accommodate performers; rather the multiple sounds from a recording are fed into the chamber (usually via speakers at one end of the room, but sometimes simply through an opening to the recording space), with a microphone picking up the reverberated sound from the room giving the effect of a live performance. In Figure 4.1, for example, as a

Figure 4.1 Recording drums with ambience, Parr Street Studios, Liverpool
Photo courtesy of Tony Draper

The Studio Sound-Space   65

drummer is playing, the reverberated sound of the drum kit is being picked up by a microphone in a stone-lined room immediately behind the drummer. Through adjusting the position of the microphone within the echo chamber relative to the sound source, the sound of the echo chamber could be modified. The fact that these echo chambers were custom-built meant each had a unique sound and so, through their use for sound enhancement on recordings, provided a unique sound on the recordings emanating from each studio (Simons 2004).

As noted, the need for echo chambers in many ways arose from the "dry" sound of recordings that was resulting from main recording rooms in which sound was carefully controlled and in which singers and musicians were isolated in booths. Echo chambers could be used to provide some ambience to the recordings. Prior to the construction of echo chambers (and in studios too small to allow for the construction of a chamber) sound engineers had to find innovative ways of getting a "live" sound, often using stairwells, corridors or tiled bathrooms for recording (see Horning 2012)—spaces where there was a natural reverberation.

Today, the relatively expensive and time-consuming construction of live echo chambers is largely considered unnecessary as reverb can be created through the use of digital reverb effects. This means that even in very small recording studios, engineers can achieve similar "live" sounds (Simons 2004). Indeed, it could be more generally argued that the development of new digital sound processors and effects units, combined with small isolation chambers that completely isolate sound, have significantly reduced the importance of properly acoustically treated rooms, allowing even very small studios to achieve the types of sounds only previously achievable in large studios.

However, although to some degree most modern recording of music can be undertaken in a small project studio, the physical size of the acoustic space continues to determine the types of recording projects for which a studio is suitable. While project studios may be able to accommodate the recording of vocals and individual small instruments, larger studio rooms are required to record drums, given that they require space and/or specialist sound isolation when being recorded (although electronic or sampled drums in some instances remove this need). Similarly, recording an electric guitar through an electric amplifier requires isolation due to the volume of the sound produced (although amplifier simulation is possible using processors or software-based guitar amp simulators). Furthermore, as we shall see in the following section, "live" recording involving rhythm sections (drums, bass guitar, rhythm guitar) or even entire bands remain important in particular genres, and large live rooms are required to accommodate this. As one interviewee explained:

> If you're recording a band you need an environment that is acoustically treated because bands make a lot of noise. You need a big enough space

to record drums and a big enough space where you're going to have a few variations and options of different guitar amplifiers and bass amplifiers and stuff like that.

(Interview 10, male engineer, thirties)

Thus, although the rise of multi-track technologies has resulted in a trend away from large, live rooms (and the subsequent closure of many studios) many recording studios with sizeable live rooms continue to exist.

For larger groups of musicians, in particular orchestras, very large rooms are required. Although many of the largest studios have now closed, a few such rooms do still exist, especially to provide the large spaces required for the recording of orchestral music for film soundtracks and television. In New York, Right Track on 38th Street has a 4,600-square-foot[1] orchestral studio (Simons 2004). In London, Abbey Road's Studio One has a floor area of 4,908 square feet and Studio Two 2,131 square feet; while AIR Studio's Lyndhurst Hall (Figure 4.2) provides 3,229 square feet for orchestral recording sessions. In Los Angeles, Capitol Studios' largest recording space, Studio A, has more than 1,500 square feet of floor space. Acoustic design remains highly important in these spaces, with the aim of giving a "concert-hall"

Figure 4.2 Lyndhurst Hall, AIR Recording Studios, London
Source: Author

The Studio Sound-Space   67

ambiance to recordings; AIR Studio's Lyndhurst Hall, for example, is a converted Church and has attendant acoustic properties.

As with other studios, technology continues to challenge their viability, in particular mobile recording equipment allowing recordings "on location" in spaces such as churches at a fraction of the cost of hiring a major studio. However, as such spaces are not acoustically treated and "sealed," noise leaking into these locations from outside—for example, a car passing during a quiet element of a performance, or a pigeon on a window ledge—can present significant challenges to recording.

4.2   ISOLATED AUDIOSCAPES AND "LIVE" SOUNDSCAPES

As Williams (2012) notes, the architecture of the recording studio is divided into two main types of space: the control room where technicians reside; and the performance space inhabited by the musicians. The control room, he suggests, is a sound-space that exists through speakers—a singular *audioscape* in which everyone present hears the same sounds. The performance space, traditionally, is a sound-space that exists through the live performance of the musicians as they perform—a singular *soundscape* in which the musicians playing together hear the same shared sound.

However, the prominence of a singular performance soundscape has been challenged by the rise of multi-tracking, which, in creating the desire to isolate particular sounds during a performance (Box 4.1) brought about

---

Box 4.1   The impact of multi-tracking on studio design and live recording

Even when we had eight tracks, sessions were still done live. But by the early 1970s we had 16 tracks—which suddenly gave us the ability to put all of the instruments on separate tracks. Initially it didn't work, because there was too much bleed between the instruments, the result of studios being designed to actually enhance the concept of live performance. So, in a further attempt to really isolate the instruments, in order to take full advantage of the 16-track technology, they started to deaden the studios. . . . The idea was that, with that many tracks, you could really control things, you could create something by having the ability to isolate and replace entire sections of a song . . .

And in order to pull it off, you had to also re-think the way the studio was constructed—because up until that point, you didn't have the wherewithal to really hone those parts individually. So in turn they began this new studio prototype: one where leakage could be maintained, if not completely eliminated. It was a tremendous change in the method of modern recording up to that point.

Source: Producer-engineer and studio designer Chris Huston, quoted in Simons (2004, 15–16)

68 *Inside the Studio*

divisions within the performance space (Williams 2007). This is often achieved through the use of sound baffles and moveable walls, which can be placed around performers and/or instruments and amplifiers to isolate the sounds of individual instruments and/or voices (Figure 4.3) reducing unwanted "leakage" of sound out to other microphones in the room. While these provide a level of isolation of sounds, if carefully arranged they still allow musicians to be close to one another in a shared physical space if not in a singular shared soundscape. Even greater separation is achieved through the use of isolation booths, which are designed to completely eliminate the leakage of musical sounds. However, as Williams (2007) argues, while these booths completely isolate musical sounds, they also have the consequence of completely isolating musicians from one another.

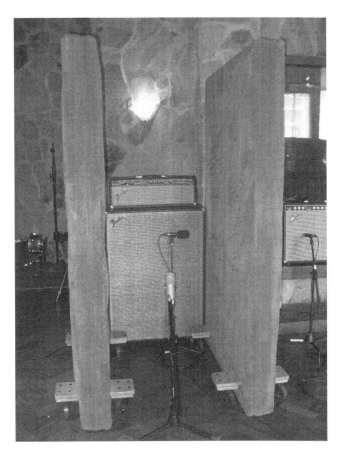

Figure 4.3 Baffles around a bass guitar amplifier to prevent sound leakage
Source: Author

Williams (2012) suggests that when musicians become separated and acoustically isolated from one another in this way, a singular soundscape no longer exists, but rather is replaced instead by multiple isolated soundscapes. An alternative soundscape is created for each musician through the use of headphones, which Williams argues is more akin to audioscape of the control room. The headphones allow musicians to hear what is being played, or has been played, by other musicians. So, for example, a lead guitarist or vocalist of a band may perform with the sound of the pre-recorded rhythm section (drums, bass guitar, rhythm guitar) playing through their headphones. Headphone mixes can be tailored to the individual musician, for example by making certain elements more prominent in the headphones and other less prominent. Therefore, as Williams suggests, although headphones allow musicians to bridge the physical divides between them, in the case of multiple headphone mixes each isolated audioscape appears autonomous to the musician who inhabits it. Spatially and sonically, musicians and their producers increasingly "compose" their music in solitude, rather than it being a product of live performance and experimentation. Thus in this way the technological calculation of recording studios discourage live performance, alienating musical performers from collective acts of music-making (Porcello 2002). Therefore, as Born suggests, the recording studio becomes a site of rationalised and alienated musical labour, which is "evident in the way that tracks are built up through a sequence of separated, often individual takes in which any possibility of co-present aesthetic response and mutuality is lost" (2005, 26).

As Williams (2012) notes, headphones usually become the focus of a musician's discomfort in the studio. The first instance of this dissatisfaction, he argues, concerns the sound of their instrument or voice as mediated by technology and the engineer, compared to how the instrument or voice sounds naturally within the room. But there is a more significant element of dissatisfaction that should be recognised, and which is the way in which the isolation of musicians fundamentally impacts on the performance of a musician or vocalist. For most bands, their careers are spent rehearsing and playing live together. As a result, the process of recording as isolated individuals in the studio using headphones creates a sterile and fragmented environment. As noted in the previous chapter, for bands and musicians who are used to playing together in a live setting in which an audience provides energy and feedback on the performance, performing in the recording studio is a strange and sometimes uncomfortable experience, and one which is exacerbated when the musicians are isolated from one another:

> . . . the worst, most sterile environment that you can ever place a performer into is the studio. For someone who's used to either doing it on their own or being in front of a huge stadium of people and getting the energy off that—you don't put them in a room like a studio, with people with headphones on and say, "Give me everything you've got." It is a really difficult environment for the artist.
>
> (Producer Frank Filipetti, quoted in Massey 2000, 8)

70 *Inside the Studio*

In a live performance situation, players share an acoustic space allowing the use of spatial, aural and visual cues (Crooks 2012). These are vital to the spontaneity, speculation, improvisation and even mistakes that characterise the "now" of live performance (Morton 2005). Similarly, performances in the studio involve spontaneity and improvisation. However, if musicians are isolated from one another, the interaction that characterises live performance is absent, including the visual cues and eye contact that are so central to creativity and spontaneity, impacting on the ability of musicians to perform (Box 4.2); as

---

Box 4.2 Rock 'n' roll recorded "live": Oasis and the recording of *Definitely Maybe*

Tony McCaroll, a drummer with the band Oasis, recalls the different experiences of the band when recording individually when compared to recording together live in the studio. Their first experience of the recording studio came at Monnow Valley recording studio in Monmouth, Wales, where the band began recording their debut album *Definitely Maybe*. Here, the producer Dave Bachelor got each member of the band to record their parts of song arrangements individually:

> The producer had us recording our individual pieces in separate rooms away from each other. It just wasn't right. For three years we had rehearsed and recorded together. The eye contact and feel was as important as the music itself. It was what we had become accustomed to. Without this energy, the music sounded soulless. Day after day we would record, only to be bitterly disappointed when we played back the results in the evening.

After 18 days of recording, the band had the recording for only one song complete. The decision was taken to move the band to a different studio—Sawmill Studios, also in Wales—to work with a different producer, Mark Coyle. Here the approach to recording was very different, with the band playing together live in the studio. As McCarroll describes, this way of performing felt much more natural to the band, resulting in a more enjoyable recording process and recording songs much more quickly:

> Creation had obviously decided that the experiences at Monnow Valley were not to be repeated. Their plan had the desired effect. During the next week we recorded again as a band in the same room, unlike in Monnow Valley. It was a re-creation of the set-up we'd had in both the rehearsal room and Bootle, and we had that feel back, that understanding a nod or a wink could bring back, that spark. We began to trawl through the new batch of songs and laid down "Shakermaker", "Up in the Sky", "Digsy's Dinner" and "Rock 'n' Roll Star" in quick succession. It was obvious that it worked when we played as a unit and it didn't when we didn't, so we ploughed on. Next we completed "Live Forever". The song was a joy to record.

Source: Extracts from McCaroll (2011, 121–123)

Moorefield argues ". . . the spontaneity, the groove found in a good live group is lost; the resulting music may sound artificial, stilted, "cold" if the producer is not careful" (2010, 55). Thus when musicians are afforded this interaction within a "live" space—a single shared soundscape free of baffles, moveable walls and isolation booths (Figure 4.4)—what results is a more "live" sounding recording:

> When you have excellent players all working together at once, there is usually some friendly competition. People tend to perform to the best of their abilities. The interaction sparks additional excitement, thereby creating a more lively track. It plays a large part in the overall warmth and spirit of the recording.
> (Producer Matt Wallace, quoted in Simons 2004, 11)

> . . . playing together in the same room is, once you get rid of those headphones and you get rid of the boards between everyone and things like that, there's a certain something where, if two musicians are playing they're bouncing ideas off each other . . . it's going back to that subconscious mind, because it's too quick for you to think about it, it just happens. And yes, that really sounds good . . .
> (Interview 11, male engineer, twenties)

Figure 4.4 Recording "live," Ocean Sound Recordings, Norway

Photograph courtesy of Tony Draper

72 *Inside the Studio*

Whilst it is arguably the case that through technological development the primacy of recording has generally become asserted over live performance (Moorefield 2010), in many genres—such as jazz, country, blues, rock and folk music—live performance as a band, group or ensemble in particular urban spaces remains central to musical authenticity. As Connell and Gibson (2003) note, where music retains its local linkages and identity, it can claim authenticity, but where it becomes influenced by the economic imperatives of the music industry, it can lose this authenticity. Considering this in terms of recordings, it becomes clear that the type of highly commercialised, electronically produced recordings typical of popular music would produce a major disjuncture between producers and consumers (Connell and Gibson 2003). This presents the challenge of producing "authentic" recordings that stay true to the spirit and sound of local live performance. In response to this challenge, particular studios have developed recording practices that incorporate group performances on particular parts of the recording, most commonly the rhythm section, allowing for the signification of live performance and authenticity; at the same time, overdubbing of the lead instrument and vocals means that the sonic qualities of the recording are not compromised (Box 4.3). In some genres, such as classical and jazz, in which music is played by highly trained musicians, performances may be recorded entirely live, without overdubs and with minimal if any post-performance enhancement, capturing the live performance as realistically as possible (Moorefield 2010).

This is not always straightforward, however, and there are a number of related challenges in making studio recordings of music that reproduce the dynamic and emotional nature of live performance. For example, Bennett (2012b; no pagination) argues that "such has been the extent of technological change in the last 3 decades that an entire generation of musicians have now grown up without ever experiencing or knowing a recording process that involves a full, live performance." This lack of experience also extends to producers and engineers, many of whom may have not recorded live and as such may not have developed some of the tacit skills required to record in this way, such as microphone selection and placement. However, to record live requires producers and engineers not only with the required technical knowledge but also with an interest in the particular style of music in order to give appropriate creative direction. The producer and/or engineer of jazz music, for example, must be comfortable with the high levels of improvisation that characterise the live performance of jazz, as well as being familiar with using close-microphone placement and creating the "dead" acoustic spaces that characterise jazz recording which "in the hands of the expert engineer . . . can lead to beautiful, intimate, and detailed recordings . . ." (Crooks 2012; no pagination). The issue of microphone placement is one that is attended to in the next section of this chapter.

Box 4.3   Music mediated as live in Austin, Texas (Porcello 2002)

The Austin sound exists both at the level of musical genre and at the juncture of performance practice and sonic characteristics of the music. But more than an aesthetic, it is also a deeply political stance toward the value of local musical practices in the face of an increasingly mediated and global music industry. For most musicians in the Austin country, blues and roots rock scenes, those most closely associated with the Austin sound, live performance is the hallmark of this valuation of localness.

If the Austin sound is based in large part on the link between sincerity and live performance, then Austin musicians and bands are faced with a particular challenge when making studio recordings of their music; how to maintain the sincerity/liveness link despite a recording process that rarely relies fully—in most cases, even predominantly—on live, uninterrupted ensemble performances.

How, then, can one record the Austin sound—its liveness and sincerity audibly intact—without sacrificing the sonic aesthetics expected of contemporary sound recording?

Rarely in my experience did members of the rhythm sections of Austin bands record individually; the common approach was for the ensemble to perform and record live . . . the rhythm tracks were generated in live performance, and significant overdubbing was reserved for lead and solo instruments and voice. In the recorded Austin sound . . . the rhythm section bear much of the burden of signifying liveness, of anchoring and foregrounding the live performance/ sincerity link . . .

Source: Extracts from Porcello (2002, 70–74)

4.3   CODING THE SOUND-SPACE OF THE STUDIO

Particular recording studios have particular acoustical characteristics, often making the sound of one studio identifiable from one another (for example, through the sound of their echo chambers). Nisbett (1995) notes how recordings pick up these physical characteristics of the studio as much as those of the player, with the studio acting as a "sounding board" to instruments and its shape and size giving character to the music. These characteristics often become imprinted on the work of the artists who recorded in them (Horning 2012), as well as being imprinted more widely on to a particular place or music scene (see Chapter 5). The "sound" of a studio is however not an issue of acoustics alone, but is an outcome of the way in which particular producers and engineers working in a studio manipulate its natural acoustics (Horning 2012; Tankel 1990), or to put it another way, the way in which they "code" the sound-space

74 *Inside the Studio*

of a particular studio. This coding can be done, for example, through the careful selection and placement of microphones based on the instrument or voice to be recorded, by fixing various parameters of sound such as volume, pitch, timbre, juxtaposition, presence and attack/decay, using microphone preamplifiers (Figure 4.5), and by applying particular effects such as compression and reverberation through the use of "outboard" equipment, that is equipment that is separate from the recording console or mixing desk (Figure 4.6).

In this way, the producers and engineer can "code" not only the music but also the musical space (Tankel 1990). Thus particular sounds have become associated not only with particular studios but also with particular producers working in these studios, no one more than the American producer Phil Spector (Box 4.4).

The "art of microphoning" (Horning 2004) is a crucial craft skill for the recording studio engineer. This term refers to the careful selection and placement of microphones in the recording studio based on the instrument or voice to be recorded. As Zak notes:

> Recording microphones hear source sounds and the resulting ambience as a composite sonic image, which can be shaped by microphone choice

Figure 4.5 A studio engineer adjusting the input level on a microphone preamplifier during a recording session

Source: Author

Figure 4.6 Rack of outboard equipment including preamplifiers and effects units
Source: Author

Box 4.4   Coding the "sound" of the studio: Phil Spector's "Wall of Sound"

Working at Gold Star Studios in Los Angeles between 1958 and 1966, American record producer and songwriter Phil Spector would pioneer an innovative production technique that became known as the "Wall of Sound." Central to the development of this technique was the way in which Spector used the ambience of the recording studio, and in particular the studio's excellent echo chambers, as a "textural resource" (Zak 2001).

By recording with large ensembles and multiple instruments performing the same parts in unison with one another—not only orchestral instruments, but also instruments such as guitars which previously had not been used in ensemble playing—Spector created a dense, layered sound, which was enhanced through experimentation with the ambience of the room. As Zak notes:

> . . . parts were commonly doubled and tripled, the large group of musicians overwhelming the relatively small recording space with a wash of reverberant sound. . . . What was a kind of musical soup in the recording studio, with sounds both bleeding together in space and bleeding into one another's microphones, could be controlled by the use of multiple

76 *Inside the Studio*

> microphone inputs in the control room. The ambience of the room could thus be tailored and shaped by experimenting with different microphone placements and balances.
>
> (2001, 77)
>
> Reverberation was then added through the use of the studio's echo chambers, with the signal from the studio played into the echo chamber through speakers and picked up by microphones located in the chamber to be mixed in with the rest of the track. By using the acoustic ambience of the studio in this way, Spector's productions achieved a distinctive audio quality and resulted in a rich, complex sound. As Moorefield notes:
>
>> [Phil Spector] was using the studio as his orchestra, arranging the timbres of various voices, instruments and effects, and room tones in much the same way as a more conventional composer would employ the colours of the orchestra. . . . To him the studio was a musical instrument, to be tuned and practiced on and performed with.
>>
>> (2010, 14)
>
> *Sources*: Moorefield (2010); Zak (2001)

and placement. . . . Because the ambience imparted by a recording space is integral to a sound's aural identity, the relationship between the two is a central concern for recordists.

(2001, 76)

Knowing the characteristics of hundreds of microphones and a variety of acoustic environments is therefore an important part of the complex set of technical abilities and tacit knowledges that engineers and producers are required to have (Kealy 1990). Each studio, with its own particular acoustic qualities, and each project with its own particular musical style and instruments, will require different microphones and microphone placement (see Nisbett 1995). While placement of microphones is to a large degree dependent on a technical understanding of acoustics, it is also a skill that can only be acquired through practice and trial and error (see also Hennion 1989), leading to the development of tacit knowledge. Through such trial and error, within a given acoustic environment, the engineer must learn how to "mike-up" particular instruments and which microphones to use to get a particular sound; how to select and place microphones for recording vocals; and how to select and place microphones for a range of different recording artists from solo performers to rock bands to jazz ensembles to orchestras. Figure 4.7 and Figure 4.8 show just two examples of microphone placement for different recording situations; for recording a solo performance on guitar and vocals, and for recording drums, respectively.

Close-miking a particular instrument or vocalist will give different results to placing the microphone further away from the source of the sound. Close-miking can give a more detailed and intimate sound to the recording (see for example Crooks 2012, on recording jazz), picking up the fine detail of the sound produced, and giving the listener the impression the musician is in the room with them. Conversely, the "ambience" of the recording space can be captured and emphasised by positioning microphones some distance away from the instruments being recorded, giving the listener the impression of being in the room with the musician—a technique common on older recordings. As one interviewee described:

> . . . do I want it close-miked so it sounds like it's here, or do we want it in the room? . . . the nice thing about old recordings is you can somehow "see" the music . . . you can see the old blues guy in the room stomping his foot, playing guitar, singing at the same time.
> (Interview 13, male engineer-producer, forties)

Experiments with different combinations of microphones and various layouts can lead to unexpected and unintended outcomes, as can be

Figure 4.7 Microphoning for recording of a solo performance—guitar and vocals

Photograph courtesy of Katie Tavini

Figure 4.8 Setting up microphones to record drums
Photograph courtesy of Katie Tavini

seen with Toni Visconti's work with David Bowie at Hansa Ton Studio in Berlin (Box 4.5). Microphoning is then a creative, artistic skill. In research undertaken by E.T. Canby in 1956, one engineer noted that they considered "the art of microphoning as the equal of any another interpretive art . . . the plain fact is that microphoning is an art unto itself with its own laws, principles, and its own special culture" (quoted in Kealy 1990, 209). More recently however, the digitalisation of recording, and the associated increase in the number of project studios with small acoustic spaces, sometimes limited to a single vocal booth, has resulted in microphoning skills being less prevalent amongst studio engineers. As noted in Chapter 2, Gibson suggests that the digitisation of studios and the ability to manipulate sound waves digitally changed the kinds of skills required from engineers so that "long years of experience in certain acoustic spaces, and with different kinds of microphones, became less important to being able to tweak a sound recording within a software programme" (2005, 198). Such an assertion is supported by one interviewee who noted how "a lot of engineers have grown up with computers these days and they don't necessarily have miking-up skills" and described himself as an "old school guy . . . I know how to mike-up stuff" (Interview 1, male engineer, thirties).

Box 4.5   Producer Toni Visconti's microphone techniques (Moorefield 2010)

Working in Berlin's Hansa Ton Studio, which featured a huge main recording room which had once been a banquet hall for Nazi leaders, [Toni] Visconti employed complex, imaginative recording techniques which are still talked about and often imitated. The most obvious, immediately audible feature of his sound is the cavernous room ambience. . . . He set up drums, bass and guitar at opposite end of the banquet-hall-turned-tracking-room, . . . placed mikes at various distances and rolled tape. The result is hard-rocking get-up-and-move drum sound heard on hits such as Iggy Pop's 1977 *Lust for Life* . . .

A more sophisticated technique unique to Visconti was the placement of three microphones at various distances from vocalist Bowie. Each mike was linked to a gate set to open only when the signal was within a certain volume. If Bowie sang softly, only the close mike was operational; at medium volume, the second mike ten feet away kicked in; full-throated singing would open up the third gate. The effect, which can easily be heard on the title track of *Heroes*, is to add more room tone (natural ambience) the more the singer projects.

Source: Extract from Moorefield (2010, 51–52)

4.4   THE SOUND-SPACE OF THE MASTERING STUDIO

The sound-space of the studio is also of crucial importance in the process of mastering. Unlike the recording studio, in which the sound-space is organised around recording, in the mastering studio the sound-space is organised around listening, due to the way in which mastering engineers need to be able to listen to music at high volumes and at high levels of detail, in order to make very fine changes to music and vocals. Thus they require studio spaces with particularly high levels of acoustic treatment and expensive monitoring equipment (speakers). This acts to concentrate the process into a relatively small number of studios that are organised and constructed specifically to undertake this process. Arguably, these formal studio spaces, as the space in which the final creative process happens, are becoming of increasing importance when the recording process can now be undertaken in a wide range of different spaces which may or may not be acoustically treated. As two of the interviewees described:

> . . . the mastering room has tended to become the place that's actually being built acoustically properly where you can make a proper technical evaluation . . . now because you can buy really good recording equipment quite cheaply it does open the opportunity of going somewhere

80 *Inside the Studio*

really bizarre and recording. But . . . you still need this place that's going to pull it all together and get you a result.

> (Interview 3, male mastering engineer, fifties)

. . . nowadays, it's even more important . . . because they're working in facilities that are not especially acoustically well-treated and well set-up. Then this is the last chance that anybody really has to check out their stuff in a proper environment, where the acoustics are good, the monitoring is good, the engineer knows those speakers, that monitoring, inside out, can pick up any issues that may be a problem, and put them right.

> (Interview 18, male mastering engineer, fifties)

The above quote highlights the need for mastering engineers to develop a very intimate knowledge of the acoustic space in which they are working. This acts to lock particular mastering engineers into particular recording spaces (see Chapter 7). As one interviewee described:

. . . engineers tend to move from studio to studio with projects, whereas mastering engineers only ever work in the room that they work. So you know how things should sound in your room and that's the key thing. We're the common denominator; we're the bit where somebody is really familiar with their environment . . .

> (Interview 3, male mastering engineer, fifties)

While mastering engineers may be familiar with the technical equipment found across different mastering studios, interview responses suggested that it takes some time for an engineer to get used to the particular acoustics of a new mastering studio space. As one mastering engineer described, ". . . if I move to another room I'm all over the place and it can take me a week, sometimes longer, to accustom to be able to do the kind of work I do for the mastering work. It would take quite a while to accustom myself to that" (Interview 6, male mastering engineer, fifties). Another interviewee suggested that it might take as long as six months to a year to become familiar with the acoustics and monitoring of another mastering studio. This highlights how mastering engineers must become intimately familiar with the space in which they are working. Within this space, mastering engineers find a particular and very specific position at which to work and listen, a position in the space of the room in relation to the monitors where acoustics mean the sound is at its optimum (Figure 4.9): ". . . we know what a good record should sound like . . . I know what if I walk over there the bass is heavy, and I walk back there the bass is wrong, I've got to be in this sort of area" (Interview 6, male mastering engineer, fifties).

Figure 4.9   Mastering room, Master+ mastering studio, Rennes, France

By Masterplus (Master+) [CC-BY-SA-3.0 (http://creativecommons.org/licenses/by-sa/3.0) or GFDL (http://www.gnu.org/copyleft/fdl.html)], via Wikimedia Commons.

4.5   CONCLUSION: THE STUDIO SOUND-SPACE IN THE DIGITAL AGE

With reference to studio sound-space, Horning (2012) discusses "the end of space," arguing that from the 1960s increasing experimentation with new electronic sounds that had no use for natural acoustics resulted in acoustically dead recording environments, as well as resulting in the closure of many studios with large recording spaces. As the development of multi-tracking allowed for increasing levels of musical creativity through composition, and required increasing control over the recording process, the idea of "studio as instrument," originally based around the idea of experimenting with acoustics treatments in the studio to alter sound, would shift firmly on to the technologies of the control room, as discussed in Chapter 2. Technology has further undermined the viability of studios with large acoustic spaces through the development of computer software which can simulate the ambience of an array of different sound-spaces; as Zak notes "the image of cathedral, a concert hall, or a cavern can be drawn by sound that is actually produced in a small room" (2001, 77).

The continued value of live recording to particular genres counters to some degree negative arguments about the future of recording studios and

82 *Inside the Studio*

sound-spaces. Horning's argument that, due to the adoption by consumers of more portable lo-fi listening devices (see Chapter 8), there is "a generation of listeners who have never heard the sound of the room" (2012, 41) may well be true. However, the same generation will most certainly have heard music in live settings, and therefore will not only make judgements on the authenticity of recorded music on this basis, but will also understand the energy, improvisation and enjoyment inherent in performance and expect this to be recreated "on record." As has been argued in this chapter, small, isolating recording environments fail to provide the conditions necessary for this; rather, larger rooms are required where musicians are able to play together in a singular shared soundscape. Thus larger studios with live rooms remain important, as to do the ability of producers and engineers to code and shape these acoustic spaces.

NOTE

1. To give a sense of the size of these spaces, it requires a studio of over approximately 3,000 square feet to accommodate a full orchestra, which may contain anywhere between approximately 70 and 100 musicians.

Part II

Beyond the Studio

5   Recording Studios in Urban Music Scenes

The second section of the book moves from considering the work that takes place *within* the space of the recording studio, to consider music production and creativity that extends *beyond* the studio. Although recording studios are often regarded in the popular imagination as a closed and guarded environment (Warner 2003), it is not only the relationships operating *inside* the studio that affect creative moments. Recording studios are at once insulated spaces of creativity, isolated from the world outside, and spaces influenced directly by the *wider contexts* in which the studios operate. A relational approach emphasises that when considering musical creativity, it is not only important to study in detail the physical places in which it occurs, but also to consider the wider networks of creativity within which it is situated. It is to this task that the following three chapters attend, across a range of spatial scales.

This particular chapter is concerned with musical creativity and production at the scale of the city, and in particular the ways in which urban geography is a crucial mediating factor in the production and consumption of music. The city provides the physical places which offer spaces for musical creativity. While certain spaces—including recording studios—are specifically organised for this purpose, music is produced in many urban spaces, from the bedroom, garage or home studio (Connell and Gibson 2003); to community and youth centres (Hoyler and Mager 2005); to street corners (Toop 2000) and clubs (Todorović and Bakir 2005). However, music is not only made *in* urban spaces, but also *for* urban spaces. Specific sites link the production and consumption of music, for example night clubs and concert halls, but also abandoned and reclaimed spaces such as empty warehouses and former factories (Gibson 1999) and public spaces like the street.

Consideration is given in the chapter to recording studios as being embedded within urban centres of musical creativity, and in particular the role recording studios play in the development of urban music scenes. The development of urban music scenes in particular locations is evidence of the way in which cities can sustain networks that foster and support musical creativity, networks which come together in particular locales of creativity and production. These networks may persist over time—particularly in large cities

86 *Beyond the Studio*

where there is a constant renewal of the creative bloodstream, for example the urban music scenes of the big global cities of London and New York—or may exist only for a short creative episode—as is evidenced in many smaller provincial cities, for example grunge in Seattle or indie music in Manchester during the early 1990s. Thus, some cities have become associated with one particular musical scene that now no longer persists, while others provide a constant stream of musical creativity (Kloosterman 2005).

The chapter begins by considering how urban music scenes might be defined, how they arise and develop, and the economic, social and geographic components of such scenes. In particular, music scenes are seen as *arenas of socialisation*, developing around a social infrastructure that includes live music venues, cafes and bars. The second section of the chapter then considers the important role played by recording studios in the development of urban music scenes, both with regard to the development of the "sound" of music scenes and as crucial social infrastructure within scenes. Finally, extending the relational consideration of music production, the chapter considers musical creativity and performance outside the formalised space of the recording studio in the urban environment, and in particular the way in which specific urban spaces link the production and consumption of music.

5.1 URBAN MUSIC SCENES

Music is intimately tied to place, with particular forms of cultural expressions strongly linked to particular places. As Allen Scott notes more generally, "culture is a phenomenon that tends to have intensively place-specific characteristics thereby helping to differentiate places from one another" (1997, 324). With regard to music, one might consider New York's Tin Pan Alley (Furia 1992), Nashville's Music Row (Kosser 2006), Motown in Detroit in the 1960s (Quispel 2005), or the guitar music of Liverpool (Cohen 1991) and Manchester (Halfacree and Kitchin 1996) as just a few examples of how specific types of music have become associated inextricably with particular cities. As Connell and Gibson suggest, a common element of literature on popular music is a "tendency to search for links between sites and sounds, for inspirations in nature and the built environment" (2003, 91).

Such literature has in particular focused on geographical roots in, and influences of, a particular "scene" or "sound" which musicians or producers identify with. But also, it is important to recognise that "places are hugely marketable constructs" (Banks 2007, 145). In an increasingly global and increasingly saturated music market, "place" becomes a way of branding music, of identifying particular types of music from each other and invoking authenticity. In this way, "space produces as space is produced" (Leyshon et al. 1995, 425). As Gibson (2005) notes, in the global cultural economy, such local contexts are often elevated and made overt, with consumers and

Recording Studios in Urban Music Scenes 87

audiences investing meaning in such associations and marketers playing up links to particular places to establish musical credibility. As with other cultural products, then, the city is used as a *symbolic resource* for marketing music:

> ... cultural-products industries compete increasingly on crowded global markets, and that success in this competition is aided where the monopoly powers of place are mobilised to the maximum implicit and explicit branding of products.
>
> (Scott 1997, 329)

The link between music and place is most commonly described in terms of the development of a "music scene." Florida and Jackson suggest that the term music scene was originally used to describe "the geographic concentrations of specific kinds of musical genres that evolved in mid-twentieth-century musical centres like New Orleans jazz, Nashville country, Memphis soul, Detroit Motown and Chicago blues" (2010, 311). They suggest that musicians show a tendency to concentrate in these geographical creative centres. Similarly, Bennett and Peterson define a music scene as "the context in which clusters of producers, musicians and fans collectively share their common musical tastes and collectively distinguish themselves from others" (2004, 1).

For Currid (2007a), such a scene arises once communities and subcultures begin to come together in particular niches focused around clustered creatives in a particular location. One can think of music scenes, then, as arising when musicians with shared artistic sensibilities come together in particular locations in search of inspiration and mutual learning, to relate to one another, and to create and consume music. Straw (1991) identifies scenes as created and produced through *alliances* of musical preferences, constrained or enabled by power relations across space. Similarly, Crossley (2008, 2009) emphasises the importance of social networks to the development of music scenes, with music scenes entailing a network of actors who belong to and participate in it, and who must meet, influence and inspire each other.

While certain cities have developed an intimate relationship with music, and are celebrated as distinctive sites of productions for particular forms of music, cities are not however single homogeneous entities. Certain neighbourhoods and places within these cities are identifiable places of particular music scenes and particular forms of musical creativity, containing specific spaces of musical production and consumption. Musical creativity will be influenced by both the physical landscape and cultural diversity of particular neighbourhoods (Hubbard 2006; see also Drake 2003). As Straw (1991) suggests, local musical creativity is cosmopolitan yet fluid, loose, transitory and geographically dispersed in nature. Diverse neighbourhoods provide the opportunity for the mutual exchange of musical styles and practices

88 *Beyond the Studio*

amongst different cultural groups, increasing wider exposure to a set of *atonal ensembles* of diverse musical cultural expressions (Said 1990).

Musical creativity from cultural fusion in and across such neighbourhoods has produced some of the most successful and influential genres of music. Hip hop, for example, finds its roots in the Caribbean but materialised as a distinct genre when mixed with urban musical cultures in Western cities. Emerging in the deprived inner-city neighbourhoods of U.S. cities, in particular the Harlem and South Bronx neighbourhoods of New York, hip hop was, and remains, intense in its territoriality, and in particular in its focus on the *ghetto* as both a real and imagined space (Connell and Gibson 2003). Similarly, Allen and Wilcken (2001) describe how in New York Caribbean-American musicians have a history of interaction with African-Americans, which has resulted in the fusion of musical styles in the form of *Salsa* and *Soca*, as well as hip hop. Jazeel's (2005) examination of British-Asian soundscapes emanating from the U.K. highlights the new soundscapes that develop when musical creatives draw on fluid, transnational cultural and technological influences in both their work and life. Jazeel draws on the example of the British-Asian musician and producer Talvin Singh to highlight how the mixing of cultures results in music that is difficult to place:

> His sound combines tabla and turntable, sitar and sampler, it is a sound that emerges from his Brick Lane studio in London's East End, is played on the dance floors of hip UK and US clubs. . . . His beats, tones, and chords, however, evoke geographical imaginations of Asia and elsewhere. Singh's sound belies easy placement.
>
> (Jazeel 2005, 234)

City diversity is seen to be a significant factor in encouraging creative individuals to locate to a particular city (Jacobs 1961; Florida 2002; Hubbard 2006), contributing to an open, dynamic and cool "people climate." Nowhere is this more marked than in the buzzing, heterogeneous, ethnically diverse and tolerant neighbourhoods of cities (Helms and Phleps 2007). Certain neighbourhoods within certain cities act as magnets for talented individuals from across the globe (Scott 1999a); musicians and other artists have a historical tendency to concentrate in the creative and bohemian enclaves of particular cities in search of inspiration and experience (see for example Lloyd 2006, on the Wicker Park neighbourhood of Chicago, and Foord 1999, on the Hackney area of London). The development of a particular creative tradition, it is argued, is due to a place being continuously attractive over a relatively long period of time. Törnqvist suggests that "new ideas are built upon a capital of experiences gathered through interaction with one's surroundings" and that "processes of renewal cannot develop in empty space for long without stimulation and new outside impulses" (2004, 4). Individuals with unique skills and creativity are from this perspective seen as the main prerequisite for the maintenance and renewal of creative networks.

Recording Studios in Urban Music Scenes   89

However, the development of a music scene does not rest solely on the clustering of musicians in particular areas of cities. Rather, it requires the coming together of those producing the music—including musical *and* business talent—and those consuming the music, in a physical space. A music scene develops around supporting networks of musicians, other creatives, audiences and music industry players, and by a presence of a cultural and economic infrastructure; that is to say that is to say that music scenes "have overlapping and mutually reinforcing economic, social and geographic components" (Florida and Jackson 2010, 318). Music scenes can thus be seen as:

> . . . geographic locations that bring together musical and business talent (e.g. agents, managers, taste-makers, gate-keepers, critics, and sophisticated consumers) across social networks and physical space (neighbourhoods, communities, club, music stores, recording studios, and venues) . . . a music scene is a geographically delimited market in microcosm rooted in location.
>
> (Florida and Jackson 2010, 311)

As Connell and Gibson (2003) suggest, "cultural space" can be carved out of wider social space through musical praxis and the alliances that support musical scenes and performance spaces. This suggests that music scenes and associated spatial agglomerations in the music industry are important due to the way in which they function not only as pools of skills (and capital), but also as *arenas of socialization* (Scott 1999a). As Grabher (2002a) notes personal networks seem to be strongly, although not exclusively, rooted in a particular locality, particularly in the creative realm. Research on the music industry, for example, has highlighted the importance of geographical proximity and face-to-face interaction in the development of personal and social networks and relationships, the dynamics of which are built around informality and trust (Watson 2008). Such findings support accounts that have developed in economic geography regarding the way in which spatial agglomerations function as potent frameworks of cultural reproduction (Scott 1999a) and learning (see Asheim 2002).

The term local "buzz" (Storper and Venables 2004) is often used to refer to the frequently used networks of information and communication developed through face-to-face contact within a cluster. This contact allows for the transfer of the types of tacit knowledge that are difficult to transfer without face-to-face contact. Bathelt et al. (2004) suggest that this knowledge can be understood in a meaningful way because the same shared values, attitudes, interpretative schemes and institutional and economic frameworks are shared by those working in the same location[1]. With regard to music, this is particularly important given that production in the music industry is a transactional, information-rich and highly discursive process (Leyshon et al. 1998). Furthermore, it is considered that relationships of trust are based on

90 *Beyond the Studio*

the shared experience of repeated interactions and transactions (see Gordon and McCann 2003; Wolfe and Gertler 2004).

Local social infrastructure is of particular importance in this respect. Social spaces such as cafés, bars, pubs and clubs, and live music venues within particular areas of cities are spaces in which musicians may meet, collaborate and exchange creative experiences. Musicians may share practice rooms and studios, or appear on the same live music bill, but they may also meet through chance encounters when drinking in the same bars and clubs (Box 5.1; see also Luckman et al. 2008; Cohen and Lashua 2010; Cummins-Russell and Rantisi 2012). Music industry professionals may likewise meet

---

Box 5.1   Live music venues and Manchester's post/punk music scene

In his 2009 account of social networks dynamics in the development of the post/punk music scene between 1976–1980, Crossley explains the importance of particular live music events to the development of the social networks:

> Punk nights and venues were particularly important to the process of network formation because they were time-spaces in which many of the key actors in the network first met and forged ties. In the context of *the Squat, the Ranch, the Factory; the Electric Circus* and the *Manchester Musicians Collective*, amongst others, a network of would-be musicians, promoters, producers and journalists began to hook up.
>
> (2009, 39)

Crossley highlights numerous different instances of social connections and friendships arising from particular events. Drawing on the work of Feld (1981, 1982), Crossley notes how these venues become "foci" for the development of networks, with people of shared interests being drawn to the same places and events, where they are more likely to meet and, given their shared interests, to form bonds:

> ... punk events and venues draw together those actors within a geographical area who share an interest in punk. A punk network formed because punk venues and events brought punks into contact.
>
> (2009, 40)

For Crossley, for cultural production to occur, actors with the relevant talents and resources must find one another; they must meet, interacted and influence one another. We can then take Crossley's study as an important empirical example of how live music venues act as a key arena for the socialisation that is so crucial to the development of a music scene.

Sources: Crossley (2009)

and exchange experience and information in informal ways (see for example Currid 2007a, 2007b), as well as within more formal music industry networks. The dynamics of social relationships are built around an informality that blurs the business-social divide and transgresses the boundaries of firms (see for example Watson 2008). These often fragile networks of links and relationships come together in these spaces to form creative *ecologies* (see Grabher 2001a, 2002a) that provide local support for creativity and help solidify the presence of music scenes:

> The most famous scenes have all built upon local support, and featured particularly vibrant combinations of venues, local production and methods of information flow and exchange. Infrastructures of musical exchange solidify the presence of scenes, providing concrete spaces and emphasising cultural meaning for participants.
>
> (Connell and Gibson 2003, 102)

Pubs and clubs retain a particular importance in local music scenes due to the way in which they act not only as social spaces for musicians, but also remain the main sites for engagement with live music and as such are central to the development of scenes (Shuker 1994). Much has been written on the role of live music venues in shaping urban music scenes and giving value to local music in a global market, especially in an Australian context[2]. Gallan and Gibson, for example, argue that the history of Australian live music is a history of pubs, with pubs and clubs playing "a central role in providing spaces for musical performance" and acting as "a training ground for new bands and fostering the development of unique styles of local live musical production and consumption" (2013, 174), that is to say they are sites which nurture and support local performers. In these venues, consumers and record companies can see the music performed in a physical space (as opposed to the fluid space of the internet), serving to distinguish the authenticity of the musician or band and their musical product.

In his discussion of the "Oz Rock" tradition in Sydney, Homan (2000) suggests that the fact that live music venues have come to be seen as the "natural" site of local music production and consumption is an example of the way in which the connections between music and place are *constructed*. Over time, live music venues often become the focal points for particular subcultures and alternative social groups. In their study of the Oxford Tavern in Wollongong, Australia, for example, Gallan and Gibson (2013) emphasise the "prolonged intricate relationships" that were crucial to establishing the space as a focal point for the city's alternative and punk live music scene and a site of local and original live musical performance and creativity.

Music scenes arise then where talent concentrates (both musicians and music industry personnel) and where there is supporting infrastructure that

92 Beyond the Studio

includes not only formal music industry infrastructure (recording studios, for example) but also a social infrastructure that facilitates meetings between talent and audiences (especially live music venues). Indeed, Connell and Gibson (2003) suggest that everyday links with audiences and other musicians are perhaps more important to the inspiration of musical creativity than urban cultural diversity. Such an assertion seems to hold when one considers the role of live music venues in the development of music scenes. In New York in the 1920s and 1930s, for example, jazz would become centred in the city in uptown Harlem, where an upsurge of musical creativity, centred on a number of live jazz venues such as the Cotton Club, the Shalamar and the Paradise, attracted an array of new talent to the city (Simons 2004). Much more recently, in Birmingham, U.K., the British Bhangra music industry has grown due to a key concentration of music talent and expertise; the presence of key record labels, studios and distribution companies; and, importantly, a culture of live DJ performance (see Dudrah 2007). Similarly, in Manchester, the existence of local record labels, promotional facilities, venues and clubs—in particular the infamous Haçienda nightclub—spurred the development of the "Madchester" scene (Halfacree and Kitchin 1996). Returning to New York, a major commercial centre for Caribbean jazz and popular music has grown up around an unparalleled network of performance venues, as well as record companies, recording studios and broadcasters (Allen and Wilcken 2001).

For the creation of a music scene, it is however not enough alone to have an environment that is supportive of creativity. In examining local musical creativity and music industries, we must also recognise the role of supply and demand in the local economy. For local music industries and infrastructure to be economically successful or even viable, there must be a sufficient number of customers, and density of human capital and resources to economise on production costs (Andersson and Andersson 2006), to make production profitable. Large live music venues, for example, have high fixed costs. While live music performance are recognised as a key source of revenue in the music industry (Williamson and Cloonan 2007), especially at a time when music sales continue to suffer from online file sharing, venues must be able to attract a sufficient number of consumers within a distance that allows ease of travel to the venue. Larger music venues are therefore almost exclusively located in cities with considerable population density (Andersson and Andersson 2006). Demand within local markets is then crucial to the economic viability of the music industry. Furthermore, while new technologies may empower musicians within studios, it cannot guarantee commercial success. Almost all music that is commercially successful has to pass through urban spaces, in which cultural innovators practice their vocations on products for both localised consumption and also distribution to more remote places (Krims 2007). Musicians may find it difficult to sell music without "going through" particular places with their supporting industry infrastructure.

5.2 THE ROLE OF RECORDING STUDIOS IN URBAN MUSIC SCENES

As noted above, the recorded music industry is, for the most part, an urban phenomenon, and recording studios as a key part of any localised musical economy tend also to be located in cities. One can point to a number of specific economic reasons for this. First, recording studios, especially large facilities, can have large fixed costs from continuous investment in new technologies, and therefore must be able to attract a sufficient number of musicians and producers to use the studio in order to cover these costs. Therefore the largest and most successful studios are predominantly located in cities, where the density of musicians is likely to be highest. Second, related to this, musical recording in the late 1960s became recentralised in cities and strongly reconnected to the music industry as the new technology demanded considerable investments in studios and skilled personnel that only major record companies could afford. Recording studios, then, could no longer be understood solely as enabling spaces of musical creativity, but also as spaces to centralise, control and channel creativity (Toynbee 2000) in and through major cities and through corporate networks. While this centralisation has been significantly challenged by the development of digital technologies that are affordable to a general consumer market, as well as technologies that allow the linking together of recording studios in distant locations and thus seemingly obviate the need for co-location in cities, recording today still remains a largely urban phenomenon (see Chapters 6, 7 and 8).

But one can also point to cultural reasons for recording studios predominantly being located in large cities. As was argued earlier, large cities have large influxes and through-flows of people, resulting in a constant renewal of the creative bloodstream. Furthermore, diverse neighbourhoods of cities are home to many different ethnicities and cultural backgrounds, resulting in the convergence and mixing of different forms of cultural and artistic expression. This is significant in terms of a city's musical creativity. Simons (2004), for example, describes how the development of a large cluster of recording studios in New York went hand-in-hand with the unique musical palate emerging from the convergence of cultures in the city. This would result in the song-writing community on New York's East 14th Street that famously became famously known as "Tin Pan Alley," and later the songwriters of the Brill Building at 1619 Broadway. A tight concentration of recording studios would emerge in a small area of between Broadway and Sixth Avenue, including many world-famous recording studios such as A&R Studio 1, Mira Sound, Columbia Studios A and B and Atlantic Studios 1, 2 and 3.

To develop a full understanding of the role of recording studios in the development and maintenance of urban music scenes, then, one must look beyond the economics and economic geography of the musical economy. One must also look to develop an understanding of recording studios as musical

94 *Beyond the Studio*

and social spaces that both shape the musical scenes in which they are embedded through particular musical sounds, styles and aesthetics; and which are themselves influenced by these scenes. As Matsue (2009) argues with specific reference to the Tokyo hardcore scene, recording studios offer necessary spaces for *performance* of a scene; they are sites where musicianship culminates and which enhance a sense of locality in music scenes (see also Condry 1999 on Japanese hip-hop). In particular, Matsue asserts the importance of the "spatially reinforced intimacy" (2009, 65) that recording studios provide, "offering rooms for further intimate socializing among members of bands" (2009, 144). Thus, as has been emphasised in earlier chapters, studios are more than physical or technological spaces, but inclusive social spaces of collaboration, a "sanctuary" for musical performance and creativity:

> The fact that these studios were little more than converted radiator shops (Sun Studio in Memphis) or fruit and vegetable refrigerators (J&M Studio in New Orleans) makes the recordings that came out of them, like "Great Balls of Fire" or "Blueberry Hill" all the more magical. Perhaps most significant, the studio provided a backdrop for more than mere hit making. It was a space, a sanctuary, where blacks and whites labored daily as artistic collaborators.
>
> (Cogan and Clark 2003, 12)

Recording studios are at once insulated spaces of creativity, isolated from the city outside, and spaces influenced directly by the wider urban contexts in which they operate. As such, they become an important focus for musical activity, and an intimate relationship thus comes to exist between a neighbourhood, city or region and its recording studios through musical creativity (see for example Box 5.2 on Stax Records in Memphis, Tennessee). As Simons describes:

> For decades, recording studios reflected the unique vibrations of the regions they inhabited. The soul kitchens of Memphis and Muscle Shoals reverberated with the southern hybrid of country and R&B; the boogie-woogie and barrelhouse piano riffs emerging from Cosimo Mattasa's New Orleans studio gave listeners an earful of the energy coming off the streets outside.
>
> (2004, 18)

As Théberge (2004) asserts, studios exist in neither a musical or cultural vacuum, and music scenes, local aesthetics, musicians and skilled labour play an important role in the development of approaches to recording and an influence on the resulting sounds. Gibson (2005) argues that studios rely on the cities that host them, both to supply a stream of musicians, and to add credence to them, whilst also providing a stimulating social environment for their workers.

Box 5.2 The neighbourhood studio: The case of Stax Records

The American record label Stax Records, which would become famous for its role in the creation of the Southern soul and Memphis soul music styles, was founded in 1957 as Satellite Records in Memphis, Tennessee (it would be renamed Stax Records in 1961). Although it was known for the production of black music, the label was founded by two white business people, and early releases were country music, rockabilly and straight pop records. It would be staff producer Chips Moman who would play the crucial role in the development of Stax as a black rhythm and blues label, through opening Satellite Studios in the former Capitol Theatre, at 926 East McLemore Avenue in South Memphis. As Bowman notes:

> According to Chips Moman, it was he and songwriting friend Paul Richey who found the theater while deliberately scouring black neighborhoods looking for a suitable building. "I wanted it in a black community," claims Moman. "That's the music that I wanted to do."
>
> (1997, 8)

This decision would prove to be of crucial importance to the development of the Southern soul and Memphis soul music styles, which would emerge from the neighbourhood in which the studio was located. As Bowman describes:

> The label benefitted from a number of fortuitous circumstances with regard to this new found direction. Perhaps the most important was the fact that Satellite's studio was located in the heart of what was fast becoming a black ghetto. Significantly, Satellite's first salaried songwriter, David Porter, worked at the Jones' Big D grocery right across the street from the studio. Two other early arrives, Booker T. Jones and saxophonist Gilbert Caple also lived in the neighborhood. Similar stories abound with regard to the arrival of other Satellite/Stax singers, instrumentalists, songwriters, producers, engineers, and office staff.
>
> (1997, 10)

As Bowman suggests, not only was Stax an integral part of the community in which it was located, but much of what would become Stax records and the Stax "sound" came straight out of the community.

Sources: Bowman (1997)

Perhaps the clearest manifestation of this relationship in musical terms is the way in which the certain sounds, associated with specific studios, particular producers or musicians, become associated with a particular place or scene in which the studio is located (Pinch and Bijsterveld 2004). Table 5.1 lists a number of urban music scenes whose development was centred on

Table 5.1 Urban recording studios and "sounds" of the city (adapted from Gibson 2005, 201)

City and period	Recording studios	"Sound" associated with the city and recording studio (and prominent artists associated with sound)	Significant producers and engineers
Kingston 1950s–1980s	Studio One, King Tubby's Studio	Reggae (Bob Marley and the Wailers, Lee "Scratch" Perry); ska, dub	Clement Seymour "Coxsone" Dodd, Osbourne Ruddock
Los Angeles 1950s–1960s	Capitol Studios, United Western, Sunset Sound	Jazz/pop (Frank Sinatra, Dean Martin); west coast pop and rock (Beach Boys, Doors)	Brian Wilson, Paul A. Rothchild and Bruce Botnick
Memphis 1950s–1970s	Sun Studios, Stax Records	Memphis blues; soul music (Ottis Reading)	Sam Phillips
London 1960s–1970s	Abbey Road	"Swingin' London" (The Beatles)	George Martin and Geoff Emerick
Detroit 1960s	Motown, Tamla	The "Motown" sound (The Temptations, Marvin Gaye, Gladys Knight & the Pips)	Norman Whitfield
Nashville 1960s–present	RCA Studio B, WSM Studios, Castle Studios	"The Nashville sound" subgenre of country music (Jim Reeves, Patsy Cline) and "Countrypolitan" (Lynn Anderson, Kenny Rogers)	Chet Atkins, Owen Bradley, Bob Ferguson, Bill Porter, Billy Sherrill
Philadelphia 1970s	Sigma Sound Studios	The "Philly sound": soul, disco, funk	Joseph Tarsia
New York 1970s	The Record Plant, A&R Studios, Scepter Studios, Electric Lady Studios	New York punk (New York Dolls, The Velvet Underground, The Stooges, The Ramones, Patti Smith)	Craig Leon, John Cale, Todd Rundgren, Shadow Morton
Berlin 1970s–present	Hansa Studios	Punk/garage/gothic rock/glam rock (David Bowie, Iggy Pop)	Toni Visconti
Manchester 1990s	Cargo Studios, Pennine Studios, Strawberry Studios	The "Madchester" scene— a mix of alternative rock, psychedelic rock and dance music (Joy Division, New Order, Stone Roses, Happy Mondays)	Martin Hannett

(Continued)

Table 5.1 (Continued)

City and period	Recording studios	"Sound" associated with the city and recording studio (and prominent artists associated with sound)	Significant producers and engineers
Tampa 1980s-1990s	Morrisound Studios	Death metal (Morbid Angel, Obituary)	Scott Burns
Gothenburg 1990s	Studio Fredman	The "Gothenburg sound": melodic death metal (At the Gates, In Flames, Dark Tranquillity)	Fredrik Nordstrom
Seattle 1990s	Bad Animals Studio, Reciprocol Recording Studio	"Seattle grunge" (Nirvana, Pearl Jam)	Jack Endino, Rich Hinklin

one or more specific recording studios. This includes many significant music scenes from the 1950s to the 1990s, and is demonstrative of the importance of particular studios, and of particular producers, to the development of urban music scenes.

In the 1960s in Jamaica, for example, the recording studio and record label "Studio One" would become central to the development of the distinct sounds of reggae music. Its characteristic sound would come from the way the studio was engineered by producer Clement Seymour "Coxsone" Dodd. Dodd balanced sounds in a unique way based on the studio room, which meant that his sound could not be replicated elsewhere (Bradley 2001). He also chose key musical directors, and by keeping them on a wage helped to retain a distinctive sound. His studio was an open, creative environment, and the only studio in which musicians and singers could smoke weed (Bradley 2001). It was therefore seen as an environment that was sympathetic to creative concerns of Jamaican musical talent—a crucial social space in the development of a music scene. A much more recent example is the death metal music scene which emerged in Tampa, Florida, around the Morrisound Studios and producer Scott Burns, music which would later be appropriated into a melodic subgenre as part of the "Gothenburg sound" emerging around Studio Fredman and its principal producer/engineer Fredrik Nordstrom (Box 5.3). As was noted earlier, in the global cultural economy, such local contexts are often elevated and made overt, with consumers and audiences investing meaning in such associations (Gibson 2005).

Further, for Scott (1999a) the recording studio is a sort of microcosm of a much more extensive domain of activities in the creative field. As Krims (2007) describes, the attraction of creative workers to a city supports

98 Beyond the Studio

**Box 5.3   Recording studios in music scenes: The case
of Death Metal (Dunn 2004)**

Throughout the late 1980s and early 1990s, Tampa, Florida, was the first
death metal "hotspot." . . . The main magnet to the Tampa area was Morrisound Studios and producer Scott Burns whose production and engineering work "played a crucial part in creating the 'clean', precise guitar sounds
that dominated Death Metal in that era" (Harris 2000). Bands from as far as
Canada and Brazil travelled to Florida to capitalize on the high-quality production of Morrisound. As Christie comments, "life in Florida did not revolve
around any significant social scene, but dozens of bands had their albums
produced or engineered by Scott Burns and the staff at Tampa's Morrisound
studios" (2003, 242). Morrisound studios was thus critical in establishing the
Tampa sound, which was widely copied by death metal bands elsewhere in the
United States and other countries.

   The melodic direction of European (mostly Swedish) death metal bands
in the 1990s challenged the boundaries of the genre for many metal fans. . . .
Although several important bands associated with this sound originate from
Stockholm, Gothenburg has become labeled by fans, the music press music
press, and record labels as the "home" of this specific style. One reason for
this labeling is that, similar to Tampa, Gothenburg is also the location of
an important studio—Studio Fredman—and principal producer/engineer,
Fredrik Nordstrom. Like Scott Burns, Nordstrom is credited with shaping a particular sound through the production of key melodic death metal
albums. . . . Studio Fredman has served as key factor in the development of
an identifiable Gothenburg Sound.

Source: Extracts from Dunn (2004, 114–115)

---

a different infrastructure, which in turn may correspond to concomitant
developments in musical life in those same places. The location of studios
within large cities thus reflects the locational preferences of musicians and
skilled workers from throughout the music industry including the producers
and sound engineers critical to the studios.

5.3   OUTSIDE THE STUDIO: MUSICAL CREATIVITY
AND PERFORMANCE IN THE CITY

Given that the title of this book makes explicit reference to cultural
production *beyond* the studio, it is important to recognise that while
recording studios are amongst the most formal and conspicuous spaces
of musical creativity, urban creative musical spaces may take a variety
of forms and occupy a range of material spaces in diverse settings, from

Recording Studios in Urban Music Scenes   99

bedrooms and garages to street corners, clubs, dance halls and ware-houses. As Gibson notes:

> Wild variants and cross blends, from major subcultural styles such as hip hop, reggae, punk, heavy metal, "indie" rock and techno, to the specialised niches of acid house, speed garage, drum and bass, acid jazz, speed metal, dub, industrial techno, ragga, lounge and trance, occupy discrete social and material spaces in diverse settings . . .
>
> (1999, 20)

In the 1920s and 1930s in North America, for example, big band swing music developed into a distinct genre through being played in large urban dance halls. As Southern blacks migrated to northern cities, their dance traditions fused with European traditional formal ballroom dancing, resulting in a new dance form known as the Lindy Hop (Rogers 1998). As the best bands followed the dancers, and developed swing music suited to the "dancers" needs, the dancers in turn followed the best bands and created dance moves that emphasised the musicality of the emerging "swing" music. Harlem, with its dense concentration of speakeasies and dance halls, nightclubs and ballrooms, became the epicentre for this new dance form. In particular, it was the Savoy Ballroom, spiritual home to some of the most famous personalities of the time, such as the "swing master" Chick Webb and dancers Norma Miller and Frankie Manning (see Ward and Burns 2000), that acted as the key space for musical creativity and consumption.

Similarly, in the 1950s and 1960s in the Pacific Northwest Region of North America, a distinctive musical style called the Northwest Sound developed around the key social institution of teenage dance, as both a social event and an opportunity to hear live music. As Gill (1993) describes, the music at these dances captured and created the excitement, power and illicitness of the events, as well as reflecting the physicality of the work life of the Northwest. The urban spaces at the centre of these local social activities were "big band"-era ballrooms, where promoters presented local groups. These groups developed local dance hall alternatives to the rock 'n' roll being written in a factory style in New York, which was produced in a layered and artificial style that made the music difficult to reproduce in a live setting. The creative process was driven by the need to produce music which young people could dance to when played live in the dance halls. The sound they created was necessarily elemental and energetic, loud and hard-edged with a driving dance beat (Gill 1993). These examples show how dance-beat oriented people, through their preferences and demands from the dance floors of a specific set of urban spaces, directly influenced the development of the musical styles of big band swing and the Northwest Sound.

In Jamaica, from the 1930s to the 1950s, a vibrant big band jazz scene also thrived, amongst affluent city-dwellers. In high-class clubs and hotels, bands played American jazz standards, as well as adapting pan-Caribbean

100 *Beyond the Studio*

forms (Katz 2003). However, poor working-class Jamaicans could not afford these smart venues. Instead, their entertainment came from "sound systems," large sets of sound equipment that were played at high volume at dance events. Small areas accommodated an extraordinary number of open-air and dance hall venues (Bradley 2001). "Sound men" would confront each other with their sound sets, aiming to play the most exclusive music. From these battles, certain personalities, such as Tom the Great Sebastian and Duke Vin, would rise to prominence as legendary sound men through being adventurous and playing the most varied selections of music to attract the largest audiences. As Katz (2003) describes, sound "clashes" were waged to establish dominance of an area, with the dancing public making clear which of the rivals they felt had a superior selection. For Bradley:

> There was always much more of a connection between a Jamaican dee-jay and his crowd than the idea of a disco or night-club might imply. A good dance would be a group experience; a mutual-appreciation society between deejay and disciples.
>
> (Bradley 2001, 10)

Audiences had a direct influence on the music being played by the sound men and thus on the music being created in, and imported into, Jamaica's embryonic home-grown music industry. In Jamaican dance halls, systems of sound amplification would allow the development of a new genre of music known variously as dancehall, dub and ragga, involving live talking impro-visations against the background of recorded music. This genre developed as DJs adjusted lyrics and music in line with instant feedback from audiences (Cooper 2004). The music of the sound systems would act to inspire the next generation of Jamaican music artists, and were crucial to the evolution of world-renowned reggae scenes. As Bradley surmises:

> . . . everything that is Jamaican music today can be traced back to those first sound-system operations. Today, more than forty years later, the sound system remains the mainstay of the Jamaican music industry. . . . Thus musical evolution remains, quite literally, by popular request.
>
> (Bradley 2001, 11)

The sound system technologies pioneered in Jamaica would have a fun-damental technological influence on the evolution of rap and hip hop music in North America through migration. The hip hop music genre that emerged from the deprived areas of North American cities has become one of the most globally appropriated, resonating with urban social conditions across the world. Hoyler and Mager (2005), for example, examine the built envi-ronment of youth clubs and community centres as key sites of creativity and performance in the creation of "first generation" hip hop communi-ties in Germany. They highlight these spaces as being "multifunctional and

Recording Studios in Urban Music Scenes 101

palimpsestic—re-usable and re-writeable—for purposes as diverse as live concerts, theatre performances, exhibitions, lectures, discotheques or hip hop jams" (Hoyler and Mager 2005, 252). These clubs and centres facilitated cultural interaction and became the focal meeting points for hip hop artists in the same neighbourhood or town, allowing the communication of ideas about personal experience, creativity, musical production technologies, and also a space in which to perform. This led to the formation of sustainable networks in the form of friendships, information flows, musical collaborations and joint cultural productions (Hoyler and Mager 2005). These networks in turn were central to the establishment of infrastructures such as specialised magazines, stores, record labels and studios, which played a key role in creating, reproducing and distributing German hip hop music (Hoyler and Mager 2005).

The advent of club cultures, raves and other forms of dance music has predicated certain urban spaces being symbolically transformed by music (see, for example, Gibson 1999, on the subversive sites of rave culture in Sydney, Australia, and Ingham et al. 1999, on warehouse parties in Blackburn, U.K.). This is due to the ways in which dance music producers have traditionally been quick to embrace new technologies and modes of production. Dance music focuses on DJs using and mixing pre-recorded material in a live environment, mediating "fragments of other texts from diverse geographical contexts in re-combined forms" (Gibson 1999, 25). Using available technologies to compose new sounds, dance music creativity links directly to the spontaneous moments of live performance, and spaces of performance are at once spaces of production and consumption of dance music. In such instances, as Wood et al. assert, ". . . music making is a material practice: it is embodied and technologised; it is staged; it takes place" (2007, 869).

However, as Gibson (1999) and Ingham et al. (1999) describe, unlike more commercial forms of dance music performance that have permeated more widely into many diverse spaces of production and consumption, rave and "acid house" performances deliberately took place in large abandoned spaces, often previously used for industrial and manufacturing production such as old warehouses and factories, turning the cracks in urban landscapes into temporary *lived* spaces and *imaginative* landscapes:

> While "rock" and "indie" scenes often mythologise particular performance and production sites in an historical context (Abbey Road, Woodstock, etc.), establishing fixed locations with rich traditions . . . the idealised "rave" occupies space momentarily, before such industry narratives are solidified. Such events rely on the uniqueness of particular sites, and the transient ways in which otherwise ordinary spaces are transformed . . .
>
> (Gibson 1999, 22)

These spaces are more than simply containers of activity; they are symbolic resources (see Sarup 1996). These unregulated spaces, when combined

102 Beyond the Studio

with music, and in many instances illegal drugs, particularly ecstasy (see Critcher 2000; Glover 2003), provide the setting for a temporary culture of hedonism, physical abandon, euphoria and escape from everyday *real world* identities (McRobbie 1994; Goulding et al. 2002). They are at once spaces of fixity, making use of permanent spaces in the urban environment of particular cities, and spaces of cultural and technological flows, as DJs and audiences enter into these spaces to transform them into places of creativity, performance and consumption. However, as Critcher (2000) describes, due to questions over the legality of place and measures to control raves and drug taking, by 1993 warehouse raves had virtually become extinct in the U.K. Instead, rave culture diversified into legal venues and became incorporated into the structure of the night club industry and wider dance music culture (see for example Hesmondhalgh 1998).

Fraser and Ettlinger (2008) provide an analysis of British drum 'n' bass (D&B) music, one of a number of musical forms that emerged from the rave scene in the 1990s. Characterised by a dub plate culture, in which music producers give unsigned records to DJs, innovation occurs again in a wide variety of spaces ranging from those that are physically fixed, such as recording studios and homes, to collaborations in virtual space. However, "learning also occurs on the dance floor in raves, which become a testing ground, a laboratory, even a marketplace in which new, often unsigned music is played and consumed" (Fraser and Ettlinger 2008, 1649). The authors argue that "D&B events rarely occur in places designed for the music" (Fraser and Ettlinger 2008, 1649), a conclusion that again underlines the importance of an urban environment that provides multiple locations for the expression of alternative musical creativity.

5.4 CONCLUSIONS

This chapter has highlighted the "mutually generative relations between music and place" (Leyshon et al. 1995), and described how musical creativity in cities is realised—and accordingly how music scenes develop—through the mixing, encounters and contacts between people within and across particular spaces and places. Certain spaces and particular neighbourhoods within cities have become identifiable places of musical creativity; in particular it is in the more diverse neighbourhoods of cities that creative moments are more likely to spark, through the mutual exchange of musical styles and practices among different cultural groups. Diversity alone is however not sufficient to sustain creativity. The presence of supporting networks is crucial in this respect, fostering and driving creativity in such neighbourhoods. These networks include musicians and creatives, music industry players, and live music venues and audiences, as well as the cafes, bars and clubs where musicians and music industry professionals may meet, collaborate and exchange creative experiences.

In particular, the chapter has emphasised the role that recording studios play in creating the "sound" of particular music scenes. More than simply pieces of economic infrastructure, much like live music venues recording studios are important spaces of socialisation in music scenes, acting as a focal point for networks of musicians and musical creativity. Furthermore, the work of particular producers and engineers in particular studios has shown to be central to the development of the "sound" of a scene; as was highlighted in Chapter 4, each producer or engineer draws on the unique acoustic characteristics of a studio and a particular palate of technologies to create a particular style of sound. In turn, their work becomes key to the association that develops between particular types of music and particular cities, an association frequently used in marketing to distinguish musical products on an increasingly global music market.

NOTES

1. There is however a developing concern in economic geography that this focus may reinforce a set of powerful spatial discourses (Allen 2000), which privilege one spatial scale for analysing knowledge (see Bunnell and Coe 2001), resulting in clusters being viewed as impermeable producers and containers of knowledge. As Wolfe and Gertler (2004) suggest, a large component of the knowledge inputs to local production may be drawn from well outside the local cluster.
2. See, for example, Homan (2000, 2002) and Gibson and Homan (2004) on live music scenes in inner-city Sydney; Luckman et al. (2008) on the live music scene of Darwin, Australia; and Gallan (2012) and Gallan and Gibson (2013) on the live music scene of Wollongong, Australia.

6 Recording Studios in Project Networks (1)

The Networked Studio

As we have seen throughout the preceding chapters, recording studios can be considered as *relational* spaces of creativity, both inside the space of the studio and beyond. The previous chapter, for example, argued that the idea of the recording studio as a relational space extends beyond the insulated space of the studio to the (mostly) urban settings in which studios are located. However, the relationality of the recording studio extends further than this; it extends beyond the urban (or non-urban) locations in which they are based, out into interurban networks at a global scale.

Alongside developments in technologies and computer software for recording, as outlined in Chapter 1, there has been the relatively recent development of networking technologies that allow the sharing of digital music files and simultaneous real-time virtual collaboration between recording studios in geographically distant locations. Recording studios have increasingly adopted such networking technologies (and record producers and recording engineers have accordingly adopted a particular set of [net]working practices around these technologies), in part to reduce production costs, but also to expand and coordinate their activities on a global scale and service a highly mobile clientele of recording artists, producers and engineers (Théberge 2004). The result is the development of new relational geographies of music creativity operating across multiple spatial scales.

It is these new relational geographies with which this chapter is concerned. The chapter is organised into three sections. The first section of the chapter sets the economic context behind the networking of studios, examining the project-based nature of work in the music industry, and specifically the production of musical recordings as a form of market-based temporary project work that links studios together into project networks. The second section then briefly considers the Internet-based technologies which are enabling new forms and intensities and networking between studios. Building on these two sections as context, the chapter then moves on to consider the nature of creative collaboration at-distance, in particular focusing on the (net)working practices and communication strategies adopted by producers and engineers to build and maintain creative relationships.

6.1 PROJECT NETWORKS IN THE MUSIC INDUSTRY

A "project" can be defined as a system of production that is constituted by different skill holders; economic, social and cultural agents with specialized and complementary competencies collaborating over a pre-determined period in order to complete a pre-specified and usually complex task (Lundin and Söderholm 1995), where the complexity of the task necessitates the coordination of multidisciplinary skills, which it is not economically efficient to bring together on a permanent basis (Lorenzen and Frederiksen 2005). Such temporary project systems are not a new phenomenon, having always been present in certain industries (Asheim 2002), particularly in those industries now considered as involving "old media," such as the music industry, and also including the film industry (see for example DeFillippi and Arthur 1998; Blair et al. 2001). In the case of music production, every new music album, whether physically produced on a CD or produced as a digital product, can be seen as a discrete product innovation with new content, which is created in a temporary project that brings together highly specialized complementary human resources, including musicians, studio producers and engineers, as well as record company executives and sales and marketing specialists (Lorenzen and Frederiksen 2005).

Whereas much of the literature on projects has focused upon "project teams," in which skilled actors are employed within the same firm, in the music industry, projects are carried out mainly in the market. In "market-based" projects, participating skill holders are employed in different firms or may be freelancers (Lorenzen and Frederickson 2005). If we consider the process of recording, for example, it is one that requires skilled labour in the form of studio producers and engineers, with the appropriate technical skills, tacit knowledge and appropriate aesthetic appreciation for a project. Producers and engineers are no longer typically employed on a permanent basis by a single recording studio (see Chapter 9). Therefore, many will have no long-term association with any one recording studio or any one record company, but rather carry out their work in creative project networks that transcend the boundaries of firms (Lorenzen and Frederickson 2005). It is these individuals, with unique skills and high levels of creativity, that are the main prerequisite for the maintenance and renewal of these creative networks (Törnqvist 2004) and thus for project-based working in the music industry.

Activities in temporary projects are dominated by individual knowledge embodied in these highly mobile project members (Asheim 2002; Grabher 2002a). As these embodied creative knowledges are for sale on the labour market, any competitor can potentially draw on competencies that have developed (see Lam 2000). In most cases it is the record company that plays the coordinating role in bringing together recording professionals onto projects as required for a particular recording project; in order to produce successful products on increasingly global markets, record companies must be able to draw on relevant knowledge bases for the relevant part of the

106 *Beyond the Studio*

value chain in production (Asheim 2002), and draw essential competencies into the firm as individual projects require. For example, as the recording industry cannot ultimately control what is going to be commercially successful, larger firms often have attempted to monopolize access to the best recording facilities and most talented engineers and producers (Negus 1992).

The above discussion suggests that the knowledge base required to produce a recorded musical product is largely external to the record company. In some cases, it may not even be internal to the music industry (Asheim 2002), for example the increasing synergies found between music companies and ICT firms, such as those described by Power and Jansson (2004) in a growing music services industry in Stockholm, exploiting the opportunities offered by new internet and mobile technologies and digital music platforms. With the rise of "new media," focused around innovative new technologies and the internet, we are increasingly seeing the technologies and practices of these new media cross-fertilizing with old media industries such as the music industry. This is impacting on the dynamics of project-based working; in the case of the recorded music industry, for example, the potential for project-based production that spans geographic space has undoubtedly been enhanced by new internet technologies.

Recordings as Projects

Musical recordings are essentially "one-off" projects that bring together, temporarily in space and time, a group of skilled professionals to undertake a project with the definite end product of a music track or full album. Recording projects resemble a conventional form of "managed" project, in that they tend to have a budget allocated by the record company, who also appoints a manager who oversees the project (often, the producer). Management of these creative projects is however very challenging, with the record company needing to retain control of the project and ensure satisfactory progression whilst at the same time allowing the creative talent—the musicians and studio producers and engineers—the creative freedom required to produce the required standard of product. When to terminate the project is, however, a record company decision, whether this is once the project is completed, or if it is considered to be progressing unsatisfactorily.

Although these projects are essentially one-offs, as personal networks are built, further projects may be undertaken involving recurrent collaboration (Grabher 2002a, 2002b). As Grabher (2002c) suggests, projects operate in a "milieu" of recurrent collaboration that, after several project cycles, fills a pool of resources and "gels" talent into latent networks. This is due to the way in which new projects tend to draw on core members of successful prior projects. Chains of repeated cooperation are held together, or indeed cut-off, by the reputation members gained, or lost, in previous collaborations. This is especially the case given that musicians often make choices for themselves regarding the cost and location of production (Jones 2002) and the producers and engineers who will work on their recording project, a decision that will be down to a combination of previous experience on projects, personal and professional networks, and the individual reputation of producers and engineers.

The personal and professional creative networks associated with project working are increasingly spanning the globe, resulting in geographically far-flung project collaborations (see for example, Cole's 2008 study of animated film production in Europe). In the case of the music industry, new technologies that network studios in geographically distant locations enable musical recording projects to be coordinated on a global scale and so allow for projects to draw on creatives in geographically dispersed locations.[1] Ties between record companies, musicians and specialized producers and engineers reach out between musically creative cities across the globe, and each individual recording project may involve a range of different studios, often in geographically dispersed locations. The effect of this is to bring studios together in shared project networks, linked through mobility—either through the physical mobility of producers, engineers and/or artists as they travel between studios; or through the mobility of recordings as they are transferred digitally. Thus, we are seeing the development of new relational geographies of musical creativity across multiple spatial scales, and the formation of global urban networks of musical production. An example of such a geographically dispersed recording network is shown in Figure 6.1, for the album *Tonight* by Franz Ferdinand, released on Domino Records/Epic Records in January 2009. The network of recording for this particular album is dispersed across six studios in six cities, including cities in the U.K. (London, Bristol, Glasgow), the U.S. (Los Angeles, Phoenix) and Canada (Vancouver).

Figure 6.1 Example album project network: Franz Ferdinand *Tonight* (Domino Records/Epic Records, 2009) City codes: BR—Bristol; GL—Glasgow; LA—Los Angeles; LN—London; PH—Phoenix; VN—Vancouver

Reproduced from the article "The World According to iTunes: Mapping Urban Networks of Music Production" by Allan Watson, published in *Global Networks* 12 (4): 446–466 (John Wiley & Sons)

108 *Beyond the Studio*

Although linking studios in this way makes recording projects both more complex to manage and more expensive, using a number of different studios during a recording project can bring a number of significant advantages, not least to be able to select a studio based on its suitability for a particular aspect of the production. As we have seen in Chapter 4, different recording studios have different types of recording equipment and different acoustic spaces that will suit different types of music and different stages of the recording process. As one interviewee described:

> ... sometimes it is different studios for different parts of the recording. So you might go to a big studio to record drums to get that initial rhythm section down, and then you might go to a smaller place so that you can just fine tune it ... sit there, recording guitars. ... And then you might go to another studio that's really good for mixing, that's got loads of outboard equipment and you don't need the big live room because you're mixing, so you go somewhere else for that. And then you'll go somewhere else entirely to give it to the mastering engineer. And the advantage, I guess, is that there's ... the gear's specifically good for that part of the recording process, and also because you've got different experts, so as it passes between the studios, the speakers are different, they're going to bring out different overtones that you might not have heard at the place before, and you've got different experts that are giving their little bit to the project.
>
> (Interview 11, male engineer, twenties)

Some studios have a palate of technologies focused on vintage analogue recording equipment, which is considered to give a warm and full sound to guitar-based music. Other studios specialise in the mastering of music rather than recording, which requires a very different palate of technical equipment. Furthermore, different studios will employ staff with particular technical skills or, in the case of freelance labour, particular producers or engineers will prefer to work in particular studios. Therefore, recordings will often move between studios to take advantage of particular technologies or particular "experts" who may specialise in particular types of music or be specialist in using or programming particular technologies. The advantages of this type of project working in terms of the creative outcome of the project were expressed by two interviewees, one noting that "sometimes it's really profitable to have an album move round lots of studios, because you get lots of people's opinions and lots of ears, different ears on the project" (Interview 11, male engineer, twenties), while the other noted that "people will come here for one track when recording an album ... usually the plan is to record in several different places to get different vibes and different flavours for different songs" (Interview 1, male engineer-producer, thirties). Thus from any one recording project, there can emerge a range of songs with different aesthetics that have been produced in different studios, by different producers and engineers, and using different technologies.

6.2 NEW TECHNOLOGIES FOR NETWORKING

As Théberge describes, in recent years, various forces within and outside the music industry, in particular hardware and software suppliers and Internet service providers, have created techniques and tools that allow recording studios in remote locations to be networked in "ever more complex and intimate ways" (2004, 759). This, he argues, has given rise to "network studios," which in their attempt to service a highly mobile clientele (recording artists, producers and engineers) have "increasingly adopted recording technologies and practices that enable them to expand and co-ordinate their activities on a global scale" (2004, 761).

Two developments have been particularly important in this respect. Firstly, the spread of high-speed internet and the development of the File Transfer Protocol (FTP) for the transfer of files from one computer to another over the Internet now allow for digital files to be shared remotely between studios in geographically dispersed locations. One interviewee, a mastering engineer and owner-operator of a mastering studio in London, explained how there had been a distinct shift in the way work was coming in to the studio, such that the percentage of their work now being received via digital networking was "quite high, it's got to be like 95, 96 per cent of the stuff that I'm working on is either going via our FTP server or is coming in as You Send It, digital deliver files" (Interview 3, male mastering engineer, fifties). Secondly, the development of Digital Audio Workstations, and in particular the commonality of these DAWs, means that not only can files be shared, but sent in a common format which allows files to be opened and worked on in most studios, before being saved and then transferred on, opening up new possibilities for project work across geographical space (Box 6.1). Furthermore, these technologies are not exclusive to professional recording studios. With the increasing availability of high-speed broadband in personal homes, networking technologies are now also available to producers and musicians working in home studios, linking even the smallest of studios into geographically dispersed networks of production.

Aside from FTP, perhaps the most significant development in networking technology that has impacted on the work of recording studios is Integrated Services Digital Network (ISDN). ISDN is a set of communication standards for the simultaneous digital transmission of voice, video, data and other network services over the traditional circuits of the public switched telephone network. For recording studios, the key feature of ISDN—the integration of speech and data on the same lines—has enabled the development of technologies for simultaneous recording that allow musicians, producers and engineers to collaborate in real-time and at distance. In the U.K., one of the earliest major studios to invest in ISDN capability was AIR recording studios in London, which in the 1990s invested in installing ISDN in each of its studio rooms, believing it to be an area of technology that would become increasingly important in the future (see Cunningham 1998). In 1995, for the first time a single

110 *Beyond the Studio*

Box 6.1 A collaborative, transnational music recording project: "Veiga, Veiga"

Crowdy and Neuenfeldt (2003) describe the production of the track "Veiga, Veiga" recorded by Henry (Seaman) Dan in 2003 involving at-a-distance collaboration between songwriters, musicians and producers based in Australia (Cairns, Sydney and Thursday Island) and Papua New Guinea (Port Moresby). While the authors' interest lies across the aesthetic, technological and cultural processes informing the production, of particular interest to the discussion presented in this chapter is the enabling role played by technology. In this respect, shared recording technology between studios is crucial—in this the case multi-track digital recording software Pro-Tools. This enabled the sharing of work between collaborators in a digitised format. The engineer and co-producer of the recording project, Nigel Pegrum, notes that:

> Obviously we have to establish between the different locations which are going to be handling the recorded material that there is some sort of common system . . . in this particular case it was made easier because the other locations, PNG and Macquarie University, run Protools. There are different versions of Protools but to my knowledge all versions can open files of this fairly simple nature and work on them and then pass them on in a useful form.

What made this particular recording project particularly challenging was that, as a result of a production schedule involving a variety of audio elements with a variety of collaborators in a variety of locations, different versions of the song circulated at once with certain stages incomplete. Project participants did not know what had been recorded elsewhere. As a result, Crowdy and Neuenfeldt note that "the final structure and aesthetics of the song remained malleable and unknown to individual collaborators until the final stages" (2003; no pagination), with the challenge falling to engineer and co-producer Nigel Pegrum to construct the final track from the various files circulated during the project. Perhaps unusually, in the case of this project, working files were not sent between studios using e-mail or FTP. Rather, the files were written on to CDs which were couriered back-and-forth between recording and mixing locations in Australia and Papua New Guinea. Nigel Pegrum explains why Internet file transfers were not used:

> [Pro-Tools is] purely the operating platform but there are several possible problem areas, one of which is the transferring of the digital information between locations. We decided to courier a CD containing the information from studio to studio. It may seem to people who are used to the world of email and Internet transfers [to be] a rather cumbersome way of doing it. But I was concerned that information could be corrupted in the course of transferring it.

As Crowdy and Neuenfeldt suggest, this collaborative recording project demonstrates how at-a-distance collaboration is facilitated by the new media technology of recording programs such as Pro-Tools.

was recorded and mixed simultaneously when Japanese guitarist Hotei at Singapore's Form Studios was linked to Jesus Jones at Real World Studios near Bath in the U.K., a distance of over 7,000 miles and covering two different time zones, via Solid State Logic's WorldNet system (Cunningham 1998). Two interviewees working in larger studios with ISDN technologies gave some examples of simultaneous collaborative working at-distance; the first described how "we had an American producer listening in to voice over sessions, so they're listening and the actor's doing the line to the voiceover. And they direct it from there" (Interview 8, male engineer, twenties), while the second gives the example of an orchestral recording project for a film score:

> So I'm there in London, I've got an audio feed that's going to three places . . . got the audio feed and we've got then a Skype call or an iChat call where we can talk to each other . . . so we can have a conversation in just about real time about the music . . . I can be recording something for somebody in London and there can be three different people have a conversation about it.
>
> (Interview 2, male engineer, thirties)

Three particular advantages to remote collaboration might be identified. Firstly, a number of interviewees explained how internet networking technologies had extended out their client bases into other geographic territories, markets that it would have otherwise been difficult to penetrate without a physical studio presence. As one interviewee explained:

> . . . the internet's also broadened out the client base. I've had work in from the Netherlands, from Turkey, from Australia, from America, which wouldn't have happened in the past because sending tapes over would have been expensive and a pain. So the world is getting smaller.
>
> (Interview 3, male mastering engineer, fifties)

The second advantage, and related to the above, is the ability to send recordings to studios located in cities in different time zones, meaning that working can take place across time zones (Box 6.2). As one interviewee noted about the use of internet technologies, "I'll use the time zone, so I'll use people in New York or LA. So I go to bed they continue, wake up in the morning, pick it up again, and that's great, that's a really expedient way of working" (Interview 12, male engineer-producer, forties).

Finally, a significant potential advantage of remote working technologies is the reduction and perhaps even removal of the need for travel. This is especially advantageous when project teams are large, as was described by one interviewee in the context of orchestral recording:

> It's not ideal, but it does mean that they don't have to fly over. That's the thing with a big film score, you're getting composer, composer assistant, music editor, music assistant, director, director's assistant, two or three

112   *Beyond the Studio*

Box 6.2   ISDN-working across time zones: The case of h2o Enterprises, London (Robjohns 1999)

ISDN (the acronym stands for Integrated Systems Digital Network) might sound like one of those purely technical issues that perhaps doesn't really belong in the pages of a music recording magazine, but believe me, it does. And the reason it does is because it has already significantly changed the way in which music is recorded. Any situation in which high-quality audio needs to be transferred over long distances in real time, perhaps between studios around the world, or just between a radio reporter and his newsroom, is a candidate for employing an ISDN link-up.

One of the leading exponents of the use of ISDN technology in professional audio applications in the UK is the south London-based h2o organisation, founded by Andy and Robin Hilton. They claim the h2o facility to be the first purpose-built ISDN "virtual overdub" suite in the world . . . the company will typically handle between three and five ISDN sessions a day, with work from New York tending to fill in the early evening and Los Angeles in the small hours of the morning. The transfer side of h2o's business typically involves sending or receiving audition copies of album mixes, or approval copies of radio commercials. This is a particularly effective way of working when different time zones are involved. For example, if an artist is mixing an album in New York but the recording company executives are in London, using ISDN to transfer some full-quality alternative mixes overnight allows the record company execs to listen and comment before the next day's work commences back in the States. . . . In the example above, getting virtually instant feedback on a mix project allows it to be completed much more efficiently and quickly, and the time and money saved on returning to mixdown suites and resetting the console and outboard to remix a track far outweigh the modest expense of real-time ISDN transfers.

Source: Extract from article by Hugh Robjohns in *Sound on Sound Magazine*, April 1999. See also: http://www.h2o.co.uk

---

producers so there can be twelve people coming over from America to do a project sometimes, and now you don't have to do it anymore.

(Interview 2, male engineer, thirties)

It was noted by interviewees however that, alongside such advantages, there are also significant challenges and problems of working with technology that is at a relatively early stage of development. For example, a number of interviewees working with ISDN technologies for simultaneous collaboration noted that what they could actually achieve with the technologies was relatively limited. One interviewee described how:

We're nowhere close to actually being able to run a proper set of satisfying sessions real-time at the moment, and also at the moment we're

The Networked Studio   113

still in a state of flux where we're dealing with technology that "sort of works," and "sort of works" isn't great in a professional world . . .

(Interview 12, male engineer-producer, forties)

The need that arises to send a series of working files between studios and/or clients to be edited and commented upon also presents particular problems in terms of the limitations of current technologies. Not only does the editing process take time, but also large music files may take some time to upload where internet bandwidths are low, and therefore where constant reworking of files is needed, this can be extremely time-consuming, as one interviewee explained:

> . . . it is really time-consuming making changes and uploading them can take hours, can take six or seven hours to upload a single ProTools session. And then if someone comes back and says he doesn't like it, just change one thing, you have to upload it again which will take you another day. So it is not ideal yet, but I guess it all comes down to bandwidth and technology just catching up.
>
> (Interview 9, male engineer-producer, thirties)

While bandwidth and the reliability of internet connectivity can be improved, the required infrastructure can be prohibitive for all but the largest recording studios. Many studios can justify installing permanent ISDN lines, but buying all three commonly used audio codecs is prohibitively expensive unless they are in regular use. Therefore, many studios hire ISDN equipment as and when it is needed. London's two major studios, AIR Studios and Abbey Road take this approach. Moreover, both studios today use a costly high-speed internet connection provided by Sohonet, a company which provides high-speed managed internet connections for media and entertainment industries (see http://www.sohonet.co.uk; accessed 08/10/2013).

6.3 COLLABORATION AT-DISTANCE

As noted, technologies for file sharing permit new forms of remote working in the recording studio sector, linking geographically distant studios to each other in complex ways (see Théberge 2004). These developments have resulted in new forms of collaboration, that rather than being face-to-face, are at-distance and virtual. Without the face-to-face interactions which, as highlighted in the discussions of emotional labour in Chapter 3 are key to creative collaboration and the building and maintaining of relationships in the studio, remote collaboration has required studio workers to develop new strategies for collaborative working and communication with clients. A number of interviewees noted that, to compensate for the lack

114 *Beyond the Studio*

of face-to-face interactions, collaborating on a project remotely involves a constant stream of communication (usually via e-mail) as well as the need to send a whole series of working files between studios which can be edited and then commented upon. One interviewee described how one of the main problems in communicating in such a way is not getting the level of dialogue that would part of a face-to-face conversation, and how he tries to encourage such a dialogue with his clients:

> . . . it's trickier with projects over the internet because you have to do that thing by e-mail. It's "look, I'm going to send you back what I think, you don't have to say 'yes' and 'no', you can say 'yeah, I like this' or 'I don't like that' or whatever, and only once we've got to the point where you're happy, that's where I take your money. . . . Don't just feel that you have to go 'yes.'"
>
> (Interview 3, male mastering engineer, fifties)

He goes on to emphasise that while it would be much quicker to work through the creative process if the client were in the studio, it is important that despite this a dialogue be maintained with the client, in order that the client is able to communicate exactly what it is that they want from a project:

> Oh it would be so much quicker. It's much quicker if they're with you. But the important thing is to, is to still go through the process even when they're not. Because it is a, it's a dialogue process and who am I to tell an artist what they want is wrong? They've composed it, they've performed it, I'm just trying to, from my perspective present it in the best light. If there's a particular thing that they're trying to achieve and I haven't got that for them they have to be able to tell me that.
>
> (Interview 3, male mastering engineer, fifties)

There are however a number of barriers in achieving effective communication at distance, especially when using e-mail. While the above interviewee emphasises the need to go through a detailed process of dialogue when working remotely, the following interviewee expressed his frustrations when attempting to do this:

> . . . that process doesn't really happen, because by the time you have written that into an e-mail and then you read the e-mail back and you go well, that sounds a bit arrogant for me to say that, that sounds a bit like, no, actually I have to rephrase that, fucking hell . . . so maybe something might get lost.
>
> (Interview 13, male engineer-producer, forties)

In some instances, the client that may not be able to effectively communicate their requirements for a project at distance may not be a musician or a recording

The Networked Studio   115

artist, but a producer or engineer who has sent a recording digitally to another producer or engineer in another studio to be worked on, for example a recording to be mixed or mastered. One interviewee described his own experience of these difficulties and suggested that the difficulty in communicating detailed requirements at distance can put a strain on working relationships:

> . . . I have done collaboration with another producer on some of my stuff where this producer that I know and trust and I think is amazing, and I have sent him files and just let him get on with it without being in the room. And then he sends stuff back and I wasn't happy with it at all. And then it is really difficult to communicate ideas when you are not sitting there, when you are not in the room choosing sounds with people. The same thing goes for mixing tracks, sending songs to America. A lot of guys do online mixing and mastering, sending the songs off to get mixed. He is the most respected guy, he charges a fortune and if you don't like his mix, it is really hard to tell him why you don't like his mix. Trying to communicate a list of things without making it sound like you have got two hundred bullet points that you need him to change, and that puts a strain on relationships I think more than anything.
>
> (Interview 9, male engineer-producer, thirties)

Thus as creative working at distance becomes more prevalent in the industry and presents particular challenges in terms of creativity and communication, the need to build and maintain strong relationships with clients at distance—to perform *distanciated* emotional labour (see for example Bryson 2007) becomes increasingly important.

The Continued Need for Travel and Face-to-Face Collaboration

These issues highlight perhaps the most significant disadvantage of remote working—whether this be simultaneous real-time working or working via file-transfer—namely that it is inherently unsatisfactory to many producers and engineers when compared to face-to-face working in the space of the recording studio. Cunningham (1998) notes that the use of ISDN appears to be isolated at least in part due to the human need to be in the same room as each other and the intimate level of communication required between musicians to create music. Such an assertion was supported a number of interviewees. One noted that "a lot of them [recording studios] use ISDN to do their stuff. But I'm never really happy utilising that technology because, number one, you want to see the person and interact with them face to face" (Interview 5, male engineer, sixties), while another stated:

> . . . ultimately I much prefer to being face to face, I think there's something about communication that is so difficult when you're not in the

116 *Beyond the Studio*

presence of the person who is ultimately looking to you to turn their work into a masterpiece . . . essentially I much prefer working with someone and therefore I would say the face to face communication aspects and the travel aspects is quite important.

(Interview 10, male engineer, thirties)

The above quote suggests that in a time when studios are increasingly becoming networked through technologies (Théberge 2004) allowing for remote creative collaboration, travel remains important. Travel is important due to the way it facilitates face-to-face meetings (Faulconbridge et al. 2009) both with clients and collaborators, allowing for creative collaboration in cross-border recording projects, and also crucially in terms of getting future work, the building of personal social networks:

Yes I think it is going to be an important part of it because people always need to travel to get good results I think . . . Yes I think it makes a massive difference . . . I think in terms of building relationships which is what it is all going to be about. It is really, really important to just solidify your contacts for starters. And to be in the same room with the artists to make them feel comfortable and make sure that they have the support around that they need in terms of having the person that they trust in the room.

(Interview 9, male engineer-producer, thirties)

Thus, despite new communication technologies in the recording studio sector, the need for "meetingness" (Urry 2003) appears to remain in the recording studio sector. This is illustrated in the high level of mobility of many producers and engineers. In 2008, a questionnaire survey of producers and engineers working in recording studios in London was undertaken by the author. Out of a total of 64 respondents, 30 (just under 50 per cent) had worked abroad at some point during their career. Respondents were asked to provide location details of the overseas studios at which they had worked, and the information obtained is plotted in Figure 6.2.

The figure demonstrates that the geographic mobility of these engineers and producers is truly global in nature. These networks of physical movement stretch out from London across Western and Eastern Europe, North America, Pacific Asia, Australasia and Africa. The highest densities of connections through physical travel exist with Western Europe and North America. The most frequently cited destinations for project work abroad were Los Angeles and New York—demonstrating the important networks of mobility between three major centres of musical recording for Anglophone markets (see Chapter 7)—as well as Paris. Sydney, Berlin, Munich, Brussels and Rome also received multiple responses. Respondents were also asked to provide details on how the opportunity to work abroad arose. Most frequent responses made references to invitations being made based

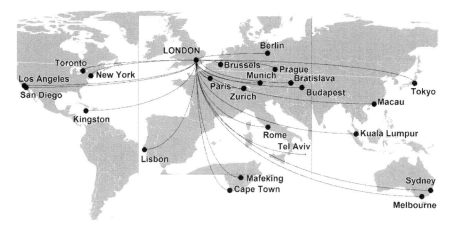

Figure 6.2 Geographic mobility of a sample of London-based recording engineers

upon either reputation or opportunities for work emerging from personal relationships developed with recording artists or other studio engineers and producers (see Chapter 10).

6.4 CONCLUSION

As was argued in the previous chapter, "studios do not exist in a musical or cultural vacuum" (Théberge 2004), but rather are intimately connected with the local music scenes, local aesthetics and music practices of the places in which they are located. Recording studios, it was argued, are a key part of the mutually constitutive relationship between place and musical identity. However, for Théberge, developments in networking technologies raise fundamental questions about the future relationships between recording studios and the local places in which they are embedded, giving rise to the notion of the "placeless" virtual studio. Viewed as simply nodes in networks, he argues, studios become "non-spaces" and "non-places"—an expression of the tendencies of economic globalisation. In the following chapter, Chapter 7, this idea of studios as "nodes" in networks is extended through a mapping of the urban networks of music production.

However, there is an inherent contradiction here in scales; while some recording studios may enable certain mobile actors to create music on a global scale, they are also likely to be used by more local independent actors to produce very localised sounds. As Théberge notes:

> the network studio can be used in such a way to reinforce the status of the studio within the 'flows' that characterize the spatial logic of the dominant economic order, or it can be used to coordinate more

118   *Beyond the Studio*

autonomous forms of genuinely collaborative production that are at once local, regional, and perhaps even global in character.

(2004, 779)

Viewed from this perspective, recording studios can be considered as articulating the local with the global, resulting in new relational geographies of music creativity and recording across multiple spatial scales. In this regard, while Théberge is undoubtedly correct in his assertion that networking tools and techniques connect studios in *complex* ways, his suggestion that they connect studios in *intimate* ways is a problematic one. The discussion presented in this chapter, based around the perspective offered by producers and engineers during interviews, suggests that while network-working has particular advantages, it lacks the intimacy of face-to-face contact, which they consider to be of central importance to creative collaboration. While producers and engineers have adopted a particular set of (net)working practices and communication strategies in an attempt to manage collaboration at-distance, including the performance of emotional labour at-distance to build and maintain creative relationships, ultimately these practices and strategies seem to be unsatisfactory. This is demonstrated through the continued importance of travel for producers and engineers.

NOTE

1. It is important to note here that the history of project work between studios stretches further back than the widespread introduction of the internet. Copies of recordings have long been sent throughout the world to be mixed and mastered in different studios by specific engineers, while mobile musicians and producers have moved between recording studios to work on particular recording projects.

7 Recording Studios in Project Networks (2)

A Global Urban Geography of Music Production

In the previous chapter, a discussion was presented of the new technologies that have given rise to the "networked studio" (Théberge 2004). These new communications and networking technologies enable musical recording projects to be coordinated on a global scale and link studios in complex ways to other studios in geographically distant locations. The chapter described how personal and professional creative networks are increasingly spanning the globe, resulting in geographically far-flung project collaborations, with projects drawing on pools of creative labour in geographically dispersed locations. As such, the production of music provides a revealing focus for research on urban networks of cultural production, due to the ways in which music production is caught up in multiple layers of networks (Connell and Gibson 2003) involving a wide range of actors in a range of locations.

Building on the discussion in the previous chapter, it is these urban networks of musical production, and specifically their global nature, with which this chapter is concerned. The chapter employs social network analysis to undertake an examination of these networks, and the importance of particular cities within these networks. The analysis is based upon data on the social connections occurring through project work. This is *relational* data linking cities with other cities, allowing us to ascertain how connected cities are to each other, rather than attributional data for specific cities (such as the number or size of a city's recording studios) which whilst interesting can tell us little about the position or power of particular cities in networks of musical production. Specifically, the chapter examines the *working flows* that occur between recording studios, based in cities across the globe, when they are part of temporary creative projects that are brought together to produce recorded music albums. The end result is a mapping of global urban networks of music production, and specifically the power and centrality of particular cities within these networks. Following a brief discussion of methodology and data collection, the chapter describes the results of the social network, which attempts to define and map the urban networks formed through creative project working in the recorded music industry; assesses the level of connectedness of particular cities; and employs a number of

120 *Beyond the Studio*

measures to determine the power and centrality of cities within networks of production for digital music markets.

7.1 SOCIAL NETWORK ANALYSIS METHODOLOGY: ASSESSING POWER AND CENTRALITY IN URBAN NETWORKS

Social network analysis provides a set of tools that can be employed to empirically assess networks between cities, through the analysis of social actors and their networks. As Dicken et al. (2001) and Yeung (2005a) suggest, a central component of such a relational analysis is recognition of the existence of differential power relations within networks. Powerful and active actors play a key role in driving networks and making things happen. Their ability to do so is dependent upon their control of key physical, political, economic, social and technological resources. However, while the control of resources is necessary in order to have power, it is not a sufficient condition for the ascription of power to an actor; rather for Yeung (2005b) power is the relational effect of the capacity to influence and the exercise of this capacity through actor-specific practice. Power can therefore be defined in terms of both position and practice within networks, a relational and emergent concept *manifested through practice*. Some actors within networks derive their capacity to influence from structural positions, whereas others may experience power through relational practice with power emergent through practice rather than being dependent upon position.

The power of particular cities within networks of production can be defined in both terms. From a structural position perspective, city power has been conceptualized in terms of power as a capacity for domination (Allen 1997), based upon a stock of resources that can be used instrumentally as power over other cities (Friedmann 1978). From a practice perspective, power has been conceptualized as a medium (Allen 1997) with a city occupying a strategic position in the world city network based not upon capacity but on its interrelations with other cities. The essence of this "networked" understanding is "power to" rather than "power over," with every city in an urban network occupying an incipient position of power (see Taylor et al. 2002).

The analysis presented in this chapter employs two different measures to assess the power of cities as central nodes of recording in the global urban networks of music production. The first measure used is Bonacich's *power-based centrality measure* (see Hanneman and Riddle 2005). In applying this measure to urban networks, centrality and power in the network is a function of the connections of the cities to which a particular city is connected. The more connected the cities to which a particular city is connected to, the more central the city is. The less connected the cities to which a particular city is connected to, the more powerful the city is, and the less connected cities will be more dependent on it.

A Global Urban Geography of Production 121

The second measure used is *flow betweeness*. This measure is based on the proportion of the entire flow between two actors, through all of the pathways connecting them, which occurs on paths of which a given actor is a part. The measure adds up how involved the actor is in all of the flows between all other pairs of actors, as a ratio of the total flow betweeness that does not involve the actor (Hanneman and Riddle 2005). Betweeness centrality is an important indicator of control of information exchange and resource flows within a network (Knoke and Yang 2008), as the measure ascertains the extent to which an agent can play the part of a "gatekeeper" with a potential for control over others (Scott 1991). Although they may not necessarily have the most connections to other cities, those cities with a high degree of flow betweeness centrality are considered to be the most important mediators in the urban network. These cities are better situated than other cities as a result of the position that they occupy in the network (Alderson and Beckfield 2004) due to their own and their neighbour's network connections.

A core-periphery analysis is also undertaken on the valued data matrices to identify those cities belonging to the core of the network and those which belong to the periphery. The social network analysis presented in this chapter was undertaken using the UCINET social network analysis software (Borgatti et al., 2002). The network visualizations provided are derived through the embedded NetDraw visualization tool.

Data Collection

The projects on which the analysis in this chapter focuses are recorded popular music albums, defined as a group of audio tracks with a generally consistent track list across the different territories in which it is released. As was described in the previous chapter, each album is its own temporary project, consisting not only of firms (record companies), but also localities (recording studios in particular cities), and the professional and personal networks of the musicians and studio producers and engineers. Within these projects, elements of creative labour may be fixed in particular studios, with recordings being transferred digitally, or this labour may be mobile between studios in different cities. It is these movements, of both labour and recordings, which are the connections that form urban networks of musical production within the recorded music industry. Thus, in collecting data for the social network analysis described in the following section of the chapter, an event-based strategy has been employed in which network boundaries are drawn by including actors who participate in a defined set of activities occurring in specific times and places (see Knoke and Yang 2008). Each of these events, in this case temporary music industry projects (albums), has their own distinct production network, varyingly dispersed in terms of their geography. By including multiple events (albums) in the network analysis, it is possible to produce a comprehensive and inclusive network, in which many distinct networks overlap with one another.

122 *Beyond the Studio*

iTunes sales charts were chosen for analysis because iTunes is the leading player in the online downloads market. In 2008 iTunes became the largest U.S. music retailer. Databases of recording information for albums, consisting of information on the recording studios used, and the producers, engineers and mastering engineers involved in the recording, were constructed based upon the details given in the credits of albums appearing in the top-10 iTunes download charts, for the U.K., U.S. and Australian digital music markets, during the first six months of 2009. During the period of data collection, iTunes top-10 music sales charts were published online and continuously and automatically updated, and were available for most of the major national digital music markets. This allowed comparisons to be made between a range of national digital music markets. In this chapter, comparisons are made between the U.K., U.S. and Australian digital music markets. These three Anglophone markets were selected for analysis primarily due to the availability of the required data in English. An exploratory data collection exercise for a number of non-Anglophone markets including Japan revealed significant difficulties in obtaining the required data such that a full and comprehensive analysis would not have been possible for these markets.

For reasons of practicality the continuous updates to the charts could not be followed on a constant basis, and therefore the charts were analysed on a weekly basis. Data was sampled between 1 January 2009 and 31 June 2009. Only full albums released in this time period and up to one year before, and including newly released material, were included in the sample. EPs (releases containing a smaller number of tracks than a full album), compilations, "greatest hits" compilations and albums originally released over one year before the sampling date, were not included. The final databases contain data on 53 albums from the U.K. download charts, 52 albums from the U.S. download charts and 39 albums from the Australian download charts respectively. The data are coded as non-directional, i.e., there is no distinction made between "senders" and "receivers" in relationships, rather they are considered to involve mutual exchange. The data produce three symmetrical and valued matrices, one for U.K. networks of production, one for U.S. networks of production, and one for Australian networks of production with the matrices linking 36, 43 and 29 cities across the globe respectively. Inevitably a significant amount of overlap occurs between the three databases.

7.2 STUDIOS AND CITIES IN PROJECT NETWORKS: DISPERSAL AND CONCENTRATION

Examining the data collected on the recording studios in which sampled albums were produced is revealing of two trends in recording: first, the increasingly networked nature of music production; and second how the democratisation of the recording process has undermined the position of the major studios. If one looks at the 52 albums sampled from the U.S.

A Global Urban Geography of Production   123

download chart for example, they were produced across 137 different recording and mastering studios, with 20 of the albums being produced across networks of four studios or more. If one looks at recording studios only, only two studios—Chalice Recording Studios in Los Angeles (five) and Blackbird Recording in Nashville (three) were associated with more than two albums in the U.S. sample, suggesting a high level of democratisation in production. Similarly in the U.K. sample of 53 albums, just three recording studios were associated with more than two albums—again Chalice Recording Studios in Los Angeles (five), as well as Olympic Studios in London (which closed in February 2009) (five), and Sarm Studios in London (three).

If one examines where the studios in the sample are located, however, the picture is one of strong concentration. Table 7.1 ranks the top five cities based on the release of albums into the U.K. digital music market. The figures given are based on the number of albums for which studios in the city were involved in the recording "project" expressed as a percentage of the total number of albums captured from chart data. Based upon this, London is shown to be the pre-eminent centre for the output of sales-successful recorded music into the U.K. digital music market. Studios based in the city were involved in the recording projects for over 50 per cent of all the albums captured in the data. Los Angeles and New York, with 38 per cent and 36 per cent respectively, trail behind London but are far ahead of a second tier of smaller U.K., European and U.S. cities. Many other cities with individually smaller levels of output make up a third tier of production. The dominance of the global city triad of London, New York and Los Angeles in terms of sales-successful output for the U.K. digital music market is clearly highlighted by these figures.

Table 7.1   Top five cities ranked by output of albums; U.K. digital music market

Rank	City	Albums output from the city (% of total number of albums)
1	London	52%
2	Los Angeles	38%
3	New York	36%
4	Cardiff	7%
5	Bristol	5%
~	Glasgow	5%
~	Portland (MN)	5%
~	Miami	5%
~	Dublin	5%
~	Stockholm	5%

Note: A single album can be considered to be output from more than one city where the album is produced within a creative project network of cities.

124   *Beyond the Studio*

Table 7.2   Top five cities ranked by output of albums; US digital music market

Rank	City	Albums output from the city (% of total number of albums)
1	Los Angeles	58%
2	New York	46%
3	London	25%
4	Nashville	10%
5	Portland (MN)	8%

Note: A single album can be considered to be output from more than one city where the album is produced within a creative project network of cities.

Table 7.2 ranks the top five cities based on output of albums into the U.S. digital music market. In the case of the U.S. digital music market, Los Angeles is shown to be the pre-eminent centre for the output of sales-successful music, with its studios involved in the recording of almost 60 per cent of all the albums captured in the data. It is closely followed by New York, with New York studios involved in 46 per cent of the albums sampled. Contrasting with the case of the U.K. digital music market, London is significantly behind both Los Angeles and New York in terms of sales-successful output into the U.S. digital music market, accounting for 25 per cent of the albums sampled. These cities are followed in the top five cities by two more U.S. cities, Nashville and Portland (MN), accounting for 10 per cent and 8 per cent respectively.

Table 7.3 provides the same rankings for the Australian digital music market. In this case, New York and London are pre-eminent, with studios in both cities involved in over 40 per cent of all the albums captured in the data respectively. They are closely followed by Los Angeles, whose studios are involved in 38 per cent of the albums sampled. These are followed by the Australian city of Melbourne. Accounting for 13 per cent all the albums captured in the data, it is well behind the global city triad, but ahead of another Australian city, Sydney, which accounts for 8 per cent all albums. This data for the U.S. and Australian markets thus also highlights the dominance of the global city triad of London, New York and Los Angeles.

One of the key reasons for this strong level of concentration is found when attention is turned to mastering, where there is a strong level of concentration in particular studios in particular cities, which undertake mastering for an unbalanced share of the recordings sampled. In terms of the U.K. digital music market, the most significant mastering studio is Metropolis Studios based in London, followed by Sterling Sound based in

A Global Urban Geography of Production 125

Table 7.3 Top five cities ranked by output of albums; Australian digital music market

Rank	City	Albums output from the city (% of total number of albums)
1	London	41%
~	New York	41%
3	Los Angeles	38%
4	Melbourne	13%
5	Sydney	8%
~	Portland (MN)	8%

Note: A single album can be considered to be output from more than one city where the album is produced within a creative project network of cities.

Table 7.4 Top five mastering studios in networks of musical production, U.K. digital music market

Mastering studio	City	Number of albums mastered (% of total number of albums)
Metropolis Studios	London	20%
Sterling Sound	New York	13%
Bernie Grudman Mastering	Los Angeles	8%
Gateway Mastering	Portland (MN)	7%
Masterdisk	New York	7%

New York (see Table 7.4). Together, these two mastering studios account for one-third of the total number of albums sampled. In the top five these studios are joined by Bernie Grudman Mastering (Los Angeles), Masterdisk (New York) and Gateway Mastering (Portland, MN). Together these five studios account for 55 per cent of the total number of albums sampled.

In terms of the U.S. digital music market, it is a U.S.-based studio that is prominent. Sterling Sound, based in New York, dominates the list of key mastering studios (Table 7.5), accounting for 27 per cent of albums. It is followed by Bernie Grudman Mastering (Los Angeles), Gateway Mastering (Portland, MN), Marcussen Mastering (Los Angeles) and Metropolis Studios (London). Together these five studios account for 66 per cent of the total number of albums sampled, suggesting even greater concentration of the mastering process than that found in the networks of production for U.K. digital markets.

126   *Beyond the Studio*

Table 7.5   Top five mastering studios in networks of musical production, US digital music market

Mastering studio	City	Number of albums mastered (% of total number of albums)
Sterling Sound	New York	27%
Bernie Grudman Mastering	Los Angeles	13%
Gateway Mastering	Portland (MN)	10%
Marcussen Mastering	Los Angeles	8%
Metropolis Studios	London	8%

Table 7.6   Top five mastering studios in networks of musical production, Australian digital music market

Mastering studio	City	Number of albums mastered (% of total number of albums)
Sterling Sound	New York	28%
Metropolis Studios	London	10%
Bernie Grudman Mastering	Los Angeles	8%
Gateway Mastering	Portland (MN)	8%
The Exchange	London	8%

Sterling Sound in New York also dominates the list of key mastering studios for the Australian digital music market (Table 7.6), accounting for 28 per cent of albums. It is followed by Metropolis Studios (London), Bernie Grudman Mastering (Los Angeles), Gateway Mastering (Portland, MN) and The Exchange (London). Together these five studios account for 62 per cent of the total number of albums sampled. Mastering then, as a key production process, plays an important role in concentrating production in certain key cities, and in particular London, New York and Los Angeles, and does not display the same level of democratisation as for recording.

Key to the concentration of the mastering process in particular recording studios is skilled labour, specifically the mastering engineers contracted to these studios. For example, Ted Jensen, chief mastering engineer at Sterling Sound in New York, alone accounts for 15 per cent of the total number of albums sampled from the U.S. digital market, while mastering engineers John Davis and Tim Young of Metropolis Studios in London together account for the mastering of almost 20 per cent of the total number of albums sampled from the U.K. digital market. Bob Ludwig of Gateway Mastering in Portland alone accounts for 10 per cent of the total number

A *Global Urban Geography of Production*   127

of albums sampled from the U.S. digital market, and 7 per cent of those from the U.K. digital market. The prestigious nature of certain studios, and thus the concentration of the mastering in particular cities, can then be directly attributed to the skilled engineers that are working in these studios.

7.3   RECORDING STUDIOS IN GLOBAL URBAN NETWORKS OF MUSICAL PRODUCTION

Connectivity in Urban Networks

While the output data described in the previous section is useful in providing a hierarchy of studios and cities based on levels of production, it tells us little about networks of production *between* cities. The data gathered on connectivity, based on the links between cities occurring as part of creative projects, is more informative as to the configuration of global urban networks of musical production. Table 7.7 ranks the top cities in the urban networks of production for the U.K. digital music market based on their total number of connections to other cities. London, New York and Los Angeles dominate the rankings as the three most connected cities, with around three times the number of connections of the fourth placed city, Bristol. All three cities have their highest connectivity to each other, and all of the other cities have their highest connectivity with one or more of these three cities. The

Table 7.7   Top cities ranked by total number of connections, U.K. digital music market

Rank	City	Total connections	Highest connectivity
1	New York	38	9 (Los Angeles) 6 (London)
2	London	37	8 (Los Angeles) 6 (New York)
3	Los Angeles	35	9 (New York) 8 (London)
4	Bristol	12	2 (London, Glasgow)
5	Glasgow	10	2 (London, Bristol)
~	Portland (MN)	10	2 (New York)
7	Miami	9	3 (Los Angeles) 2 (New York)
8	Atlanta	8	2 (New York, Los Angeles)
~	Dublin	8	2 (New York, London)
~	Stockholm	8	2 (New York, London)

128 *Beyond the Studio*

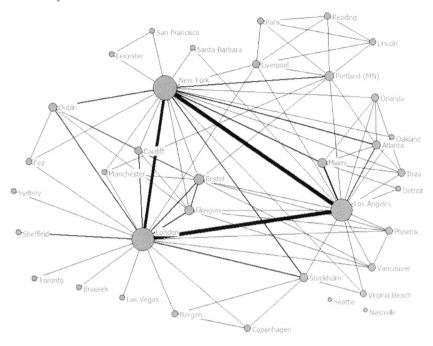

Figure 7.1   Global urban networks of recording, U.K. digital music market

strongest link between individual cities is shown to be that between New York and Los Angeles, very closely followed by the connection between London and Los Angeles. The remainder of the list consists of other smaller U.K., U.S. and European cities. Figure 7.1 provides a visual representation of the urban networks formed by these connections. The visualization displays the triad of London, New York and Los Angeles lying at the centre of network, surrounded by a web of less connected cities whose role as music recording centres is articulated through the three highly connected global cities.

Table 7.8 ranks the top cities within the urban networks of production for the U.S. digital music market, based on their total number of connections to other cities. The U.S. global city dyad of New York and Los Angeles are shown to dominate the rankings of the most connected cities. Both cities have over twice the number of connections of the third placed city, London. The two cities are shown to have an extremely strong level of connection to each other when compared to the strength of their links with other cities, having around four times more connections with each other than they have with London. Figure 7.2 provides a visual representation of the urban networks formed by these connections. The visualization displays the dyad of New York and Los Angeles lying at the centre of network of production. Contrasting with the network for the U.K. digital market shown in

A Global Urban Geography of Production 129

Table 7.8 Top cities ranked by total number of connections, U.S. digital music market

Rank	City	Total connections	Highest connectivity
1	New York	54	18 (Los Angeles) 5 (London)
2	Los Angeles	53	18 (Los Angeles) 4 (London)
3	London	23	5 (New York) 4 (Los Angeles)
4	Portland (MN)	11	3 (New York)
5	Phoenix	9	1
6	Portland (OR)	7	1
7	Vancouver	7	2 (Los Angeles)
8	Seattle	6	1

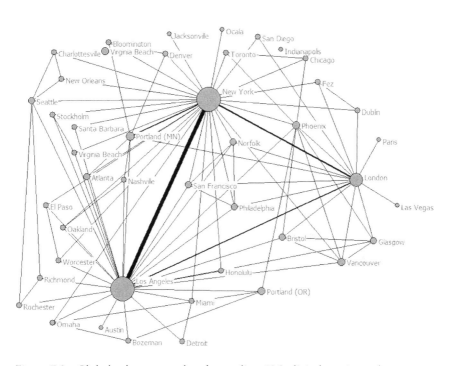

Figure 7.2 Global urban networks of recording, U.S. digital music market

Figure 7.1, London does not match these two cities in terms of importance at the centre of the network.

Table 7.9 ranks the top cities within the urban networks of production for the Australian digital music market. Mirroring the case for the U.K. market, the triad of London, New York and Los Angeles are shown to dominate the

130 *Beyond the Studio*

Table 7.9 Top cities ranked by total number of connections, Australian digital music market

Rank	City	Total connections	Highest connectivity
1	New York	27	6 (London) 5 (Los Angeles)
2	Los Angeles	23	5 (New York) 5 (London)
~	London	23	6 (New York) 5 (Los Angeles)
4	Bristol	5	1
~	Glasgow	5	1
~	Melbourne	5	1
~	Phoenix	5	1
~	Stockholm	5	2 (New York)
~	Vancouver	5	1

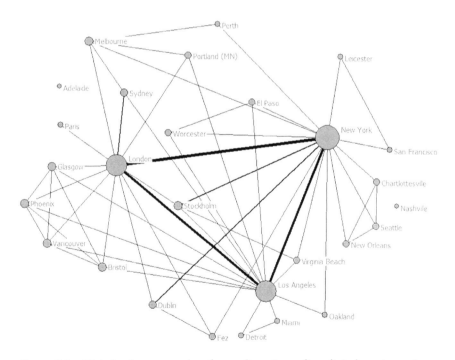

Figure 7.3 Global urban networks of recording, Australian digital music market

rankings, with New York marginally ahead of the other two cities. The highest ranked Australian city, Melbourne, has only a fraction of the number of connections of the triad. Figure 7.3 provides a visual representation of the urban networks formed by these connections. The network diagram displays a very

A Global Urban Geography of Production 131

similar configuration to that for the U.K. digital music market (Figure 7.1), with the triad of London, New York and Los Angeles lying at the centre of network.

Centrality and Power in Networks of Music Production

In the urban network of production for the U.K. digital music market, Los Angeles, whilst only the third most connected of the cities in terms of total connections, is calculated to have the highest degree of centrality, i.e., has the most connections to other cities with a high degree of connectivity, marginally above both New York and London. Although London accounts for the output of many more albums into the U.K. digital music market than Los Angeles and New York (52 per cent of albums, compared to 38 per cent and 36 per cent respectively), by this measure it is the least central of the dominant three cities.

However, in terms of power in the urban network, i.e., in terms of many cities with low degrees of connectivity being dependent upon the city, London is calculated to be the most powerful city in the network, very closely followed by New York. Los Angeles is the third most powerful city, but is shown to be far less powerful than both London and New York. London is also calculated to be the most important mediating city in the network based upon the flow betweeness centrality measure, significantly more important than New York, which is turn is a significantly more important mediator than Los Angeles. These results, outlined above and summarized in Table 7.10, are indicative of London's dominance as the most important city within the urban network of production for the U.K. digital music market.

In the urban network of production for the U.S. digital music market, New York is shown to score highest on all three measures (Table 7.10). This is despite having a weaker album output than Los Angeles (involvement in 46 per cent of total albums compared to 58 per cent), and only a marginally higher number of connections (54 compared to the 53 of Los Angeles).

Table 7.10 Centrality measure rankings for London, New York and Los Angeles

Market	City rankings; Bonacich centrality	City rankings; Bonacich power	City rankings; Flow betweeness centrality
UK	1. Los Angeles 2. New York 3. London	1. London 2. New York 3. Los Angeles	1. London 2. New York 3. Los Angeles
US	1. New York 2. Los Angeles 3. London	1. New York 2. Los Angeles 3. London	1. New York 2. Los Angeles 3. London
Australia	1. New York 2. London 3. Los Angeles	1. New York 2. Los Angeles 3. London	1. New York 2. Los Angeles 3. London

132 Beyond the Studio

Based on the Bonacich measure, New York is calculated to have the highest degree of *centrality*, i.e., has the most connections to other cities with a high degree of connectivity, although it is shown to be only marginally ahead of Los Angeles. Both cities have much higher centrality rankings than London, which in turn is significantly ahead of the fourth-placed city, Atlanta. New York is also shown to be the city with the most *power* in the urban network, i.e., in terms of many cities with low degrees of connectivity being dependent upon the city. By this measure, New York is shown to be much more powerful than Los Angeles.

Los Angeles is shown to be only marginally ahead of London in terms of power in the network, despite accounting for a much higher output of albums (involvement in 58 per cent of total albums compared to 25 per cent) and having many more connections (53 compared to the 23 of London). This highlights London's power over certain weaker cities in the urban network, cities which New York and Los Angeles may have to go through London to access. New York is also calculated to be the most important *mediating* city in the network based upon the flow betweeness centrality measure, significantly more important than Los Angeles, which is turn is a significantly more important mediator than London. These results are indicative of New York's dominance within the urban networks of production for the U.S. digital music market.

New York also scores highest on all three centrality measures for the Australian digital music market (Table 7.10) and therefore is calculated to have the highest degree of centrality, to be the most powerful city, and the most important mediating city in the network in the urban network of digital music production for the Australian market. It is however only very marginally ahead of London in terms of its centrality. Los Angeles comes ahead of London on the Bonacich power measure and flow betweeness centrality measure, despite having a marginally weaker album output, although it is below London on the Bonacich centrality measure. One interesting outcome is the score of the Australian city Melbourne on the flow betweeness centrality measure. Melbourne is positioned clearly in fourth, behind the global city triad but well ahead of other cities in the network. This demonstrates that Melbourne occupies an important position within the network as a *mediator* city, playing the part of a "gatekeeper" for access to the Australian music market.

A core-periphery analysis for the networks of production for the U.K. digital music market gives a core that contains nine of the 36 cities involved in the production of the musical outputs included in this analysis. Along with the three dominant cities of London, New York and Los Angeles, is a second tier of core cities: Atlanta, Bristol, Dublin, Glasgow, Miami and Stockholm. These cities have relatively strong ties to the three dominant cities, and to each other, when compared to peripheral cities. The same analysis for the networks of production for the U.S. digital music market gives a core that contains just five of the 43 cities included in the data. New York, Los Angeles and London are present in the core; they are joined by Atlanta

A *Global Urban Geography of Production*   133

and Portland (MN), the only second-tier core cities. All other cities in the network have relatively low connections with the core cities and each other. A core-periphery analysis for the networks of production for the Australian digital music market gives no distinct core or periphery.

7.4 CONCLUSIONS

Over these last two chapters we have seen how, enabled by new networking technologies and driven by market-based projects in the music industry, ties between record companies, musicians and specialized producers and engineers reach out between musically creative cities across the globe. This is resulting in the development of new relational geographies of music production and creativity. Through social network analysis this chapter has provided an exploration and mapping of a relatively small sample of urban networks of production within the global recorded music industry. It has emerged from the social network analysis that the spatial agglomerations of music industry firms, studios and creative labour in particular key cities remain central to music recording process in the age of digital music markets, with outstanding technical studio facilities strongly centralized in particular key cities. This is especially the case for the triad of global cities of New York, Los Angeles and London, home to very strong concentrations of record companies and recording studios (see Scott 1999b; Watson 2008).

The results of the analysis are demonstrative of the fact that the path dependence of networks of recording is intimately embedded in physical infrastructures. Musical recording in the late 1960s was recentralized in cities and strongly reconnected to the music industry as the new technology demanded considerable investments in studios and skilled personnel that only major record companies could afford. As Gibson (2005) notes, the best technology was rare, and usually found in cities with thriving music scenes, at studios such as the EMI Abbey Road Studios in London and Capitol Studios in Los Angeles. In a time of digital production and home recording, networks of music production remain material outcomes of economic processes that are localized in certain places and territories and exist over long periods of time (see Bathelt and Glückler 2003). In particular, the analysis has demonstrated how mastering as a key part of the production process plays an important role in concentrating production networks through certain key studios in certain cities. These are engineers and studios that producers, recording engineers and record companies seek out, chosen over others. It is perhaps unsurprising that the three most central and powerful mediating cities as indicated by the centrality measures—London, New York and Los Angeles—are also the three most prestigious cities in respect of mastering studios.

However, it must be noted that the strength of the outcome of the analysis in terms of the dominance of New York, Los Angeles and London, is at least

134 *Beyond the Studio*

in part due to some of the limitations of the sampling strategy and data used in this empirical analysis, which focuses solely on three Anglophone markets. If one were to undertake the same analysis for major non-Anglophone markets, especially those in Asia such as China and Japan, the resulting urban networks would likely be configured rather differently to the results presented in this chapter.

ACKNOWLEDGMENTS

Figures 7.1 to 7.3 and Tables 7.1 to 7.10 are reproduced from the article "The World According to iTunes: Mapping Urban Networks of Music Production" by Allan Watson, published in *Global Networks* 12 (4): 44–66 (John Wiley & Sons).

8 MP3s and Home Recording
The Problems of Software

This, the final chapter of Part Two, considers two key technological developments which have impacted directly on both the way recording studios operate and on their future viability as formal, professional spaces of recording. The specific technological developments being referred to are, first, the development of the MP3 software format; and second, the increased availability of software for home recording. In the first instance, both technological developments seemed fairly innocuous, even positive, developments for the music industry; the MP3 software format was a product of the development of an international standard for picture and audio files (Leyshon 2001); while the development of software based Digital Audio Workstations (DAWs) was the latest in a long line of digital and software developments giving greater ability to professional engineers and producers to manipulate sound creatively. Both developments however had somewhat unforeseen impacts.

In the case of MP3s, the development of a compressed, standard file format for music quickly resulted in the sharing of music online between listeners, the result of which was an undermining of music sales and a crisis of funding across the musical economy in which the recording studio sector is embedded. In the case of DAWs, the combination of powerful yet affordable home PCs, and the availability to consumers of the same software being used by professional studios, drastically lowered entry barriers into cultural production and would result in a rise in home recording and a huge loss of income for professional recording studios.

The purpose of this chapter is to evaluate critically the current and likely future impacts of these technological developments on the recording studio sector. To begin, the chapter considers the impact of the development of the MP3s software format on the wider musical economy, examining the resulting "crisis of reproduction" (Leyshon 2009) that would result in disastrous losses for the leading firms in the sector, and importantly with regards to the recording studio sector, a decrease in recording budgets. Further, it highlights another challenge to recording studios around the development of the MP3 format, namely a culture of "lo-fi" listening that threatens to leave current models of high-quality recording significantly

136 *Beyond the Studio*

outdated. The second section of the chapter then considers the development of home recording technologies and the rise of skilled home producers, which questions the need for industry expertise and equipment. The chapter argues that, while such technologies suggest a democratization of production, home recording is a mode of production intrinsically linked to, and dependent on, consumption (De Carvalho 2012). Finally, the chapter considers the extent to which the technologically driven democratisation of *both* production and consumption is allowing musicians to make a living from autonomous music production, and in particular the saturation of the digital marketplace for music.

8.1 MP3S AND THE "CRISIS OF REPRODUCTION" IN THE MUSIC INDUSTRY

There has long been a close relationship between the music industry and technological developments (Leyshon 2001), from early innovations in sound reproduction, through the reproductive mediums of vinyl, magnetic audiotape and compact disc (CD), each in turn providing higher quality audio playback. This relationship has largely been a positive one, with each technological development in recording medium bringing about economic benefits across the musical economy, especially to record companies and music publishing companies—for example, the reissuing of back-catalogues in new formats (see Lovering 1998)—and to electronic companies producing new reproductive equipment. Following the introduction of the CD the music industry enjoyed about 15 years of steady growth in recorded music sales (Leyshon et al. 2005). A symbiotic relationship has then existed between electronic companies who produce reproductive equipment and create consumer demand for new, higher quality audio playback, and the record companies producing music on the new medium. Indeed, one of the music industry's major corporations, Sony, is a major producer of both technology and entertainment. As Leyshon (2001) describes, given the economic benefits of these previous technological developments, the development of the internet as a vehicle for world digital distribution was largely seen as a positive one.

It is now however widely known that rather than an opportunity for economic gain, this development would present one of the most significant challenges ever faced by the music industry in terms of its profitability; indeed, it would fundamentally challenge the viability of the music industry in the form in which it had existed for many years. This challenge centred on the development of the MP3 format as an international standard (Box 8.1). At first a seemingly innocuous development, the creation of a compressed, standard file format for music, playable on most home PCs and a range of mobile music devices, would quickly result in the sharing of music online between listeners from computer to computer.

Box 8.1 The development of MP3 files (Leyshon 2001)

The reason that a world of cabled connectivity began to be perceived not as a boon but as a serious threat, not only to future profitability but, in the opinions of some industry commentators at least, to the long-term survival of established record companies, was an unforeseen and hitherto unremarkable technological development originating in the considerably less glamorous world of international standards.

This development was seemingly innocuous software programme called MPEG-1 Audio Layer 3 or, as it is better known, MP3 ... MP3 is a compression program, which reduces the size of digital audio files, making them quicker to make and easier to distribute. Compression programs analyse the profiles of digital packages to remove repetitions and redundancies of information. MP3 achieves compression through a task known as "psychoacoustic masking." The software analyses and filters sounds according to their degree of audibility to the human ear. This filtering process means that MP3 files are much smaller than conventional digital music files, so whereas as CD requires 11 megabytes (MB) of memory every minute of sound contained, an MP3 requires only 1 MB of memory of every minute of sound. Therefore, whereas a standard of three-minute CD track would require around 30MB and take around 90 minutes to download onto a computer, an MP3 file of similar length would require only 3 MB and would take only 10 minutes*.

Source: Extract from Leyshon (2001, 50–51)

* At the time of writing, the speed of a typical broadband internet connection in a home in the UK would allow a for an entire album to be downloaded in around 1 minute, while super-fast fibre-optic broadband allows for an entire album to be downloaded in around six seconds.

As Leyshon (2001) suggests, the size of these files had important consequences for their mobility, as they were small enough to be transferred from computer to computer via the "narrow-band" dial-up modem connections typical in homes in the late 1990s and early 2000s. The copying of music on CDs into MP3 format and the subsequent sharing of this music on the internet would substantially undermine sales of recorded music, impacting directly on the economic viability of the music economy, and tipping a music industry already on the verge of crisis into a full-blown "crisis of reproduction" (Leyshon 2009). Furthermore, it threatened to loosen the grip that record companies exerted over musical networks of creativity, reproduction and distribution (Leyshon 2003).

Issues around the breach of intellectual property rights and illegal copying would abruptly come to the fore with the rise of peer-to-peer file-sharing networks[1], which exposed just how heavily the music industry relied on the exploitation of copyright for generating profits. These networks, as Leyshon (2003) argues, destabilised the regime of governance that supports

138 *Beyond the Studio*

"copyright capitalism" by creating, and giving mass access to, a series of "gift economies" in which the products of the music industry were given away for free, substituting for sales. Perhaps the best known of the peer-to-peer networks were Napster, which operated between June 1999 and July 2001 and which at its peak allowed tens of millions of users to share and download music for free through a user-friendly interface (Leyshon 2003); and Kazaa, which began operating in March 2001 and which had a user based of around 140 million users with as many as four million users online at any one time (Leyshon 2009). Due to these networks, "digitized music's immateriality and hyper-mobility as code caused both the economic and legal property regimes associated with the pre-digital era to become outdated and impotent" (Born 2005, 25). In 2001, music sales fell by 5 per cent, and then by over 9 per cent in the first half of 2002, resulting in a reduction in the inflow of capital to the industry and disastrous loses for the leading firms in the sector (Leyshon et al. 2005). The outcome was a crisis of funding across the wider musical economy, resulting in significant reductions in rosters of recording artists. Associated with this, there was a significant decrease in already squeezed recording budgets, which would impact directly on recording studios, especially the major studios, resulting in a spate of studio closures (Leyshon 2009).

There are further complexities relating to copyright and MP3 file sharing that go beyond the free downloading of music for personal consumption. As discussed in Chapter 2, the development of electronic samplers from the 1980s allowed for a new form of musical creativity and composition. However, the combined availability of software-based samplers for PCs, and MP3s available freely from peer-to-peer file sharing networks, created a new online "mash-up" culture in which practitioners use audio-editing software to splice and combine songs encoded in MP3 format to produce "mashed-up" recordings (Shiga 2007). With beat, key and tempo matching now commonly available even in free software packages, anyone can mash-up different albums and hear how they sound together (Moorefield 2010). Furthermore these creations can then be shared easily and quickly through peer-to-peer file sharing services; Born (2005) for example notes how the website Ccmixter (http://ccmixter.org/) operates as a music sharing site where users can sample and mash-up music in whatever way they choose, and can then upload their own versions for others to resample. In this way, she argues that "distributed across space, time and persons, music can become an object of recurrent decomposition, composition and re-composition by a series of creative agents" (2005, 26).

An online music scene has developed around mash-ups, giving rise to mash-up stars and highly sought after creations, some of which have reached the mainstream media (Shiga 2007). Thus as Riddell (2001) predicted, a new music has arisen based on reworking of MP3 recordings pulled from the Internet, and as such "the Internet is more than just a means of distribution, it becomes a *raison d'etre* for a culture based on audio data." This type of

MP3s and Home Recording 139

self-organising "digital community network," Hughes and Lang (2003) suggest, represents a shift in power away from the large and established music industry institutions. Perhaps no mash-up better expresses the current challenge posed by digital music formats, distributed via the internet, to current models of music property rights, and to producer-consumer dichotomies, than *The Grey Album* produced by the recording artist Danger Mouse in 2004 (Box 8.2).

The impact of MP3s on the music industry, while significant, and extremely negative in the short term, is unlikely however to result in the end of the control of major companies over the music industry, for a number of reasons. First, litigation formed an important part of the response of record companies to the challenges of software formats and Internet distribution system, particularly with regards to peer-to-peer networks, and this has largely proved to be successful. In a landmark case, on 7 December 1999, the Recording Industry Association of America (RIAA) filed suit against Napster, claiming that the free service cut the sales of CDs, and in late July 2000 an injunction was ordered against Napster, which was subsequently upheld in February 2001 (McCourt and Burkart 2003). Napster shut down in July 2001 and declared bankruptcy in 2002. Legal action would follow against a range of peer-to-peer networks, and in some cases, individuals sharing large numbers of files through these networks (in the case of Kazaa users, for example).

Box 8.2   Danger Mouse's *The Grey Album*

Danger Mouse's *The Grey Album* brought together samples from an a cappella version of *The Black Album* by rap artist Jay-Z with unauthorized instrumental samples from *The White Album* by The Beatles. The album demonstrated the type of music that could be produced using software in a low-budget home studio. The album was released in limited quantities through a small number of internet outlets, with artwork for the album later posted on the Danger Mouse website. Both Jay-Z and Paul McCartney gave public statements to the effect that they were happy for their music to be sampled in this way. Indeed, the a cappella version of Jay-Z's album was explicitly released for such a purpose, and samples were used by many other producers; a Jay-Z "construction set" would also become available through peer-to-peer networks, containing 650MB of samples and remixed material for constructing mash-ups. However, given the commercial value of The Beatles' music, EMI (holders of the copyright) moved quickly to halt its distribution. This however only acted to increase the notoriety of the album, and the album became more widely available on the internet through peer-to-peer file-sharing networks.

Sources: Gunderson (2004); Rimmer (2007); Moorefield (2010)

140 *Beyond the Studio*

Second, with the debut of Apple's iTunes in 2003, as well as subscription services such as Napster 2.0 and Rhapsody, it became clear that many consumers were willing to pay for music downloads. It also became apparent that, given the few costs associated with online distribution compared to manufacturing a physical object, record companies can sell music online for a relatively low cost and yet with a higher profit margin (McLeod 2005). In 2008, the online music site iTunes became the largest music retailer in the U.S., which when considered alongside the closure of major high-street music retailers such as HMV and Virgin stores in the U.K., indicates the sea-change occurring in the way people purchase music. Furthermore, the development of copy protection technologies and anti-piracy services such as AudioLock (http://www.audiolock.net, accessed 26/02/12) began to prevent people from copying digital files and sharing them.

Through the late 2000s and into the 2010s, the revenue from online music sales would significantly increase, and the digital music market now forms an increasingly important part of the global music market. In 2012, digital music accounted for over a third of total industry revenues (35 per cent), with revenues growing from $US4.3 billion in 2008 to $US5.6 billion in 2012 (IFPI 2013), with 4.3 billion digital singles and albums being legally downloaded. In five of the top 20 markets, digital channels now account for more than 50 per cent of record companies' revenues, whilst globally record companies have licensed 37 million tracks and more than 500 digital music services worldwide (http://www.ifpi.org/facts-and-stats. php, accessed 21/02/14). Income from subscription and advertising-supported services has also grown, and now accounts for 20 per cent of record companies' global digital revenues (31 per cent in Europe) with more than 20 million people paying for music subscription services in 2012 (ibid.).

Third, as the major companies have recognised that music by-itself is decreasing in value (McLeod 2005), they have sought to diversify their activities through multimedia and other new revenue streams. Performance rights, for example (that money paid to record companies to license music to be played on radio and in public places) was the fastest growing sector in the music industry in 2012, accounting for 6 per cent of global recorded music revenues; while revenues from synchronisation deals (the use of music in TV adverts, films and brand partnerships) were worth US$337 (http:// www.ifpi.org/facts-and-stats.php, accessed 21/02/14). Thus, as Leyshon et al. suggested in 2005, the emergence of software formats represented a "tipping point" that triggered a reorganisation of the music industry towards a new business model; it is now emerging as one of reduced capital flow; smaller artist rosters (focused on those few artists with strong cross-marketing potential); a strong focus on online distribution channels and multimedia; as well as continued strict enforcement of copyright through litigation against online "piracy."

MP3s, Audio Quality and the Culture of "lo-fi"

Alongside the lost income to the music industry, and subsequently falling recording budgets and lost income to recording studios from illegal distribution of MP3 files, the MP3 format has exposed another problem with current models of professional recording today. Specifically, this relates to the fact that many recording studios are continuing to operate models of recording that reflect a drive for very high quality audio reproduction. As Leyshon (2009) argues, studios have paid the cost of overestimating consumer demand for high-fidelity playback; for example, many studios invested heavily in equipment that would produce recordings in the Dolby 5.1 format for home cinema surround sound, but the market for such recordings has been slow to take off. Ironically, as Leyshon notes, the growth in MP3 players is indicative of an opposite trend and the embracing of relatively low-fidelity playback platforms amongst consumers.

The key issue here is that MP3 by its very nature is a low quality audio format; it is created through "lossy" data compression, a data encoding method that compresses data by discarding some of it, in order to create digital files small enough for quick downloads and storage on portable devices. Additionally, the MP3 format has also changed the way in which people listen to music. Research undertaken by Universal Music in late 2012, reported in the *Telegraph Online* (Smernicki 2013), suggests that mobile devices—phones, tablets and MP3 players—are now the adult population's most preferred way of listening to music, ahead of radio, in-car listening and hi-fi. The rise of MP3 players and in particular Apple's iPod means that people tend to listen to music through the type of relatively low-quality ear-bud audio headphones supplied with these devices. Put simply, sound quality has been lost to the convenience of buying, storing and listening to digital music. The way in which these issues play out for recording studios is summed up in Figure 8.1, which demonstrates how those studios using, and indeed continuing to invest in expensive analogue equipment, are producing music at a sound quality that is at odds with the way people are listening to music.

The low audio quality of the MP3 digital music format is not the first lo-fi challenge to a recording industry which seems to have been constantly in pursuit of higher audio quality. In the 1960s, most people listened to popular music on car radios and small transistor radios with very small, low quality speakers. As Moorefield (2010) describes, Motown producer Berry Gordy and producer Mike McClian began listening to mixes on small speakers, in order to produce music that would sound good when listened to in this way—the result was music that was ever so slightly distorted but sounded bright through small speakers, projecting the energy of a performance. Thus as Moorefield notes, "physical properties, then, or the materiality of the medium, are an influence on sculpting the frequency space, and thus on what can be called the electronic orchestration of a recording at the

142 Beyond the Studio

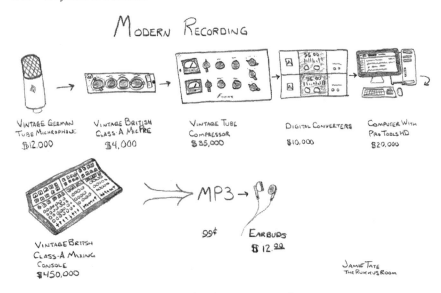

Figure 8.1 The issue of recording for the MP3 music format
Drawing courtesy of Jamie Tate, www.rukkusroom.com

mixing board" (2010, 23). In this respect then, the recent introduction of the "Mastered for iTunes" tools and guidelines (Box 8.3) which state that, when creating a master, mastering engineers should "take into account the limitations and characteristics of the medium or destination format, as well as the listening environment" represents the latest attempt to mix and master music in such a way that it sounds good in a particular format.

Box 8.3 Apple's "Mastered for iTunes"

In February 2012, Apple created a dedicated new section on the iTunes store called "Mastered for iTunes" with the tagline of "music as the artist and sound engineer intended" and promising improved digital audio quality to give a listening experience closer to CD quality than regular iTunes Plus files. *Rolling Stone* magazine reported that Apple created Mastered for iTunes when leading producer Rick Rubin publicly expressed a frustration with his inability to make the Red Hot Chili Peppers' I'm With You sound as dynamic in the Apple AAC format (equivalent to MP3) as it did on a CD. Rubin would subsequently work with Apple to develop a higher-than-usual bit rate, which when sent to iTunes for encoding, sounded better than a typical compressed audio file.

Released alongside this was a technology brief containing a set of related guidelines for mixing and mastering engineers to help them in creating the best-sounding tracks possible when music is converted to the lossy 256Kbps

MP3s and Home Recording   143

audio format commonly used in the iTunes Store, along with a free set of encoding free tools in a format compatible with Apple's Logic Pro software. The technology guide makes specific reference to the need to master for the destination format and listener environment:

> When creating a master, mastering engineers take into account the limitations and characteristics of the medium or destination format, as well as the listening environment of their audience. For example, a master created for vinyl is unlikely to be listened to in an airplane or car, and therefore is often mastered for a listening environment where a listener can hear and appreciate a wider dynamic range. Similarly, a master created for a club environment might take into account the noisiness of the intended listening environment. Because iTunes Plus is a highly portable format, its files have the potential to be listened to in a wide range of different settings. So while one listener may be using white ear buds while riding in a loud subway car, another may wind up listening intently to a Bach cantata on AirPlay-equipped Bowers and Wilkins speakers or on a similarly equipped Denon receiver in a home media room.

Source: http://www.apple.com/itunes/mastered-for-itunes/ (accessed 10/03/2013)

However, what is perhaps more significant about Mastered for iTunes is that it represents a move back towards improved sound quality for the first time since the widespread introduction of MP3s in the late 1990s. Shortly after the announcement of Mastered for iTunes, an article on the *Guardian* newspaper website (Davenport and Arthur 2012) reported that Apple was working on a new audio file format that will offer "adaptive streaming" which would provide downloads of higher-quality "high-definition" audio files from its iCloud service, dependent on the download bandwidth and storage available on the receiving device. Apple now encourages submission of 24-bit/96KHz files, which is the standard of audio produced by high-end recording studios.

In October 2013, in an article on the website of *Tape Op* magazine with the headline "The Era of Hi-res Digital Audio Is Here," Farmelo (2013) argued that "compressed audio will be outmoded as 8-track tapes" and that "new hi-fi consumer playback systems playing uncompressed digital files will soon be the norm" (no pagination). Farmelo points to two reasons why consumer demands for high quality audio will be likely to increase in the future. First was the appearance in 2013 of a series of affordable devices developed to playback high quality digital audio formats, as well as the announcement from the Sony corporation that they were not only developing hi-res digital playback devices, but were also planning to make their music catalogue available in hi-res. Such devices are designed to improve vastly on the lo-fi audio experience of iPods, laptops and mobile phones. Furthermore, as the bandwidth of both home broadband (e.g., fibre-optic) and mobile data networks increases (e.g., the introduction of 4G), and as the data storage capacity of devices also increases, it will increasingly be possible to have higher audio quality whilst maintaining the convenience of quick downloads and storage on mobile devices.

Secondly, he points to the increasing ubiquity of *on-ear* headphones as opposed to *in-ear* earphones ("ear buds"), and in particular the demand for high-quality expensive headphones. The large consumer audio-electronics firms have been quick to capitalise on this demand, including Bang & Olufsen (whose B6 headphones were their first headphone offering in over two decades), Bose, Denon, Sony and Phillips. These established brands compete in the market with new "designer" headphone brands including "Beats by Dre" and "Skull-Candy," which not only provide high-quality audio listening but which are also seen as a fashion statement. Such headphones are now available not only in specialist electronics stores but also in many supermarkets, with stores typically having headphones out on display and allowing consumers to test headphones by plugging in their own mobile music devices (Figure 8.2). At the time of writing, high-end headphones typically range in cost from £150 to £600, with some headphones available for as much as £2,000. Farmelo suggests that "the very notion that there is better sound to be had, and that it might cost some money, sends a strong message into a market" (2013; no pagination).

Figure 8.2 A range of high-quality headphones on display in a supermarket
Source: Author

If the move to hi-res digital music formats and playback devices were to take off (for example, in the same way that hi-definition television and movies have been adopted by consumers) there is a potential economic boost that may come to the music industry through the reissuing of back catalogues in a new hi-res format, much like the boost in income experienced with the CD format. Furthermore, in the previously mentioned article in the *Guardian* by Davenport and Arthur (2012), it was suggested that the real winners would be mastering studios: "It's payday for mastering engineers. . . . There could be calls for thousands of albums to be remastered, and at over £1,000 to master a mainstream album, it's going to be a healthy boost for the recording industry" (Davenport and Arthur 2012; no pagination). There is a strong potential benefit for recording studios also, in that the move back towards the high quality of audio that listeners used to be accustomed to with CDs should also act to increase the need to record, mix and master, in high-end recording studios that have expensive high-end audio equipment and offer high levels of audio quality throughout the entire recording process.

8.2   THE RISE OF HOME RECORDING

As was noted in Chapter 1, the shift to digital software-enabled recording has significantly reduced the cost of entry-level recording equipment, which has improved the quality and capacity of home recording (Leyshon 2009) and drastically lowered entry barriers into cultural production[2] (Hracs et al. 2013). In particular, the proliferation of DAWs on personal computers has brought into the home those recording practices that were considered the norm in studio production, such a multitrack recording (Théberge 1997), and removed the need for multiple expensive items of recording equipment:

> At once a means for recording audio, generating drum patterns, hosting software synthesizers and mixing down to a single file, the laptop encapsulates technological convergence. Indeed, with the right software it replaces the function of a host of hardware devices, including multitrack portastudios, hardware synthesizers, mixing desks, samplers, channel strips, compressors, guitar amplifiers, effects units and sound modules.
>
> (Prior 2012, 914)

In Chapter 2, the role of self-learning in developing the skills required for recording was discussed, involving both experimentation and the reading of "how to" books, websites, trade journals and magazines. Given that home recordists most frequently work alone, this self-learning is central to developing recording skills, and has been greatly aided by a proliferation of self-help guides for home recording. Jeff Strong's *Home Recording for Musicians for Dummies* and Karl Coryat's *Guerilla Home Recording: How*

146 *Beyond the Studio*

to Get a Great Sound from Any Studio are two well-known examples of such self-help guides. There are also a number of magazines available which are dedicated to home recording, such as *Computer Music* and *Future Music* (see Box 8.4). Through self-learning and the use of DAWs, so called "bedroom producers" have been able to develop skills and use recording and sound manipulation techniques that in the past had been the preserve of audio workers working in professional studios. As one interviewee exclaimed, "nowadays I mean what you can do from your own bedroom is unbelievable. So everyone's a producer, and everyone's an engineer now" (Interview 10, male engineer, thirties). Therefore, as Homer argues, in dispensing with the expertise of professional studio producers and engineers, "the home recording artist seems to have thrown the established hierarchy of music making into question and redefined notions of what skills are needed to create outstanding tracks" (2009, 90). Furthermore, given that DAW software, in particular Avid Technology's Pro-Tools, are standard in both professional and home studios, one might now question the need for recording "professionals":

> With sound editing software such as Pro Tools now being used by both professionals and home recording artists, there remains the question as to how far a strong literacy for such packages can in itself go towards making good music or whether there is still a place for industry expertise and equipment.
>
> (Homer 2009, 90)

Box 8.4　Home recording and the music technology press (Bennett 2012a)

A significant amount of magazines and periodicals began post-1990; these publications, many of which are still in print today, often concentrate wholly on computer music production and home-studio recording. Three main titles, among many others, are *Computer Music* (est. 1998), *Future Music* (est. 1992) and *Music Tech Magazine* (est. 2003). All these magazines concentrate almost entirely on home and project studio set-ups, often featuring "giveaways" such as free sample CDs, plug-in demos and other small "add-on" programs. The main content focuses on DAWS (Digital Audio Workstations) and each month features large articles with "tips and tricks" for operating software sequencers. The magazines focus wholly on Avid's Pro Tools, Apple's Logic and Steinberg's Cubase, as well as budget sequencers and audio programmes such as Reason, Fruityloops and Ableton Live. Equipment advertising makes up a large proportion of the content, in addition to reviews. Online versions of the magazines contain forums, reviews and blogs.

Source: Extract from Bennett (2012a, 122)

MP3s and Home Recording 147

In response to these challenges, professional producers and engineers often seek to defend the "value-added" that comes from recording in a professional recording studio, and, according to Cole (2011, 451) have "relied on their cultural capital" to portray the project and home studio owner as a mere consumer of mass technology and as "somebody who thinks they know what they are doing, but really don't." It is common to point to the limits of the self-learning of home recordists (see Chapter 2) in terms of the type of knowledge that can be gained. In particular, they point to the importance of tacit skills that they are required to have; what Zak (2001) terms "experienced technique" and the importance of which Horning (2004) argues has not diminished even in the technologically sophisticated recording studio (c.f. Gibson 2005). Such tacit skills, it is argued, are best learnt through the form of collaborative learning when an engineer or producer is able to work alongside a more experienced colleague. Similarly, the importance of having the experienced, and objective, ear of a producer on a record is often emphasised as a key benefit of recording in a professional studio, and one which is essential to producing commercially successful music.

However, there is little doubt that highly creative music with reasonable sound quality, and which finds demand amongst consumers, can be made in home studios. There are numerous examples, especially in electronic music, from mash-up artists like Danger Mouse, to mainstream artists such as Moby. Moby's album *Play*, released in 1999, was entirely recorded at the artist's home studio (based around a computer running the Cubase DAW), and was only sent away from the studio for mastering (Sound on Sound 2000). For Gunderson (2004; no pagination), "mash-up" artists such as Danger Mouse have "shown how the recording industry has been rendered superfluous by advances in music production technology." While an extremely technologically deterministic statement (the like of which have become widespread as home recording technologies have become widely available), there is little doubt that these technologies have increasingly liberated musicians from the traditional recording studio and allowed artists to experiment with recording technologies and techniques that would have been considered too unconventional in the past (Gunderson 2004). As producer John X notes "You can say that experience is important, but the kids are going to bring a whole new thing to the table because they don't have any of the rules that we have been taught" (quoted in Massey 2000, 316).

The Cost of Home Recording

For the major companies of the industry, and for many recording artists, there remains, and is likely to remain, the belief that recording in a professional recording studio is a necessary requirement for producing music that can be marketed and sold. However, even amongst this core clientele recording studios are losing business, in that developments in home recording studio technologies are encouraging artists who do use professional studios to

148 *Beyond the Studio*

do considerable amounts of pre-studio preparation work before entering the studio. Thus this reduces the time for which professional recording studios are booked. With large professional studios typically charging daily rates of around £800–£1500 per day (Homer 2009) the economic benefits of pre-production work are evident. In some instances, musicians may not enter recording studios at all. Take the afore mentioned example of the album *Play* by Moby, for instance, which was entirely recorded at the artist's home studio. While there was little need to use a professional studio as most of the album was based around samples from existing sources rather than recording of instruments, time was also a key factor. The album took a year to produce, which is possible in a home studio, but which would result in prohibitive costs was a professional studio to be used. The song "Why does my heart feel so bad," for example, took several months to get to the point of being "compositionally finished" and ready for mixing (Sound on Sound 2000). This highlights one of the major benefits of home recording, namely that it removes the time and financial constraints that can be detrimental to musical creativity in the professional studio (see Chapter 2).

There are the undoubtedly economic advantages for artists to record at home in terms of avoiding large recording studio fees. However, it is also important to recognise that setting up a home studio is by no means a "cheap" option, as purchasing the equipment to set up a home recording studio can be very expensive. Although, as De Carvalho (2012) suggests, a musician may be able to set up a home studio for a minimum average of around US$500, this really is a bare minimum cost. At the time of writing, customer versions of leading DAWS such as ProTools 11 cost in the order of £550. Further, De Carvalho (2012) argues that the discourse of home recording assumes that, given the accessibility of home recording, anyone can and thus should concentrate on reaching a professional sound at home. This discourse, he suggests, seems to be formed by "prescriptions, guides and norms" for how to record music at home. Karl Coryat's *Guerrilla Home Recording: How to Get a Great Sound from Any Studio (No Matter How Weird or Cheap Your Gear Is)* for example, suggests that "Guerilla home recording is the pursuit of professional sound in ways that don't require you to spend a lot of money" (Coryat 2008, 5). In reality, taking into account the purchase of both the necessary software and hardware (for example, computers, microphones, digital amplifiers) required to make high quality records, a musician might need to spend £2,000 or more in total on the minimum required set up (Homer 2009). If a musician were after a professional-sounding recording, studio equipment might cost in the order of £4,000, and rise above £8,000 if a musician wanted to offer professional recording services from a home studio (De Carvalho 2012).

With Protools and other DAWs providing a consistent software platform across commercial and home recording studios, the difference in audio quality—that which makes a recording sound "professional"—is the quality of other peripheral equipment, including microphones, microphone preamps

MP3s and Home Recording 149

and also the quality of monitoring (speakers) to get a full idea of the sounds being recorded and mixed (especially low-end). Good microphones can be particularly expensive, yet are absolutely crucial to recording quality vocals and when recording acoustic instruments and drums. Therefore, even if a home recordist were to overcome the space and acoustic issues associated with recording drums, for example, say by acoustically treating a garage, having an appropriate number and quality of microphones would become an issue due to cost. As one interviewee described:

> I think that's one of the reasons why people still record in these kinds of studios, because that's one of the things you can't do at home, unless you make a big investment in gear . . . even just miking up a drum kit, normally you might use twelve or even sixteen microphones on the drum kit. And when each of those mikes is about a thousand pounds . . . it gets amazingly expensive.
>
> (Interview 11, male engineer, twenties)

Similar issues are encountered with amplifiers for recording guitars. In a studio, an electric guitar would typically be played through an amplifier, the output of which would be recorded through one or more microphones. In a home studio, expensive amplifiers and microphones can be replaced with digital "pod" preamplifiers linked to a computer, allowing the computer to emulate an amplifier, and also removing the need for large acoustic spaces. However, these digital pods which aim to mimic particular sounds are not perfect in their replication of these sounds; as Moorefield argues "anyone who has played in a hard-rock band or listened to the recordings of Jimi Hendrix knows the difference in sound between a screaming Marshall stack full of vacuum tubes gone critical and the widely available approximations thereof which employ digital circuits" (2010, 76).

All of this brings into question the true level of democratisation brought about by home recording, when this democratisation is "intrinsically linked to and dependent on *consumption*" (De Carvalho 2012; no pagination; emphasis in original). Cheaper DAW software options are available, for example, but these tend to have limited functionality; "nearly free" DAWs such as the open source Audacity recording software, Apple's GarageBand or Cocko's Reaper, for example, tend to have limited functionality unless the user purchases upgrades or license (De Carvalho 2012). More recently, cheap but highly limited recording software has begun to appear in the form of apps for mobile devices; NovLegLLC's Pro-studio app, for example, which claims to provide a "mobile recording studio in your pocket" (http://novleg.com/, accessed 09/12/13), and which offers four tracks of audio recording and the importing and exporting of sound files, costs just US$9.99. However, it is highly unlikely, at least at the time of writing, that a professional sounding recording could be produced through a mobile phone.

150 *Beyond the Studio*

8.3 DEMOCRATISED PRODUCTION AND CONSUMPTION: DROWNING IN A SEA OF NOISE?

Two key issues have emerged from this chapter with regards to the democratisation of the production and consumption of music. First, digital technologies have drastically lowered entry barriers into cultural production (Hracs et al. 2013) and thus democratised the production process. In the case of the music industry, home recording technologies now enable musicians to record and produce music outside of the "formal" industry, that is to say without the need for record companies or recording studios. Second, these technologies have also acted to democratise distribution and consumption, for example through online file sharing. Thus, in theory, as McLeod argues, "the means of producing and distributing music has shifted to individual artists, which means one does not need a major label contract to reach thousands of people" (2005, 527).

However, as Hracs et al. argue, this democratisation has resulted in a contemporary marketplace for cultural products that is "characterized by infinite choice and intense competition" (2013, 1144), and one in which the oversupply of music is particularly acute. They point to the example of the major online music retail site, Apple's iTunes, as an example, given that it offers users access to more than 18 million songs. So, therefore, while digital technologies allow musicians and producers to create music outside of professional recording studios, there is the question of what happens to this music *after* it is recorded. While digital technologies have given home producers the ability to create music as a digital file, and online distribution services such as TuneCore (http://www.tunecore.com, accessed 26/02/14) enable artists to sell their work in major digital stores like iTunes, Amazon MP3, Google Play and Spotify, these online marketplaces for music are highly saturated.

As Connell and Gibson (2003) note, local artists engaging in DIY music production compete with thousands of other similar artists, all seeking success as small-scale entrepreneurs, such that much of the music that is released becomes lost in a "sea" of digital noise. Furthermore, the chances of a home musician being noticed amongst the crowd are likely to be less than those who have signed to a record company and who have recorded as part of more formal networks of production, both because of the control the major corporations have over the major channels of distribution and consumption, and because of access to leading record producers in professional studios:

> . . . I don't think that our stars of tomorrow are going to come from people making tapes in their bedroom. I think there's a certain rite of passage you have to go through; there are several steps before a person can get to people like us. I hate to say this—it's not elitism, it's just the way the whole world is set up.
>
> (Producer Toni Visconti, quoted in Massey 2000, 6)

For these reasons, more romantic visions of the democratisation of music production, distribution and consumption are open to challenge. Connell and Gibson (2003), for example, highlight the example of Byron Bay, in New South Wales in Australia, a small rural centre of alternative culture, in which a culture of DIY production has been enhanced by digital home recording technologies. They highlight how internet promotion and distribution became extremely popular in the region, with the internet strongly identified by musicians, promoters and labels as a means of overcoming corporate distribution. However, they note that these new technologies did not constitute a panacea to dilemmas associated with the Byron Bay music scene, and that considerable problems remained. In particular, as well as production quality, they point to issues with promotion and distribution as demonstrative of how technology alone could not guarantee success of the musicians:

> . . . most Byron Bay musicians were unlikely to sell enough units to make a reliable living, even with the supposedly limitless space of the World Wide Web. Bands were able to record a CD and create websites, but found it difficult to be able to convince other sites to provide links, in order for people to access, enjoy and eventually purchase their music. As one musician put it "there are lots of bands around with boxes of unsold CDs still sitting under their beds."
>
> (Connell and Gibson 2003, 262)

Further, Connell and Gibson note how "music commodities produced by local musicians were rarely purchased without consumers already having seen the live performance" (2003, 262) and that the purchase of music often formed an adjunct to the event. One of the most prominent examples of this can be found in the case of the U.K. band the Arctic Monkeys. The commercial success of the band is widely considered to rest on a new model of DIY success in the music industry (Morey 2009), one in which a substantial fan base for the band was developed based upon the free distribution of their songs on the internet. However, the origin of these "free" songs was actually from copies of a demo[3] CD given away by the band to fans after gigs (Morey 2009), and which would subsequently be distributed by these fans through online file sharing. In this sense, a sizeable fan base already existed before the music spread across the internet. This not only highlights the importance of local live music venues in building a music scene (as discussed in Chapter 7), but also the importance of building an audience and fan base through live performance. Being able to perform in the most popular music venues is far from straight forward, however; musicians must navigate the complexities of a venue booking system that often involves local booking agents who act as important "gatekeepers" for night spaces (see Gallan 2012), as well as significant corporate influence on venues to book particular acts.

152   *Beyond the Studio*

8.4 CONCLUSIONS

It has been argued in this chapter that technological developments—specifically the development of the MP3 software format and affordable home recording software—have had two major direct and negative impacts on the recording studio sector. First, the falling recording budgets of record companies have resulted in severe economic pressures for studios, and in particular on larger recording studios that have traditionally relied on recording projects commissioned and funded by these companies. Second, the development of low-cost software technologies has allowed musicians to produce high-quality recordings in home studios. These two factors, and especially the later, have undermined the previously privileged position held by recording studios in networks of recording:

> In dispensing with much of the creative process that established their reputation and by relegating professional input to post-production, digital and home technologies have no doubt caused significant damage to the authority of the traditional studio set-up.
>
> (Homer 2009, 93)

As Leyshon argues, these developments have contributed to the reduced demand for studio time, resulting in "a spate of studio closures, redundancies, and underemployment within musical agglomerations" (2009, 1309). However, while studio closures do seem to be widespread, this needs to be balanced against increased opportunities for individual producers to run their own smaller project studios. Théberge (2012), for example, reports data from the U.S. census that shows an increase both in the number of commercial studios and people involved in sound recording between 1997 and 2002.

Technologically deterministic statements regarding the end of the control of major corporations and professional recording studios over networks of recording have, however, so far proven to be largely unfounded. As Cole argues, while project studios and home studios have "altered the structure of the music recording field, challenged capital's monopoly, and led the recording industry to hemorrhage profit" the music industry remains a multimillion dollar industry of enormous power, and as such "existing systems of power and inequality continue to structure actor's practices" (2011, 459). Furthermore, postulations like those by Gundserson that a "bedroom producer can create a professional sounding album with a personal computer alone" (2004; no pagination) cannot be applied universally. Recordings made in home recording studios via cheap microphones, soundcards and digital pods may be found wanting on audio quality, even if they are mastered in a professional studio. As Bennett (2012a) notes, while budget digital technologies have undoubtedly become more accessible to non-professional consumers, so that on the one hand a democratization of technology has occurred, the high-cost technologies remain almost wholly in the realm of professional recording studios. Accordingly, if consumer demand for high quality audio increases as new "high definition" audio file formats and playback devices are developed, the result may be a reconcentration of recording in professional studios.

NOTES

1. For a detailed discussion of peer-to-peer networks on the internet, and the different new business models adopted by internet start-ups, see Leyshon (2003).
2. As Homer (2009) emphasises, while new technologies have encouraged a greater accessibility to creativity, home recording has always had an influence on the music industry, and this can be seen in the history of music-making in the latter half of the twentieth century. By way of an example he points to Hebdige's (1979) work on the "do-it-yourself" philosophy that defined 1970s punk against the mainstream pop and rock of the same period.
3. Furthermore, these demos, while not of the audio quality of subsequent commercial releases, were not rough demos produced in a home studio as is commonly thought, but were demos produced in a small recording studio in Sheffield with producer Alan Smyth, and so were demos of a good production quality.

Part III

Working and Networking in the Recording Studio Sector

9 Changing Employment Relations and Experiences of Work

The final section of the book is concerned with a different yet related set of relations in the contemporary recording studio sector: employment relations. In particular, it is concerned with recent negative developments in these relations that are, in part, an outcome of the negative impacts of technological developments outlined in the previous chapter. Specifically, the two chapters in this section will examine the changes in employment relations that are impacting directly on the way in which recording professionals perform their jobs and their experiences of work and employment. The first chapter of the section, Chapter 9, describes these changing employment relations and considers the experiences of work and employment amongst producers and engineers, while Chapter 10 examines the strategies adopted by producers and engineers to gain work and maintain employment.

As noted in the preceding chapter two key technological developments—the MP3 software format and technologies for home recording—have challenged the economic viability of the recording studio sector, and in particular the large, company-owned facilities and the centralised in-house production facilities that marked the early days of music recording. In particular, falling recording budgets of record companies have resulted in severe economic pressures for studios, and especially these larger recording studios, that have traditionally relied on recording projects commissioned and funded by these companies. The result of these challenges has been a series of high-profile studio closures and redundancies. However, what is perhaps less well recognised is that, in those studios that do remain, changes in employment relations are resulting in a rise in temporary and flexible patterns of freelance-based project work (see Lorenzen and Frederiksen 2005). Such work is marked by volatile and insecure employment, low wages and long working hours. These are developments which mirror changes in the contemporary creative and media industries more widely (see McRobbie 2002; McGuigan 2010); poor pay, long hours, bulimic patterns of working and profound experiences of insecurity and anxiety about finding work, all recognised characteristics of these industries (Jones 1996; Gill and Pratt 2008; Hesmondhalgh and Baker 2010).

158   *Working and Networking*

It is these developments in employment relations and experiences with which this particular chapter is concerned. The chapter begins with an outline of the changing employment relations in the sector and the factors driving the rise in freelance working. In particular, the discussion focuses on employment uncertainty and the precarious nature of work in the sector. Following this, the chapter considers the related issues of exploitation, exhausting work regimes and internships. The chapter then moves on to discuss the rewards of studio work and questions the viability of careers in the sector.

9.1   CHANGING EMPLOYMENT RELATIONS AND THE GROWTH OF EMPLOYMENT UNCERTAINTY

As Leyshon (2009) details, employment in the recording studio sector before the 1970s was dominated by bureaucratic careers, with producers and engineers working as salaried employees of recording studios. However, since the 1970s, there has been a shift amongst producers and engineers to freelance status. This, Leyshon argues, was driven in part by the growing celebrity status of some producers, and the possibility of making much more money than the relatively modest incomes on offer to producers and engineers contracted to studios:

> By trading in on their past successes and becoming self-employed, producers and engineers could pursue entrepreneurial careers with significantly larger incomes, based in large part on being remunerated by a share of the profits from the sales of the record they produced and engineered.
>
> (Leyshon 2009, 1322)

Also important in this respect was the growth in the number of independent studios. The trend towards freelancing that began in the 1970s has been given fresh impetus more recently by developments in affordable computer-based recording technologies that have facilitated the growth of small "project" studios and home studios (Leyshon 2009). Contracted salaried positions are now rare in the recording studio sector. This is the case even in the largest of studios, which have recently been moving towards more flexible and freelance models of employment. What has developed is a new relationship between employee and employer in which employers no longer accept responsibility for the employment and development of the workforce, but rather have a relationship with the employee that is transactional, contractual and short-term (see du Gay et al. 1996). In 2006, for example, AIR Studios in London took all of their recording engineers off the studio payroll, effectively forcing them to become freelance. As Leyshon (2009) describes, many engineers, particularly in larger studios, are now

Changing Employment Relations 159

classed as "retained" staff, getting paid a small salary to be available to work for the studio, with their pay increasing when there is work to do, which is funded out of the fees paid by the client. When not working at the studio at which they are retained, they act as freelance engineers, obtaining work at other studios.

This situation has led to the development of new employment relations between retained and freelance engineers and recording studios: where engineers gain work, they bring projects to that particular studio, and where the studio gains work they will recommend that particular engineer. Such strategies then aim to draw a competitive advantage from the network of contacts and industry reputation of both parties, although this is by no means straightforward:

> Well it is difficult because the studio that I work for understands that a client will build a relationship with an engineer . . . essentially they will build a relationship with an engineer because that's who they're sitting in the studio with. And so it is difficult from that point of view because the client has to remain the property of the studio. However, as an engineer what you're likely to earn from a client through the studio is probably about a third as what you're likely to earn with that client that comes back to you. So it's all about a really strong relationship with my manager because she understands that eventually that the client will sort of belong to the engineer, but at the same time you have to keep that relationship coming through the studio.
>
> (Interview 10, male engineer, thirties)

Furthermore, while such arrangements might suggest something of a symbiotic relationship, these new employment relations are often balanced unevenly towards recording studios. In paying staff a retainer only or moving staff on to freelance contracts, the financial risks of not obtaining work are effectively passed to the workforce (Dex et al. 2000), leaving individuals with a heightened level of responsibility for their individual destinies, but in an "ambiguous position *vis-à-vis* power to determine them" (Ekinsmyth 2002, 239; see also Ekinsmyth 1999).

In the recording studio sector, the demands being placed upon workers in terms of their self-reliance and resourcefulness by these changing employment relations (see Entwistle and Wissinger 2006) are best illustrated through the "entrepreneurial" producer or engineer who must increasingly not only perform creative tasks, but also a range of business tasks including searching for work, self-marketing and managing the finances of small studio facilities. These demands go hand-in-hand with short tenure employment and constant employment uncertainty; that is to say it is "precarious" employment (see Murdock 2003; Neilson and Rossiter 2005; Ross 2008) marked by "structured job insecurity" (Blair et al. 2001, 174). In such a precarious work environment, job seeking becomes relentless in order to

160 *Working and Networking*

sustain sufficient employment (Patterson 2001), and there is the periodic risk of being out of work (Neff et al. 2005); as one interviewee noted how it can be "suddenly three months with nothing, which you know if you don't have a lot of backing it goes quickly, the money you do have" (Interview 13, male engineer-producer, forties). This type of precarious employment is of course not unique to the recording studio sector or the music industry, rather it is a noted characteristic of employment in the creative industries more generally (see Gill and Pratt 2008; also Murdock 2003), as well as in other project-based industries (see for example Vinodrai 2006) and in industries where temporary contracts are common (see for example McDowell et al. 2009).

As Banks (2007) notes, workers navigating the precarious terrain of a more flexible economy must often juggle multiple jobs; when studio work is not available, it is often necessary for producers and engineers to find alternative incomes. In the case of some of the major studios, these demands on producers and engineers are being managed through the setting up of management companies to obtain and manage work for their retained and freelance engineers (Box 9.1). One interviewee described how he was "very much freelance, although they [the recording studio] act as my management company and give me work through the studio" (Interview 8, male engineer, twenties), while another described the benefit of having a manager:

> I'm getting more work, but there's less work around now, so it gets more complicated. There's finding the work, or you have to lower your fees, but that's why it's good having a manager because they can fight for little things for you and they get more money for you . . . although I pay twenty per cent or whatever it is to her to be my manager I probably earned at least that much more . . .
>
> (Interview 2, male engineer, thirties)

Box 9.1   The rise of producer management companies

One key aspect of the change in employment relations in the recording studio sector has been the rise of management companies who represent rosters of producers and engineers. These take both the form of "independent" management companies, representing freelance producers and engineers, and management companies set up by major recording studios to represent those producers and engineer who were previously permanent employees but who have been taken off the studio payroll and made retained and/or freelance staff.

In Europe, one of the largest independent management companies is Stephen Budd management. Set up in 1988, it was one of the first entities to focus purely on the sales, management and career development of record producers and songwriters (http://www.record-producers.com/index.shtml, accessed 22/04/12). The company now represents around 25 of the world's leading producers, mixers and songwriters. On a smaller scale, in the U.S., the

Los Angeles based Brightman Music (http://brightmanmusic.com, accessed 22/04/12) is a producer management company which manages six renowned music producers and engineers. Similarly, Gotham Producer Management, with offices in London and New York, was started with "a vision to be a boutique management company small enough to really focus on a very select few producers and engineers" (http://www.gothamproducers.com, accessed 22/04/12), and represents six producers and engineers.

In the U.K., two major recording studios have set up management companies. In 2007, the AIR Management Company (http://air-management.co.uk, accessed 22/04/12) was created in its current form through the merger of AIR Studios and Strongroom Studios, which resulted in the amalgamation of their respective management companies. Today, the company represents a total of 10 producers and engineers. Similarly, the Miloco Studios group now represents at a professional level 16 engineers who were mostly trained by the studio group (http://www.miloco.co.uk/engineers, accessed 22/04/12).

Amongst those engineers who were not able to maintain themselves financially on studio work alone, there were a number of different types of employment taken to supplement income. For some, supplementary employment was broadly related to their "core" studio work, for example working in retail outlets specialising in musical equipment and teaching on music production courses. For others, relatively unrelated yet very flexible home-based work (such as marking exam scripts for examination boards) was seen as a way to supplement income without disrupting their key focus on the core work. For a few, studio work was not their core work but rather work which fitted around a more stable "day job." Such a position is an uncomfortable one for many in respect to their "identity" vis-à-vis other producers and engineers, in that taking on more conventional nine-to-five work is often regarded as "selling out":

> So I've had to well, sell-out some people may say, or find other ways to supplement my income because essentially working as an engineer, especially when you're working, when your work comes through a studio, it is very difficult to earn a lot of money . . .
>
> (Interview 10, male engineer, thirties)

The main exception to the growing freelance and independent models of employment remains mastering, which as Leyshon suggests is the "the last remnant of the traditional model of recording studio provision" (2009, 1318), with mastering engineers largely permanently contracted to specific mastering studios. Referring back to the earlier example of AIR Studios in London, for example, while recording engineers are now freelance, mastering engineers remain permanent contracted employees of the studio. Through interviews, it became apparent that within the recording studio

162 *Working and Networking*

sector, it is widely considered that because of the nature of the work that they perform, mastering engineers work a more standard nine-to-five, five days per week pattern and therefore do not submit to the irregular, punishing work regimes experiences by recording engineers and producers, as described in the following section.

9.2 EXHAUSTING WORK REGIMES AND EARLY CAREER EXPLOITATION

Bulimic patterns of working in which "idle periods with no work can give way to periods that require intense activity" (Gill and Pratt 2008, 17) are common in studio work. Periods which are light on work, resulting in little or no pay for retained and freelance engineers, are mirrored by periods of punishing overwork when studios are busy (Leyshon 2009). As producer and engineer Phill Brown describes:

> It became common practice to work for 15 to 18 hours in a solid stretch, with food breaks in the control room. At weekends there were often 24-hour sessions. The most extreme example occurred one weekend when I was working with my brother Terry and the band Freedom. We started work on a Saturday afternoon and the session became quite complicated. Before long we were working with three 4-track machines and creating tape phasing while mixing. We eventually emerged at 7 a.m. on Monday morning, 40 hours later . . . I was working between 80 and 100 hours a week.
>
> (Brown 2010, 6–7)

Such work regimes are extremely demanding on producers and engineers, affecting the engineers both mentally and physically, and often having a very damaging impact on personal relationships away from the studio environment. As Gill and Pratt suggest, the extraordinarily long hours worked by cultural workers as part of stop-go bulimic patterns of working often exerts a heavy cost on, or even prohibits, relationships outside work with friends, partners and families, and has "attendant impacts on sleep, diet, health and social life" (2008, 17). One engineer explained how "I've seen loads of people whose relationships have been killed by it," going on to say of his relationship with his own girlfriend, "it's come pretty close with us as well" (Interview 8, male engineer, twenties). Another engineer, who now owns his own private studio, explained his experiences of coping with the demands of freelance engineering: ". . . I was freelancing at the [studio name omitted] for a couple of years and then I didn't exactly have a nervous breakdown, I had a physical breakdown . . . I overdid it, and it completely destroyed me" (Interview 17, male engineer-producer, forties).

Changing Employment Relations   163

This exhausting work regime is often met with relatively poor financial rewards, especially for engineers. As Leyshon (2009) describes, engineers receive relatively low salaries, suggesting that in 2005/06 the average starting salary for an engineer in central London was £12,000, about half national average annual earnings. Moreover, the contracts of engineers can be quite exploitive, often resulting in engineers not being paid for all of the hours they work. One interviewee described his own experiences of this:

> . . . we were really take advantage of quite a lot, where there was all sorts of dubious practice going on . . . you got paid for 150 hours a month which is quite a lot, but you only got overtime after 200 hours. So it was a big 50 hour block which you wouldn't get paid for.
>
> (Interview 8, male engineer, twenties)

However, a number of interviewees did note that working as a freelance engineer has particular advantages in this respect over being a salaried engineer. One interviewee noted how his decision to become a freelance engineer had been in part based on his previous experience of salaried work and the pressures of taking work as and when a studio dictated, explaining how "I think with the whole freelance thing, not that I turned down much work, but the opportunity to turn down work, not burn out and not be expected to be on call permanently. It was quite a big factor in the decision," going on to say that "I have had a couple of times when I've been offered permanent work but it's never really worked out to be better for me" (Interview 8, male engineer, twenties). Similarly, another interviewee explained of his decision to work as a freelance engineer was based on the challenges of working as a salaried engineer in a pressurised environment with often little scope for personal career development:

> . . . whenever I thought about applying to big studios for very little money, really crazy hours, and then thinking that literally I'd have to be spending a year or a couple of years working my way up to a semi-reasonable position . . . I felt I didn't really want to spend time doing that.
>
> (Interview 10, male engineer, thirties)

Perhaps the starkest examples of exploitation found in the sector relate to the informal internships taken by those looking to begin a career in the recording studio sector. In recent times, the massification of higher education, in particular in music technology courses, has filled a gap left by a lack of the apprentices previously found in larger studios (Théberge 2012) and created a new "post-degree vocational need" (Guile 2009) because although studying for a degree provides a grounding for new entrants to the labour market, it rarely provides an "expectation or understanding of what was required in vocational contexts" (Raffo et al. 2000, 223). In the recording studio sector, this type of vocational experience is most commonly gained

164 *Working and Networking*

through internships and work experience placements that "offer aspiring entrants opportunities to work with experienced professionals on commercial projects" (Guile 2009, 762). Two of the interviewees described the value of such experience:

> . . . my course taught me how to do things like how a microphone worked and stuff but when I started working with these guys that had been making these incredible records for years and years and years I realised that I actually didn't know anything at all. And so then I started learning how to listen to music and make music . . .
>
> (Interview 15, male engineer, thirties)

> . . . once I finished university I was like, well, if I'm going to work in studios professionally I need to go down to London, I needed to come to a studio with some really good gear . . . I wanted to come and learn what good audio sounded like and work on some really nice equipment with some good bands.
>
> (Interview 10, male engineer, thirties)

However, while the rise in university courses has in part been a result of the almost-collapse of the apprenticeship system in the recording studio sector due to the closure of many larger studios, the same collapse means that it is extremely difficult for graduates to gain appropriate work experience. Competition for such positions within studios, especially the leading studios, is fierce. One interviewee described his own attempts to secure a position, saying that "[I] sent out hundreds of CVs, got ten per cent replies, one acceptance . . .", while a second described how "[I] did the usual thing that most people do is started applying at studios to be a tea boy and a runner and assistant or whatever. . . . I applied to hundreds of studios basically and spent ages trying to get jobs" (Interview 14, male engineer, thirties). Many prospective engineers accept that the best way to secure an early foothold in the recording studio sector is to participate in such unpaid activities, essentially providing free labour which becomes "masked" in the form of "internships" (Holt and Lapenta 2010). Competition is fierce even though many positions do not involve payment; as one interviewee described, "the amount of CVs that come in from people who are happy to work for absolutely no money at all is quite amazing" (Interview 10, male engineer, thirties).

One interviewee, reflecting on the growing number of sound engineering/music technology courses being offered by universities, stated that "I do worry about a lot of these media courses because I, these poor kids are doing three-year courses on something they should be doing in the evenings around something solid . . . to come out and expect to have a job is very silly" (Interview 12, male engineer-producer, forties). Another interviewee, a veteran studio engineer with experience in training young engineers, described how he has to explain the demands of the role to young aspiring engineers:

Changing Employment Relations   165

Normally I read the riot act to young people that come in, students. And I say to them, basically, write-off the next two years of your life . . . short of you dying, short of you actually getting married on that day . . . or you're incapacitated by being knocked down by a car or whatever, there are no other excuses that you cannot work when the work is there.

(Interview 5, male engineer, sixties)

For many junior engineers, whether they have any formal training/education in sound engineering or not, their "formal" career in the recording studio sector begins as a runner, or "tea boy." These tea boys/runners form part of a distinct hierarchy within recording studios; as one interviewee noted, "I think one of the most important things for people that are coming into the business and want to be engineers and want to work in studios, there's a very distinct hierarchy" (Participant 11, male studio engineer, N1). The hierarchy consists of, at the top end, studio managers, producers and chief engineers, down through senior engineers, engineers, and assistant engineers. At the very bottom of the hierarchies sit tea boys/runners, who do a range of jobs from setting up microphones and looking after the phones to making tea and cleaning the toilets. In assisting the people above them, these workers are subject to the "often brutal power relations" (Leyshon 2009, 1316) that frequently play out in recording studios, with high demands being placed on them to perform both technical and menial tasks and work exhausting hours. One interviewee, an experienced producer, described his experience of these power relations playing out in recording studios in the 1980s:

. . . work in a studio was equivalent to now working in a kitchen with Gordon Ramsay. It was that type of environment, where you'd have an engineer producer who was just a complete b**tard and get upset about the smallest things that didn't matter.

(Interview 19, male producer, forties)

However, he goes on to note that "that's all pretty much gone now." Moreover, a number of interviewees did express sympathy towards the position of these workers, with one engineer noting that "I am always quite careful about how I treat them [tea boys/runners] . . . they're working on very low if no money at all and they also want to feel like they're being treated nicely" (Interview 10, male engineer, thirties). Another interviewee, who had not followed the standard career path as a junior engineer, described his admiration of those who do:

. . . it's quite boring to do, I mean I admire the kind of tea boy assistant job, they are amazing people, very disciplined, first there and last to go because they have to do all the boring work, all the copying after the sessions are done and then they have to be here first thing in the morning again . . . they are amazing people.

(Interview 13, male engineer-producer, forties)

166 *Working and Networking*

Whatever the conditions to which tea boys/runners are subjected, the role is an extremely important one in the early careers of aspiring studio engineers, in that it gives experience of working with technical equipment, of the social and economic realities of studio work, and allows the development of networks of contacts that will be vital to any future career. As one interviewee describes:

> . . . the first few years you put in as a tea boy are the years where you get to show the industry, even though you don't get that many opportunities to do it, but you get to show them what you're capable of. Even if it's just if you're left for five minutes to record something and then you do it and the producer comes back and they'll go, "Oh, that's good. Thanks for that." And obviously you're establishing a network. Working in a big studio as a tea boy, you're establishing a good looking CV because big studios are trapping all the artists who are big name artists. You might just be making tea for them, but that's very important. And you're also establishing a network so you can say, "Oh yeah, I did work with [name omitted] and you've even got his phone number or whatever."
>
> (Interview 17, male engineer-producer, forties)

As is highlighted in the above quote, tea boys/runners must be patient in waiting for opportunities to work in a technical capacity on recording projects; as Frenette notes of music industry internships more generally "the aspirant's transition from layperson to skilled worker is a slow and challenging process" (2013, 369). Alongside more menial tasks, tea boys/runners will also "get to sit in on sessions and use the equipment where there's any downtime and learn what you can from there" (Interview 14, male engineer, thirties). This gives them a vital opportunity to practice and develop their technical skills, such that they can put themselves in position to be able to work on paid recording sessions.

While for some the internship may be a gradual process of personal development, for others the opportunity to work on recording projects presents itself in a more immediate fashion, presenting significant challenges. One interviewee noted how "within a year the house engineer left and they said "well you can do it" so I just ended up engineering, not knowing really what I was doing and having to learn very quickly how it all worked really" (Interview 15, male engineer, thirties). Similar situations were experienced by two other interviewees, who described how:

> . . . within three weeks of being there, one of the engineers was ill and couldn't turn up for the session. And my boss said, when I got there, "do the session." And then I said, "well, I'm only seventeen." I came in off the street basically. He said "no, no, come do it. There's no one to do it." So I ended up doing it. And I just happened to be very good at it. And it went very well.
>
> (Interview 5, male engineer, sixties)

Changing Employment Relations 167

. . . the steep learning curve bit for me was when I first came in as a tea boy . . . and I just helped out, set up microphones and all the rest of it. The main guy was still there and he came in one day and we had a band in and he said "right I'm going now" and the band look worried and I looked very worried and I just had to get on with it. That was the big moment.

(Interview 16, male engineer, fifties)

The outcome of such internships for aspiring engineers is however highly uncertain. Mirroring internships in the music industry more widely, very few aspirants will secure work in recording studios; as Frenette notes, "in the context of a highly competitive labour market without a clear, formal mechanism for entry, interns perform provisional labour; internships are temporary, conditional, and ambiguous" (2013, 389). This is exacerbated by the fact that very few contracted posts are on offer in recording studios. A lucky few who are able to display a combination of willingness and competency may be offered a retained position by a studio. But for many aspirants their only option is to try to obtain work as part of an increasingly saturated pool of freelance engineers. For some, their experience of the demands of studio work may cause them to rethink their career aspirations.

9.3   THE REWARDS OF STUDIO WORK

While there are many examples of "chronic exploitation" (McGuigan 2010) in the sector, it is important to note that the situation is much more complicated than one of simple exploitation (see Hesmondhalgh 2010). As Terranova argues, this "free labour" is "simultaneously voluntarily given and unwanted, enjoyed and exploited" (2004, 74), and there exists an intimate connection between the process of subjectification and subjection (Ursell 2000). The question then becomes one of why, despite high levels of employment uncertainty and often exploitive and exhausting work regimes, people continue to want work in the recording studio sector. If one looks to the literature, it is frequently suggested that cultural work is invariably more than a job; rather it is a labour of love. Therefore, as Hesmondhalgh and Baker (2010) assert, pleasure in work is closely linked to self-exploitation.

Much like is found in other creative sectors, record producers and engineers have a strong creative and emotional attachment to their work. For many, the main "reward" from their work is not money (as noted earlier, pay is often relatively poor) but from the chance to make music: ". . . it is rewarding and I mean I wouldn't be in it for any other reason, the pay is really poor enough that the main reason I have for sticking with it is because I actually make music on a daily basis which is a dream . . ." (Interview 10, male engineer, thirties). This is not to say that financial reward is unimportant, however. Indeed, in the recording sector, there is the prospect of high

168 *Working and Networking*

financial reward for those whose work obtains notable commercial success; much as is found in the creative industries more widely (Taylor and Littleton 2008). In the case of two of the interviewees, commercial success had brought enough financial reward to allow them to invest money in building their own recording facilities. Financial reward is an important incentive for those working in the sector.

Producers and engineers perform both technical and creative roles in the studio, and many of the interviewees noted that they prided themselves on their high levels of technical competency and knowledge. Reward then also comes from the knowledge of a "job well done" in a technical sense, as well as often in overcoming the engineering challenges that particular recording projects present, and the often varied nature of projects. For many producers and engineers, it is clear that their work plays a significant part in how they define themselves as individuals. Some interviewees recognised that their job was generally seen by outsiders as being "cool" and suggested they played on this in social settings (for example "name-dropping" famous clientele), while others valued being part of "insider" communities of "audiophiles" and recording "gear geeks" fuelled by a "technoporn" music technology press (see Bennett 2012a). In these ways, work becomes a central part of the individualized identity projects and life narratives (see Giddens 1991) of these individuals.

9.4   QUESTIONING THE VIABILITY OF CAREERS IN THE RECORDING STUDIO SECTOR

Such positive experiences of work are however tempered by the expectation of high levels of uncertainty and insecurity surrounding employment, and associated exhausting work regimes—arguably the major forces shaping work lives in project-based creative and media industries (see Christopherson 2002). Ross notes that while a few cultural workers will thrive under these conditions, "most will subsist, neither as employers or employees, in a limbo of uncertainty, juggling their options, massaging their contacts, never knowing where their next project or source of income is coming from" (Ross 2008, 36). The resultant cycle of "feast and famine," Ross argues, is familiar to anyone whose livelihood folds into the creative economy.

For Dex et al. (2000) the extent to which individuals are able to cope with this uncertainty will influence the viability of cultural and creative workforces to sustain their potential and quality of the product in a wide range of project-based creative industries. Indeed, the low salaries and exhausting regimes associated with being a recording engineer were cited by some of the interviewees as reasons why, despite the many rewarding aspects of their work, they were considering career changes. There were two interviewees who were particularly candid in their discussions regarding making this decision. Both were male engineers in their thirties, and both retained to

Changing Employment Relations 169

particular studios, one on a part-time basis and another on a full-time basis. The first interviewee, who held a part-time job outside of the recording sector alongside his part-time work as a recording engineer, explained how the decision to start a family had caused him to rethink his career as an engineer, due to the need to earn more money to support a family:

> . . . a thing I'm going through at the moment actually is working out whether I can carry on doing this. Actually just recently I've got a full time job now [outside the music industry], so I'm going to have to cut back on the stuff I'm doing here, which is not ideal from a long-term being an engineer point of view, but to be honest the money side of it is going to be better so I'm going to be more comfortable and more able to pay my bills. We're expecting a child in December so . . .
>
> (Interview 14, male engineer, thirties)

The second interviewee had spent his career as an engineer at a successful and well-reputed recording studio, and as such felt he had been quite privileged in terms of working on commercially successful recording projects with high-profile musicians and producers. However, rather than inspiring him to further develop his career and reputation to emulate these producers, observing them within and outside of the studio environment had made him question the value, both economically and personally, or pursuing the career into his forties. He describes how:

> I've worked with a lot of really successful producers and engineers and people who've been in the industry for a lot longer than I have and all of them without fail, have usually dysfunctional home lives. They're usually ill, they usually have really bad diets, they have alcohol problems, drug problems and all kinds of stuff. None of them have made that much money, it's not like I'm interested in really making loads of money, but enough money to survive. And so you kind of think, well hang on, if I stay around for another ten years . . . if you look at the people who are at that level you would end up at, you kind of go, well, do I actually want to be like that?
>
> (Interview 15, male engineer, thirties)

9.5 CONCLUSION

This chapter has considered the subjective experiences of record producers and engineers of changing employment relations and working conditions in the recording studio sector of the musical economy. It has identified how new employment strategies are balanced unevenly towards recording studios, moving the pressure of obtaining work, and the financial risk of not doing so, away from the studio management and on to producers and engineers. As such, these new employment relations are characterised by constant employment uncertainty for freelance studio workers. This uncertainty is often combined with punishing yet bulimic work regimes which are rewarded, for many, with little or no pay. Both for new and experienced producers and engineers, the sector is revealed as an increasingly difficult one in which to find and maintain gainful employment, and for many an increasingly exploitive one. Yet, the individuality afforded to producers and engineers by digital technologies, and the potential symbolic and financial rewards on offer to those who can successfully follow a career in music production, means that it remains an attractive and much sought after career.

10 Networking, Reputation Building and Getting Work

The previous chapter provided an examination of the impacts of changing employment relations in the recording studio sector on the experiences of work amongst producers and engineers. In particular, the chapter considered reducing employment security and eroding working conditions that have gone hand-in-hand with increasing freelance employment and patterns of project work that are more temporary and flexible. As in other cultural and creative industries, studio workers are engaged in insecure, casualised or irregular labour; "precarious" employment marked by structured job insecurity. This chapter builds on the previous chapter through an examination of the strategies adopted by producers and engineers to cope with this increasing precarity. In particular, the chapter considers the importance of networking in developing *social capital* and *networked reputation*, both of which it is suggested are crucial assets in obtaining work in a sector increasingly marked by structured job insecurity.

The chapter is structured in three main sections. The first section considers the importance of social networks to winning work in the recording studio sector. In particular, it highlights how recording studio producers and engineers actively network in order to build a stock of "social capital," understood as a relational resource capability that is vital to being in continuous paid employment. Then following this, the second section considers how producers and engineers build reputation, considered central to getting work in the music industry and as a stabilising feature of an otherwise uncertain business. In particular, the section highlights the ways in which reputation is spread through word of mouth and becomes a networked asset for producers and engineers. The third section then moves on to discuss the little-recognised importance of emotional labour in the building of networked reputation and to winning work in a precarious environment, arguing that emotions are a key means by which clients legitimate studio producers and engineers.

172 *Working and Networking*

10.1 ACTIVE NETWORKING AND BUILDING "SOCIAL CAPITAL"

As noted in the previous chapter, a key feature of the cultural and creative industries is informal, insecure and discontinuous employment (Jones 1996), with increasing numbers of cultural and creative workers engaged in insecure, casualised or irregular labour (Gill and Pratt 2008). Necessarily, when high levels of uncertainty regarding employment exist, job seeking becomes relentless in order to sustain sufficient employment, even during times of employment (Patterson 2001; Hesmondhalgh and Baker 2010). Networking is a proactive strategy commonly used for getting work in labour markets where a lot of hiring happens informally through contacts (Coulson 2012). In this regard, social mechanisms are considered to assume a particularly important role in the allocation of work in the cultural and creative industries (Baumann 2002). Randle and Culkin (2009) argue that, for freelancers working in such industries, the development of a good network of personal contacts is vital in finding work, as when work is scarce the quality of these networks may determine whether a freelance career continues or ends.

Thus in an "economy of favours" (Ursell 2000, 822) it is often personal networks, rather than formal firm contractual networks, that provide the basic social infrastructure for finding employment. For example, in her study of new media, Christopherson highlights how media workers "overwhelmingly depend on personal networks to make employment matches" (2002, 2011). As McGuigan notes, "frantic networking is a salient feature of such working life" (2010, 333). In their study of the British film industry, Blair et al. (2001) found that the majority of workers heard about work opportunities from someone they had worked with before. Similarly, the importance of social networks of contacts to hearing about and winning work was made particularly clear through the responses of three interviewees, one of which had moved to London from abroad and two that were considering moving away from London to work abroad. In the first case, a now London-based engineer-producer and studio owner had originally moved from Sydney, Australia, to work in London. His account tells of how the technical skills he developed in Sydney were worth little when he arrived in London as he did not have an established network of contacts through which he could obtain work:

> After doing six solid years [in Sydney], three years of making tea and then three years of starting to engineer projects, I was probably in a good position to have most of the skills to make a record. But what I didn't have is any support network when I came to London. So I then went for a year or two without any work at all . . . So I'd got to the point where I was too experienced to be tea-boying but I wasn't established in London. And so that was probably, in retrospect, quite

Reputation Building and Getting Work   173

an awkward place to be because I had to build things up from the start. What I would have done if I could have gone back and done it again is just gone straight into studios and just said "I want to be tea boy. I want to work for nothing."

(Interview 17, male engineer-producer, forties)

The above quote highlights how a lack of personal networks can make new entry into a new project ecology very difficult (see also Johns 2010, on the film and television industry in Manchester), and how leaving an established regional network of contacts to move elsewhere can come at a cost to career development (see also Christopherson 2002, on new media workers). Supporting this finding, another of the interviewees was acutely aware of the problems associated with lacking a network of contacts. He described how he had worked with a leading American producer on a recording project in London, who had subsequently offered him work out in the U.S. However, he felt that he would be lacking a social network that would give him sufficient work outside the few times that the producer would require his engineering services:

I worked with an American producer . . . he wanted me to go over and work with him in the states . . . it would have been a great opportunity but then it would have been hard because if I wasn't working with him I would have no contacts at all . . . I'd have to start making contacts, going round, asking for work and all that kind of stuff, which is fine but I think it would have been really difficult for a couple of years.

(Interview 15, male engineer, thirties)

For this interviewee, building a network of contacts to gain sufficient work would then effectively require him to begin his career again from the beginning, despite the reputation he had developed in London. In the case of another interviewee, a freelance recording engineer who had taken the decision to move from London to Melbourne, Australia, for family reasons, he had already travelled out there on a short visit and worked free of charge in an attempt to build a network of contacts before moving permanently. Here he describes building network reputation as gaining "cred" (credibility) which would allow him to get work on projects when he moved to Melbourne permanently:

. . . I thought well I'll try and make some contacts . . . I had a friend there who already knew a studio and I did some research on the internet . . . I put a couple of ads on bulletin boards and things as said, look, anyone up for doing some recording, you don't have to pay me, I'll finish things off in London. All you have to pay for is the studio and I'll come and work for you for nothing. And two people responded and two people took me up on it . . . I didn't get paid for that but it got me in with the

174 *Working and Networking*

studio out there . . . and hopefully . . . when we do move over there then I'll be able to get some work there . . . I'm hoping that I might get a little bit of a resume behind myself [so] that when I go out there eventually I will have enough cred . . . I'll be out there and have a bit of cred behind [me] I might be able to get some decent stuff in straight away and see where we go from there really.

(Interview 8, male engineer, twenties)

The case of the above interviewee highlights the way in which networking is an active, ongoing and conscious process in which producers and engineers knowingly and instrumentally engage. Blair (2009) terms this "active networking," arguing that "individuals consciously act to make and maintain contacts with other individuals and groups, assuming that a variety of forms of information or opportunities for work will be more readily available as a consequence" (Blair 2009, 122). Forming networks, then, is a deliberate action involving conscious consideration of the potential usefulness of the selected individuals in the network (Coulson 2012). In the case of the above interviewee, who would continue to work on a freelance basis in Melbourne, the establishment and maintenance of a network of contacts through which opportunities of work become available is of particular importance to reducing employment uncertainty. As Blair (2009) asserts:

Freelancers operating in this manner build up a large number of contacts on whom they draw for information and for job opportunities. The reduction of employment uncertainty, rather than taking place through a fixed set of working relationships, is more dependent upon a wide net of contacts in positions either to recommend, set up a job or offer a job directly.

(Blair 2009, 131)

Following Bourdieu (1986), we can understand the personal networks developed by the engineers and producers as being their stock of "social capital." Social capital can be understood as a relational resource capability that is built collectively and cannot be possessed or built without the active involvement of others (Coleman 1988; Bathelt and Glückler 2005). This social capital is important in reducing the uncertainties associated with uncertain demand in project working, as strong social capital offers a set of opportunities for gaining future work that recording engineers and record producers can "draw from the quality and structure of their relations with other actors in order to pursue individual objectives" (Bathelt and Glückler 2005, 1555; see also Bathelt and Glückler 2003). Thus the higher the quality of social capital on which an engineer or producer can draw the more likely they are to be in continuous paid employment. If we take the earlier example of the interviewee who moved to London from Sydney, put in Bourdieu's

Reputation Building and Getting Work   175

terms, when he arrived in London, the interviewee lacked a sufficient stock of social capital to gain work.

The producer or engineer's own structural position (access to industry contacts, skills, education, etc.) will determine whether they are more or less capable of making the required contacts and building social capital. Accordingly the outcome of networking activity may be "more or less 'successful' depending on the resources a job seeker has prior access to as a result of their own structural position in addition to the structural position of their network of connections" (Blair 2009, 125). As one interviewee explained about one of his social circle, a producer who worked on a commercially successful recording project:

> . . . because of that [commercially successful project] he'll get a lot of work coming his way through certain people, and they'll recommend him to other people and suddenly, once you're in there with someone quite often you're in there with a lot of people.
>
> (Interview 8, male engineer, twenties)

Thus through working on a particular project and with particular people, the structural position of this particular producer has been improved, increasing his potential to develop a stock of high quality social capital.

This networking is however not just about making and maintaining contact to potential buyers of labour power and to people who can make referrals; it also includes scanning of the markets for future employment opportunities, actively selling oneself for future projects and enhancing one's employability by updating and developing skills (Haunschild and Eikhof 2009). Christopherson notes that once employed, new-media workers "spend a considerable portion of their work-week in activities related to maintaining their employability" (2002, 2011). She identifies that for some workers, as much as 20 per cent of their time was spent looking for new work. However, for McRobbie (2002) such quantitative measures perhaps ignore or underestimate time that is spent networking in industries in which workers must fashion a "useful self" and project themselves through strenuous self-activity.

10.2   BUILDING "NETWORKED" REPUTATION

Building reputation is a key part of the strenuous self-activity identified by McRobbie. Mirroring the "active networking" (Blair 2009) in which individuals act to build and maintain a network of contacts through which work becomes available, developing a reputation through a network of contacts involves active "reputation work." In his study of the Hollywood talent industry, for example, Zafirau finds that maintaining a favourable reputation is "not only an object of necessity, but a fundamental piece of

176 *Working and Networking*

the day to day work that Hollywood agents and managers do" (2008, 102). Reputation is central to getting work in the music industry and the creative industries more widely. This centrality is in large part due to the project-based and precarious nature of these industries, but also in part derives from the features of cultural and media production, specifically the very public nature of the products, transmitted or circulated to audiences of at least hundreds and sometimes millions (Hesmondhalgh and Baker 2008). As Zafirau (2008) argues, reputation is an important feature in the inter-actional contexts of work in the creative industries, due to the way it acts as a stabilising feature of an otherwise uncertain business, helping to make contacts, facilitating the development of trust within networks and marking competency (see also Murphy 2006).

For Glückler (2007), two significant types of reputation can be distin-guished (see also Glückler and Armbrüster 2003; Glückler 2005). The first is "public reputation," which is public domain information, pub-lished and communicated freely in media and press. The second type of reputation is "networked reputation." Glückler (2007) argues that repu-tation is networked when new contacts learn about each other's reputa-tion through joint trusted contacts within their social network. Following this line of argument, if we were to consider the role of networked repu-tation in the recording studio sector, it can be argued that if a producer or engineer is referred to a potential client (be they a musician, a record company or a producer) through a mutual contact, the client would be more likely to commission this producer or engineer to work on their recording project. Word-of-mouth recommendations about competency are therefore of particular importance in sectors such as the recording studio, where high levels of uncertainty prevail with regards to getting continued work. Networked reputation is particularly important. One interviewee, for example, when asked about the importance of word-of-mouth in getting new work, stated that "I think that's how we get most of our business here. The website helps. But I don't think, when people are searching for studios and things like that, I think a recommendation from a friend is a lot more valuable than all these things" (Interview 11, male engineer, twenties). Another interviewee, in response to the same questions, responded that "it is very much about creating a social circle, yeah definitely. It's very hard to get your name out there any other way because, obviously you can post yourself over the internet but how does anybody find you on the internet?" (Interview 1, male engineer-producer, thirties).

For many clients, be they a recording company, musician or recording artist, when they are taking the decision to work with a particular producer or engineer on a particular recording project, they may not have met the producer or engineer. They therefore will not have had the opportunity to engage in the usual forms of confidence-building activities that con-tribute to the development of trust in more traditional, enduring forms of

Reputation Building and Getting Work   177

organisation (Grabher 2001b). Rather, they will know them by their reputation, and it is this reputation that will be the basis of the trust placed in a producer or engineer when they are commissioned to work on a recording project. Grabher (2001b) terms this "swift trust," which he describes as a category-driven trust where actors can deal with one another more as *roles* than as *individuals*. Consequently, expectations of producers and engineers are more standardised and stable and defined more in terms of tasks than personalities. One interviewee describes this relationship between reputation and the trust placed in him to undertake large-budget recording projects:

> I mean the thing I always say is there's a trust thing that happens in that when I'll be working on a, I can be recording something that someone's costing two hundred and fifty thousand pounds for example and I will never have met that person before. I might be able to have a conversation with them, but they've come to me based on my reputation.
>
> (Interview 2, male engineer, thirties)

These experience-based skills become "attached" to reputation through the portfolio of previous projects undertaken by a producer or engineer. One interviewee explained how "this is my 40th year doing this. So you build up your reputation, good or bad. But you build up a reputation over that time, of experience. And partly because of the projects that I've worked on over the years I suppose" (Interview 5, male engineer-producer, sixties). A producer or engineer's portfolio of previous projects is a crucial part a reputation that attracts work from new clients. As another interviewee noted, a track record of successful previous projects is particularly important to getting work with record companies, where success in these cases is judged by the commercial sales of the recording: "record companies pretty much all they think about is 'did he have a hit recently?' That's really all they're worried about because that obviously means that he'll have another one" (Interview 19, male producer, forties). This focus on the reputation of producers, engineers and recording studios based upon their previous commercial successes can be explained by the fact that the record companies often invest heavily in artists and need to get a good result from expensive studio time. As one interviewee explains, for record companies there is a pressing need to:

> . . . pass it to someone that you can almost guarantee a good result from. Lots of companies are investing thousands of pounds in the band . . . that's the reason a record company would hire a producer is that they're passing it on to someone who knows a little bit more about the recording side so that they can say, if we give it to him we'll definitely get a good record, doesn't matter what happens.
>
> (Interview 11, male engineer, twenties)

178   *Working and Networking*

Similarly, having invested a large amount of money in the recording process, record companies will also carefully select a mastering studio and mastering engineer who will finalise the project:

> . . . having invested however much the record company's spent in the recording and mixing . . . they're going to want to make sure that it's done absolutely right. Which is why people do get so choosy about what mastering room they use. Because if you've spent fifty grand getting it to the point where it's going to be mastered, you want to put it somewhere you're, where you're confident that your money's not being wasted.
>
> (Interview 3, mastering engineer, fifties)

A number of interviewees noted that their reputation increased considerably following their first commercial success, resulting in a significant upward turn in their career paths in the industry. As one interviewee described:

> I ended up producing four tracks on his album and I also wrote, co-wrote with him and produced a track called [name omitted] which was number one. And from that point onwards my career just absolutely blew up . . . it was massive and that gave me the recognition.
>
> (Interview 4, male producer, forties)

Another interviewee noted how the development of such a reputation may in large part be down to chance in terms of the producer or engineer getting the initial opportunity to work on a recording project that is successful in terms of sales:

> . . . possibly by chance you've worked on a record that's done really, really well and then on, because you've done that one you get another one and because that's got [the] backing of a record company, that one's going to do well as well. So then you're now the man who's done two. And then you become the man who's done three and four. . . and so it goes.
>
> (Interview 3, male mastering engineer, fifties)

A number of the interviewees noted how this type of commercial success is often valorised over other reputational assets. As the same interviewee noted, "if you've had some success then yeah people take you more seriously," going on to say that "other guys have got bad reputations and their people still want to work with them if they're successful" (Interview 19, male producer, forties). Conversely, the work done by producers and engineers in the studio may be devalued by a record company if it is not felt that the output will have quantifiable commercial success. As one interviewee explained, "I've always felt that the most important thing, the most

Reputation Building and Getting Work   179

important people I have to please are the artists. They have to like it. But unfortunately if it's a major label and the artist likes it and the record label doesn't, they won't put it out" (Interview 16, male engineer, fifties). Thus, as was highlighted in Chapter 2, producers may act to ensure the quality of the final product above everything else, adopting a "dictatorial" approach that can see them being closed and unresponsive to the creative input being offered by the musicians or recording artists. Furthermore, a concern for success and reputation can lead some producers and engineers to be very selective about the clients they choose to work with on recording projects; one interviewee, for example, described how:

> . . . because your work goes by word of mouth, it's important that the networks that you establish are networks of musicians and artists that you want to continue working with . . . Just make sure that the clients that you're working with are the right ones that are going to maintain your reputation.
>
> (Interview 17, male engineer-producer, forties)

However, the "good work" on which reputations are built (Hesmond-halgh and Baker 2008) can be considered more widely than commercial success alone. For some studios, it is rare for any of the music recorded at the studio to go on to have quantifiable success, and thus the quality of the output must be judged by other criteria. Some producers and engineers will work for example in niche markets where total sales may only be small but reputation may be high within that niche market due to producing or engineering a hit in specialist charts. Other producers and engineers may gain a reputation based on their technical ability in the studio and the way this translates into recorded output of a particular quality. One interviewee explained how "sometimes it's the actual music itself that you can get credit for which of course you have been involved in, but sometimes people say 'oh, I love the way that was recorded'" (Interview 2, male engineer, thirties). Another example of "good work" performed in the studio is that which results in client expectations being met and thus high levels of client satisfaction, and so will result in the client returning to a studio, or a particular producer or engineer, for future recording projects; one interviewee suggested that "when people's expectations have been met, that's when they're most likely to come back" (Interview 10, male engineer, thirties).

In the same way that a positive reputation can be beneficial to a producer or engineer attracting new or repeat work, so the development of a negative reputation can be damaging in this respect, cutting off potential new lines of work. One interviewee noted how "you can't really ever have a bad day, you can't have an off day. . . . you're only as good as your last game" (Interview 2, male engineer, thirties). As Murphy (2006) asserts, trust is a subjective construct that emerges when one agent, in this instance the producer or engineer, complies with the expectancies of a relationship.

180 *Working and Networking*

Box 10.1   The pressure to not make mistakes (Brown 2010)

An assistant at a studio in New York ended his career with just one mistake. He was working on the album *Aja* by Steely Dan. After two years of recording, overdubbing and re-recording songs they were finally mixing their chosen tracks. Many of the master reels looked similar, and it was later believed that a tape had been put back in the wrong box. Consequently, instead of lining up the 2" tape machine with blank tape on the "tones" reel, the assistant mistakenly used one of the final master reels. Not realizing what he had done, he replaced the tape in its box. It was only when repeated searches for the required song had been carried out that this tape was finally loaded onto the multitrack machine and played from the top. Frequency tones filled the first four and half minutes of the tape. Just as they were about to give up and move to another reel, the last few seconds of the song they were searching for suddenly burst onto the monitors. As Walter Becker described to me at Park Gate studios in 1984, "Man, it was crazy. Don [Donald Fagen] and I were trying to lynch the guy. He was only saved when the studio manager sacked him on the spot and escorted him from the studio. He never worked in the music business again. Man, we wanted to kill him."

Source: Extract from Brown (2010, 93–94)

Thus producers and engineers work hard to maintain the "capacity trust" (Ettlinger 2003) of their clients, that is to say the client's trust in their ability for competent technical performance in the recording studio. Mistakes can be damaging in terms of a client's trust in the producer or engineer. One interviewee emphasised that "we work meticulously hard to make sure that things don't go wrong" (Interview 17, male producer-engineer, forties). Just one serious mistake may be enough to end a career, putting a huge pressure on studio workers, especially those at the beginning of their careers looking to build a reputation, not to make a mistake (Box 10.1). The sentiment that poor performance can damage a painstakingly built reputation is echoed by workers in a range of cultural industries, including film (see Blair 2001; Jones 1996) and television (see Hesmondhalgh and Baker 2008).

10.3   EMOTIONAL LABOUR, REPUTATION AND REPEAT WORK

In the previous section, the discussion of "public reputation" and "networked reputation" (Glückler 2007) was predicated on an understanding of reputation as being based on experience, technical skill and a portfolio of work. However, while this "good work" (Hesmondhalgh and Baker 2008) based around the skills of the trade is without doubt of great importance to reputation, Grabher (2001b) identifies another set of skills—"inter-personal skills"—as being important to building reputation:

> Reputation in project organization refers, first and foremost, to the techniques of the trade, particularly in settings like media, in which crucial skills are hardly codified into certificates. Second, the success of projects, more generally, depends on co- operative attitude, reliability and other inter-personal skills that, rather than objectivized in formal degrees, are bound to personal experience.
>
> (Grabher 2001b, 1329–1330)

These skills are important because feelings and emotions such as trust, mutual respect and friendship are key to reputation in networks, and can only be developed as result of closer interpersonal action (Ettlinger 2003). In Chapter 3, the concept of "emotional labour" (Hochschild 1983) was introduced and highlighted as being particularly applicable to work in the recording studio sector, due to the relational nature of creative work in the studio; it is predominantly face-to-face, collaborative and emotive. While emotional labour is of crucial importance to the maintenance of creative relationships during a given recording session, it is not however just in this respect that emotional labour is important. Interview responses highlighted that emotional labour is an important part of building a wider reputation, and is particularly important in attracting repeat work.

Repeated cooperation is of great importance to producers, engineers and recording studios; as one interviewee noted "you have to be re-booked. You can't survive on having a great CV and then having loads of one-off bookings" (Interview 4, male producer, forties). For Grabher projects operate in a "milieu of recurrent collaboration" (2001b, 1329) where clients will draw on core members of successful previous projects to serve on successor projects. Grabher argues that "project business is reputation business" (2001b, 1329) and such chains of repeated cooperation are held together by the reputation members have gained in previous collaborations. It was clear from interviews that the management of impressions and the ability to build personal relationships with clients is vital to gaining repeat work, due to the way in which studio clients look to develop a personal relationship of trust with a particular producer or engineer, and who they will then return to for future projects. Client perceptions of good service hinge on the extent to which the studio worker is helpful, supportive and conveys a sense of genuine interpersonal sensitivity and concern. In this context, emotional labour can be considered as:

> . . . a form of impression management to the extent that the labourer deliberately attempts to direct his or her behaviour towards others in order to foster certain social perceptions of both him or herself and a certain interpersonal climate.
>
> (Ashforth and Humphrey 1993, 90)

182 Working and Networking

Thus, for studio workers emotional labour becomes a part of the "intensification of the self-commodification processes by which each individual seeks to improve his/her chances of attracting gainful employment" (Ursell 2000, 807). In the recording studio sector, where formalised criteria for evaluating performance are not present, more informal, "softer" personality characteristics and symbolic attributes can become a more important means by which clients legitimate studio producers and engineers. Many clients will judge their experience of working in a studio on the atmosphere of the studio and service offered rather than the end product *per se*. As such, the higher the producer or engineer's empathetic and expressive abilities, the higher the client's satisfaction will be (see Ashforth and Humphrey 1993) and the higher the chances of gaining repeat work from that client. Furthermore, emotional labour is central to the development of relationships of "emotive trust" (Ettlinger 2003) in the recording studio:

> Feelings or emotional energies may be associated with symbolic representations of morality, trust-worthiness, or honesty, and an agent's ability to control his or her emotions, in accordance with the norms associated with a social situation, increases the probability that trust is achieved. For example, empathy is an emotional response that contributes to trust building practices . . .
>
> (Murphy 2006, 434)

Correspondingly, if a producer or engineer does not convey a sense of genuine interpersonal sensitivity and concern, or has poor empathetic and expressive abilities, the level of client satisfaction may be low, trust may not develop and potential future lines of work may become cut off: ". . . that's what a lot of people fall down on. Personal skills. They might be able to do the job properly, but if they're argumentative or whatever, then forget it. No one's going to work with you again" (Interview 5, male producer-engineer, sixties).

10.4 CONCLUSIONS

This chapter has highlighted how in "precarious" economic sectors such as the recording studio sector, it is considered that the development of a network of personal contacts is vital in finding work, as when work is scarce the quality of these networks may determine whether a freelance career continues or ends (Randle and Culkin 2009). In this chapter, the "quality" of personal networks has been considered in terms of the building of a stock of social capital and in terms of building reputation. These two related "assets," it is argued, are vital to being in continuous paid employment in such a precarious sector. Their development involves "active networking" (Blair 2009) and active "reputation work" (Zafirau 2008), an ongoing and

Reputation Building and Getting Work 183

conscious process in which producers and engineers knowingly and instrumentally engage in order to build a stock of social capital and enhance their networked reputation.

While the importance of social capital and networked reputation to maintaining employment in the "precarious" cultural and creative industries has been well recognised in literature, the importance of emotional labour in developing these "assets" has yet to be fully recognised (although see Hesmondhalgh and Baker 2008). The ability to build relationships and manage emotions was seen by record producers and recording engineers as being vital to gaining work, due to the way in which studio clients look not only to develop "capacity" trust in a producer or engineer, but also "emotive" trust (see Ettlinger 2003). A client's choice of producer or engineer thus becomes about something more than their technical competence in the studio, especially where formalised criteria for evaluating performance are not present. Informal, "softer" personality characteristics and symbolic attributes are an important means by which clients legitimate studio producers and engineers. Thus, to a significant degree, the networked reputation of a producer or engineer is built through the emotional labour they perform in the recording studio, and the resulting creative relationships and client experiences of the recording process.

However, as Hesmondhalgh and Baker (2008, 113) note, a contradiction exists here where "the pressure to deliver work that will help build one's reputation impacts on the individual's ability to do emotional labour. Yet building one's reputation hinges upon the management of emotions." In the case of record producers and engineers, pressure to finish recording projects on-time and to deliver a product which meets the expectations of a record company (i.e., commercial success), and so add to a producer's or engineer's reputation, can result in producers and engineers being more dictatorial and less collaborative in their approach to the recording process (see Chapter 2). In such situations, in attempting to enhance their own personal reputation, client satisfaction may well be lower because the producer or engineer's empathetic and expressive abilities are compromised. Thus, conversely, this can damage networked reputation and reduce opportunities for new and repeat business.

Conclusion

CULTURAL PRODUCTION INSIDE THE RECORDING STUDIO

It now remains to draw together the main themes emerging from the three parts of this book, drawing on the theoretical framework of relational economic geography, as discussed in the Introduction. As an entry point into such a discussion, it is useful to return to Chris Gibson's (2005) assessment of recording studios as *relational* spaces of creativity:

> What we hear when we listen to recorded music is not just a product of musician's creativity, but an emotive performance produced in particular spaces and through affective relations between musicians, producers, engineers and technologies.
>
> (Gibson 2005, 192)

By viewing recording studios from a relational perspective, this text has revealed how creative moments in the recording studio are produced not by the musician alone, but through the embodied relations between musicians, producers and engineers. It has been emphasised throughout this text that musical creativity in the recording studio relies on particular sets of *social relations*. Creativity in the recording studio is realised as a creative act in the recording studio through the social encounter between producer and engineer and musician/recording artist. As Horning (2004) emphasises, the recording studio is a site of collaboration between engineers and artists, where maximum creativity requires a symbiotic relationship demanding skills that are at the same time both technical and artistic. Therefore, in the recording studio record producers, sound engineers and other skilled musical professionals are as important in the production of recorded output as are the musicians or recording artists themselves (Pinch and Bijsterveld 2004); as Zak argues, they are the musicians' artistic collaborators:

> While musicians leave the traces of their emotions, experiences, and the sounds of their musical expression on tape, the composite sound image that we recognize as the musical work is fashioned by recording

engineers and producers—"performers" in their own right. They are the musicians' artistic collaborators, and their actions and aesthetic choices, too, are represented in the form of the finished work. Microphones are chosen and placed, balances are set, frequency content is shaped, performances are coached, coaxed, coerced—these are a few of the many techniques used the fashion the sound world of the recording.

(2001, 17)

An often overlooked, yet essential, element of these social and creative relations is the emotional work of producers and engineers. Record producers and recording engineers do not only provide technical and creative input and guidance to the recording process; as creative work in the studio is predominantly face-to-face, collaborative and emotive, their performance, communication and their displays of emotions are also all central to their work in the studio. Thus, in Chapter 3, it was argued that the concept of emotional labour (Hochschild 1983) is particularly applicable to work in the recording studio sector. For producers and engineers, skills with people and the ability to mediate performances through emotional working are at least equally as important as the ability to competently perform a technical role and operate complex studio equipment. Often, to do this, producers and engineers must manage the emotions of the performers to get them into a particular emotional state, eliciting strong emotions from the musician or recording artists to capture the most emotive performance possible, whilst at the same time showing sensitivity to the performance of musicians and recording artists, and inducing or suppressing particular feelings in order to sustain an outward countenance that provides the appropriate interpersonal climate (Ashforth and Humphrey 1993). Moreover, through performing emotional labour, studio workers can often be exposed to the personal emotions of their clients. Thus an important part of emotional labour is the management of client behaviour within the studio environment, which ranges from finding solutions to disputes, to dealing with inappropriate or sometimes aggressive behaviour, perhaps fuelled by alcohol and drugs.

It is, however, not just social relationships that are central to the process of creating music in the studio. In Chapter 4, for example, the importance of the material space of the studio to the process of creating music was noted. As Leyshon asserts, each recording studio is a unique recording space given "the acoustic environment in each studio often develops incrementally and organically in relation to the nature of the materials used in its construction or to subsequent experiments with baffling and other materials introduced to the studio fabric" (2009, 1320). Nisbett (1995) argues that recordings can pick up these physical characteristics of the studio as much as those of the players/artists, with the studio acting as a "sounding board" to instruments and its shape and size giving character to the music. The studio effectively becomes a musical instrument in its own right as audio engineers develop better control of the ability to manipulate sound (Horning 2004).

186   *Working and Networking*

However, just as important as the materiality of the studio in shaping music is the equipment used to record, process, edit and create sounds. Although generic equipment will be found in many studios, in addition to the variations in their acoustic environment, different studios may work with different, and in some cases distinctive and unique, palates of technologies (Leyshon 2009). As Chapters 1 and 2 emphasised, various pieces of recording equipment are used and employed by different engineers and producers in different ways and in different contexts, resulting in a variety of different sounds. Furthermore, very often technological practices result in unintended outcomes that in themselves are an important part of musical creativity and production. Taken together, creativity around technologies and acoustic spaces demonstrates how, rather than being inert spaces, studios are *material* and *technological spaces* that influence and shape human actions and social interactions. As Akrich notes, "technical objects define a framework of action together with actors and the space in which they are supposed to act" (1992, 208). Recording studios can thus be considered as "sociotechnical spaces" (Leyshon 2009), and as "machinic complexes" (Sheller 2004; Gibson 2005) housing assemblages of bodies and technologies. An intimate relationship exists between the acoustic environment of the studio, recording technologies, the producer and engineer, and musicians and their musical instruments:

> Musicians and engineers interact with technologies and acoustic spaces. Their perceptions are not of inanimate, non-human actors but of "live" spaces and technologies that mutate sound and shape a finished product, sometimes adding a special aural quality beyond the capacities of the musicians or technicians concerned.
>
> (Gibson 2005, 200)

To employ Actor Network Theory terminology (see Latour 2005), recording technologies represent crucial non-human intermediaries that "play a critical role in embodying and shaping action" (Law 1994, 383) in the production and recording of music. Thus, following Felix Guattari, the artistic practices performed by engineers and producers through the use of technologies can be considered as "machinic performances." Rather than being simply technological resources or passive actors, these technologies and their various capabilities "intervene actively to push action in unexpected directions" (Callon and Law 1997, 178), with technologies "shifting-out" functions from the bodily to the mechanical domain (Latour 1992).

CULTURAL PRODUCTION BEYOND AND BETWEEN RECORDING STUDIOS

While the materiality of studios and particular palates of technologies exist as part of an intimate relationship between the studio space and studio workers and musicians/recording artists, Chapter 6 described how

Conclusion 187

technologies also allow for the development of new relationalities *beyond* and *between* studios, enabling social actors to develop and maintain social relations that span out across geographical space (see Dicken et al. 2001). In Chapter 7, the quantitative social network analysis demonstrated how geographically distant recording studios are linked into national and global networks of music production by the working flows that pass between and through them when they are part of temporary creative projects that are brought together to produce recorded music albums. These working links are complex (see Théberge 2004) and are in part the result of both new technologies that allow for the increased mobility of recordings, as well as, in some cases, simultaneous remote working, which removes the need for physical travel of producers and engineers. However, results from this research suggest that physical mobility amongst producers, engineers and musicians/recording artists also remains important in the contemporary recording industry. This is in part due to the significant challenges and problems of working with technologies that are at a relatively early stage of development, such as simultaneous remote working via ISDN, but mainly is due to the way in which face-to-face interactions are key to creative collaboration and creative decision-making in the studio. Face-to-face interaction allows for sociality and facilitates the building and maintaining of relationships in the intimate space of the studio, relationships which may endure for a long period of time and open up particular career opportunities. Travel facilitates face-to-face meetings (Faulconbridge et al. 2009), both with clients and collaborators, and allows for creative collaboration in cross-border recording projects. Despite new communication technologies in the recording studio sector, the need for "meetingness" (Urry 2003) remains.

However, despite the importance of physical mobility and face-to-face contact highlighted in this research, at-distance working and the development of sociality at-distance are an increasingly important part of studio work. With social relations being of crucial importance, whether it is performed face-to-face in the space of the studio or at-distance through networking technologies, the rise of remote collaboration has required studio workers to develop new ways of working and communicating that allow for the development of a social relationality at-distance that is not primarily dependent on face-to-face contact. As well as finding suitable ways of communicating with clients—the use of e-mail is central in creative dialogue between musicians/recording artists and studio workers collaborating at-distance—it is also increasingly necessary for studio workers to perform "distanciated emotional labour" (see Bryson 2007), that is, emotional labour performed at a distance. However, despite the development of such a series of "coping mechanisms" for dealing with the challenges of remote working, for the majority of producers and engineers, working at-distance remains inherently unsatisfactory when compared to face-to-face working within the space of the recording studio.

188 *Working and Networking*

Therefore, as Théberge (2004, 779) asserts, what may become the most significant issue for studios as they become more integrated with one another is "the quality of the musical and social relationships that are made with and through them." Key for the economic success of recording studios is their enrolment into processes and networks of production that span geographical space. This enrolment is an outcome of the quality of the musical and social relationships that are made by record producers and studio engineers within, through and between studios (Théberge 2004), relationships that emerge and that are maintained through project-based working. This text has revealed how the ability of recording studio engineers and producers to reach across space and act at-distance, and thus enrol the studios at which they work in wider networks of production, ultimately depends upon the quality of their social relations with other actors, as well as the availability of effective technologies and development of effective creative practices. Thus, as Ettlinger (2001) argues, labour is not a passive part of the production system; but rather, through social relations, influences production processes and culture, engendering the production.

For Théberge (2004), developments in networking technologies raise fundamental questions about the future relationships between recording studios and the local places in which they are embedded, giving rise to the notion of the "placeless" virtual studio. Viewed as simply nodes in networks, he argues, studios become "non-spaces" and "non-places":

> What most interests me is the question of how we got from the idea of the "brick and mortar" recording studio—a very specific kind of place, made up of carefully engineered acoustic spaces, in which a variety of actors (artists, session musicians, producers and engineers), working with sophisticated technologies, come together to create a sound recording—to this notion of a placeless, virtual studio in which just about anyone with a computer, anywhere in the world, can participate in the recording of music.
>
> (Theberge 2004, 760)

However, far from being placeless "non-spaces," recording studios are intimately connected with the local music scenes, local aesthetics and music practices of the places in which they are located. As is argued in Chapter 5, recording studios are a key part of the mutually constitutive relationship between place and musical identity, playing a crucial role in the development of urban music scenes. More than simply pieces of economic infrastructure, recording studios are important spaces of socialisation in music scenes, acting as a focal point for networks of musicians and musical creativity. On the one hand, recording studios are insulated spaces of creativity, isolated from the city and wider world outside, which give musical creatives the conditions required to experiment and create music. Yet, they are also spaces influenced directly by the wider contexts in which the studios operate, which play an important role in the development of approaches to recording and have influence on the resulting sounds.

RECORDING STUDIOS AS ECONOMIC SPACES

It is important to recognise that, as well as being creative social and technical spaces, recording studios are also economic sites where particular sets of economic relations between employee and employer are played out. These relations have altered quite dramatically over the course of the last three decades, predominantly due to the negative impact of technological developments on the economic sustainability of recording studios. As is argued in Chapter 8, the developments of the MP3 software format and affordable home recording software have undermined the previously privileged position held by recording studios in networks of recording, reducing demand for studio time. The result of these challenges has been studio closures and redundancies, and as is argued in Chapter 9, in those that do remain, changing employment relations such that there has been a rise in temporary and flexible patterns of freelance-based project work (see Lorenzen and Frederiksen 2005) marked by volatile and insecure employment, low wages and long working hours. Contracted salaried positions are now rare in the recording studio sector, even in major studios, in which, in recent years, many engineers are moved from being permanent employees to retained staff, getting paid a small salary to be available to work for the studio, with their pay increasing when there is work to do. When not working at the studio at which they are retained, they act as freelance engineers, obtaining work at other studios. This changing situation has led to the development of a new set of employment relations between retained and freelance engineers and recording studios.

Examples of this are found in the management companies being set up by major recording studios to manage their retained and freelance engineers and producers. Implicit within this "managed" relationship between studio and engineer is that both parties promote each other to potential clients. Such strategies then aim to draw a competitive advantage from the social capital and networked reputation of both parties; however, while such arrangements might suggest something of a symbiotic relationship, these new employment relations are often balanced unevenly towards recording studios, who, in paying staff a retainer only or moving staff on to freelance contracts, move the pressure of obtaining work, and the financial risk of not doing so, away from the studio management and on to producers and engineers.

As such, it places considerable demands on their self-reliance and resourcefulness (see Entwistle and Wissinger 2006) and leaves them in a position where they are responsible for their own success or failure (see Storey et al. 2005). This in turn encourages the self-interest and self-preservation

190   *Working and Networking*

of freelance workers, who, as is described in Chapter 10, look actively to form networks and make associations through which they can win work. Findings support Hesmondhalgh and Baker's (2010) assertion that in the cultural industries there is a strong sense that the contacts which eventually lead to contracts rely on sociability, that is to say that the importance of networking reputation through the development of a social network of contacts is widely recognised. The creation of such a network of contacts involves "active networking" (Blair 2009) or active "reputation work" (Zafirau 2008), an ongoing and conscious process in which producers and engineers knowingly and instrumentally engage in order to enhance their networked reputation, building a stock of "social capital" which is related to working in particular studios. This social capital is important in reducing the uncertainties associated with uncertain demand in project working, as strong social capital offers a set of opportunities for gaining future work that recording engineers and record producers can "draw from the quality and structure of their relations with other actors in order to pursue individual objectives" (Bathelt and Glückler 2005, 1555; see also Bathelt and Glückler 2003). Thus, while these networks may indirectly advance the interests of their studio employers, they will tend to prioritise directly the personal interests above those of the employer. As such, the logics that inform the workplace and networking practices of workers in the recording studio sector cannot be understood solely in narrow economic terms or in terms of one single rationality. Rather, as Yeung argues:

> Economic actors are seen as embedded in diverse social discourses and practices, and cannot be conceived as rational and mechanistic economic entities. These actors are influenced by a broad array of hybrid relations among humans and nonhumans, and their action is significantly shaped by multiple logics and trajectories whose significance varies in different contexts.
>
> (2005b, 41)

However, as is argued in Chapter 8, technologically deterministic statements regarding the end of major professional recording studios and their influence over networks of recording have so far proven to be largely unfounded. As Cole argues, the music industry remains a multimillion dollar industry of enormous power, and as such "existing systems of power and inequality continue to structure actor's practices" (2011, 459). It was almost inevitable that the more established recording studios would respond to technological developments to protect their interests in the industry. As Théberge (2004) notes, there has been a movement towards geographical diversification or expansion through acquisitions and joint ventures, which link studios globally across the major centres of music production. The U.K.-based Miloco Studios group, for example, is the U.K.'s largest studio group and owns 19 recording and mastering studios across London, the U.K. and

Europe. These practices allow studios to both consolidate their position in existing markets and to establish a physical presence in new markets. Furthermore, if as is suggested in Chapter 8 consumer demand for high quality audio increases as new "high definition" audio file formats and playback devices are developed, the result may be a reconcentration of recording in professional studios and away from home recording.

CULTURAL PRODUCTION IN AND BEYOND THE RECORDING STUDIO: A RELATIONAL PERSPECTIVE

The research presented in this book has taken inspiration from a number of recent theoretical and empirical shifts associated with the development of a relational framework in economic geography. Adopting such an approach has allowed the development of a relational perspective on music production focused on the recording studio sector of the musical economy. This perspective has three key features. First, rather than considering the economic *structure* of the recording sector *per se*, the focus of the research has been on the placed and embodied *agency* of studio workers, that is to say the people involved in the "daily practices of work" (Ettlinger 2003) in the recording studio sector—on the technical and creative roles they perform, on their performance of emotional labour and on their networking activities. Secondly, the research has moved from a macro-scale analysis of the intra- and interstudio network patterns observable at the global scale, to a micro-scale analysis that uncovers the practices that form, maintain and sometimes inhibit or break, social networks between individuals and between recording studios. Finally, and related to the last two points, while the majority of literature on the recorded music industry has focused on record companies as the firms at the centre of production networks, privileging the firm as the central unit of analysis (see for example earlier research presented in Watson 2008), this study has focused on the social networks being built in and around recording studios, which have been presented here as important sites of trans-local work.

Through developing a relational perspective on cultural production, and applying this to the recording studio sector, the research has revealed how recording studios are constituted by a number of "spheres" of relations: social relations; material and technological relations; network relations; and economic relations. These spheres are not distinct, but overlap in complex ways, and are manifest at a multiplicity of interconnected geographical scales. It is this complexity that shapes the work of record producers and engineers. Underpinning all of above is the project-based working that is so prevalent within the recorded music industry. Operating over pre-determined periods of time to produce musical recordings, projects in the music and recording industry pull together a variety of different agents, including skilled studio workers and the studios in which they operate, into temporary

192 *Working and Networking*

networks of collaboration of varying intensities and geographical reach. At the same time, they drive competition in the sector, not only between different record companies and different recording studios, but also between individual workers in the recording studio sector. Projects thus determine creative practices, drive technological development and innovation, shape employment practices and necessitate networking and mobility. Put short, *relational working* requires *relational practice*.

These overlapping spheres of relations constitute recording studios as distinctive relational creative, social and economic spaces. In developing a relational understanding of recording studios, this text has demonstrated the ways in which creativity interacts with the physical form and material space of the recording studio, technology and the various actors in networks of creativity and production, in complex ways. The text has also looked to add to this understanding by drawing on sociological perspectives on cultural work to understand the ways in which employment relations and working conditions also influence creativity. The importance of taking a relational geographical approach to studying creative production is thus highlighted in the way that recording studios are at once sites of spatial and temporal closeness and convergence, *and* spatial and temporal distance and dispersion. Recording studios are not however unique in this respect as relational sites and spaces of creative production and project-based working. Creative practice and project-based work is inherently relational. Project-based workers, and particularly those in sectors of precarious employments such as those found in the creative industries, are active networkers, developing the social capital and networked reputation that are vital to their continued employment. The relations they develop extend over space and time with different degrees of intensity and reach, linking production sites together into networks; as Rogers argues, "even when creative practices are situated, they operate through networks and flows that link locations together" (2011, 663). As such, a wide variety of sites and spaces of creative practice and project-based work become materially emergent within "their unfolding event relations" with other sites (Marston et al. 2005, 426). A relational perspective is therefore central to progressing geographical accounts of work and production in the cultural industries, and in project-based industries more widely, due to the way in which such a perspective is sensitive to the geographical scales at which social actors and their networks operate.

Glossary

Attack: The way a sound is initiated. The closer the attack (initiation) of a sound is to the peak of a sound, the faster its attack is. A short attack produces a rapid compressed sound (e.g., a gunshot).

Auto-tune: An audio processor which disguises or corrects off-key inaccuracies, allowing vocal tracks to be perfectly tuned.

Balance: Refers to the balance of frequencies in a mix, including the balance between left and right stereo channels.

Channel: Refers to a particular audio path, usually on a console (see "console" below).

Compression: Refers to the process of lessening the dynamic range between the loudest and quietest parts of an audio signal, using a compressor.

Console: Also often referred to as a "mixing console" or "desk," this refers to a device that brings together various audio channels and provides routing for signals (also see "multi-tracking" below).

Control room: The room in a studio where the recording console and other equipment are located.

Cutting:
1. Tape editing performed by cutting the tape at the required point, and rejoining it to another section of tape, called "splicing."
2. The transfer of a recording onto vinyl record.

Decay: The decrease in amplitude of a sound when a vibrating force has been removed. The actual time it takes for a sound to diminish to silence is the "decay time." How gradual this sound decays is its "rate of decay."

Desk: See "console" above.

Digital audio workstation (DAW): An electronic system designed for recording, editing and playing back digital audio. Modern DAWs are typically software running on computers with audio interface hardware.

Dynamics processing: Processing which alters aspects of the dynamics (difference in sound level) of an audio signal.

Echo chamber: An isolated room specifically designed to give a "live" sound to recording through reverberation (see "reverb" below).

Effects: A general term for sounds generated from, and added to, existing sounds and instruments.

194 *Glossary*

Equaliser (EQ): An adjustable filter to modify the level of selected frequencies (see also "equalisation" below).

Equalisation: The adjustment of the amplitude of audio signals at particular frequencies.

Fader: A slider on a console allowing an engineer to control a gradual increase or decrease in the volume level of a channel of audio.

Fidelity: The degree of exactness with which an audio signal is copied or reproduced.

File Transfer Protocol (FTP): A standard network protocol used to transfer files from one host to another host over the Internet.

FX: See "effects" above.

Gate: A device that can be set to pass or not pass an audio signal depending on the input level.

Headphone mix: A separate mixed sound set up specifically for the headphones worn by individual musicians in the studio.

Integrated Services for Digital Network (ISDN): A set of communication standards for simultaneous digital transmission of voice, video, data and other network services over a switched telephone network.

Isolation: Using an object or material to isolate the sounds from individual instruments and/or voices to reduce unwanted "leakage" to other microphones in the room (see also "isolation booth" below).

Isolation booth: An isolation booth is a standard small room in a recording studio, which is both soundproofed to keep out external sounds. Often used for recording vocals.

Levelling: A process of adjusting audio levels so that they are consistent compared to a reference audio level.

Live room: (or "live space") Refers to the area of the studio where musicians perform with their instruments. Usually a separate space to the "control room" (see above).

Lossy compression: A data encoding method that compresses data by discarding losing some of the data. Used in the creation of MP3 files (see "MP3" below).

Loudness: A subjective measure of sound related to physical strength ("amplitude"). The perception of loudness is related to both the sound pressure level and duration of a sound.

Mastering: The process of preparing and transferring recorded audio from a source containing the final mix to a data storage device (the "master"), from which all subsequent copies will be produced.

Mash-up: A process where audio-editing software is used to splice and combine samples from existing music to produce hybrid recordings.

Mixing: (or "mixdown") The process by which multiple sounds are combined into one or more channels.

Musical Instrument Digital Interface (MIDI): A widely used standard for interconnecting electronic musical instruments and computers.

Monitors: Refers to loudspeakers used to monitor the playback of recorded audio. These are high specification loudspeakers specifically designed

Glossary 195

for audio production applications, such as recording studios, where accurate audio reproduction is crucial.

MP3: An encoding format for digital audio which provides a means of compressing a sound sequence into a very small file, to enable digital storage and transmission (see also "lossy compression").

Multi-tracking: Refers to a recording practice using a range of devices (e.g., recording console, tape machine, digital audio workstation) capable of recording multiple tracks of synchronous audio.

Noise reduction: The process of removing noise from a signal, such as white noise or noise introduced by a device's mechanism.

Outboard gear: Refers to audio equipment that exists outside of a studio's primary recording console or console-free computer-based digital recording systems.

Overdub: The adding of an audio track to previously recorded tracks.

Pitch: The "pitch" of a sound is determined by the frequency of the sound, normally grouped as low frequencies (bass), midrange frequencies and high frequencies (treble).

Preamp: A term that typically refers to a microphone preamplifier, a device that boosts a weak microphone signal to be processed by other equipment such as mixing consoles and recording devices with adequate quality.

Presence: The level to which the sounds of voices and such instruments seem "present." Presence can be increased through boosting upper mid-range frequencies.

Reverb: An abbreviation of "reverberation," the persistence of sound in a particular space after the original sound is produced.

Sampler: An electronic musical instrument that uses recordings or "samples" of sounds that are loaded or recorded into it by the user and then played back to perform or compose music.

Separation: The process of making each instrument and part easily discernible within the stereo field.

Sequencer: A programmable electronic device for storing sequences of musical notes, chords or rhythms.

Splicing: See "cutting" above.

Stem mastering: A method of mixing audio material based on creating groups of audio tracks and processing them separately prior to combining them into a final master mix.

Stereo: A method of sound reproduction that creates an illusion of directionality and audible perspective.

Synthesiser: An electronic musical instrument, typically operated by a keyboard, producing a wide variety of sounds by generating and combining signals of different frequencies.

Timbre: The character or quality of a musical sound or voice as distinct from its pitch and intensity.

Tracks: Refers to separate audio signals which have been recorded and can be played back.

References

Akrich, M. 1992. "The De-scription of Technical Objects." In Bijker, W., and J. Law. eds. *Shaping Technology—Building Society.* Cambridge, MA: MIT Press: 205–224.

Alderson, A. S., and J. Beckfield. 2004. "Power and Position in the World City System." *American Journal of Sociology* 109 (4): 811–851.

Allen, J. 1997. "Economies of Power and Space." In Lee, R., and J. Wills. eds. *Geographies of Economies.* London: Arnold: 59–70.

Allen, J. 2000. "Power/Economic Knowledge: Symbolic and Spatial Formations." In Bryson J. R., P. W. Daniels., N. Henry, and J. Pollard. eds. *Knowledge, Space, Economy.* London: Routledge: 15–33.

Allen, R., and L. Wilcken. 2001. *Island Sounds in the Global City: Caribbean Popular Music and Identity in New York.* Chicago: University of Illinois Press.

Amin, A. 2002. "Spatialities of Globalization." *Environment and Planning A* 34: 385–389.

Amin, A. 2007. "Re-Thinking the Urban Social." *City* 11: 100–114.

Amin, A., and P. Cohendet. 1999. "Learning and Adaption in Decentralized Business Networks." *Environment and Planning D: Society and Space* 17: 87–104.

Anderson K., and S. J. Smith. 2001. "Editorial: Emotional Geographies." *Transactions of the Institute of British Geographers* 26: 7–10.

Andersson, A. E., and D. E. Andersson. 2006. *The Economics of Experiences, the Arts and Entertainment.* Cheltenham: Edward Elgar.

Antcliff, V., R. Saundry, and M. Stuart. 2007. "Networks and Social Capital in the UK Television Industry the Weakness of Weak Ties." *Human Relations* 60 (2): 371–393.

Asheim, B. T. 2002. "Temporary Organizations and Spatial Embeddedness of Learning and Knowledge Creation." *Geografiska Annaler B* 84 (2): 111–124.

Ashforth, B. E., and R. H. Humphrey. 1993. "Emotional Labour in Service Roles: The Influence of Identity." *The Academy of Management Review* 18 (1): 88–115.

Attali, J. 1985. *Noise: The Political Economy of Music.* Minneapolis: University of Minnesota Press.

Banks, M. 2007. *The Politics of Cultural Work.* Basingstoke: Palgrave MacMillan.

Banks, M., A. Lovatt, J. O'Connor, and C. Raffo. 2000. "Risk and Trust in the Cultural Industries." *Geoforum* 31: 453–464.

Bathelt, H. 2006. "Geographies of Production: Growth Regimes in Spatial Perspective 3—Toward a Relational View of Economic Action and Policy." *Progress in Human Geography* 30 (2): 223–236.

Bathelt, H., and J. Glückler. 2003. "Toward a Relational Economic Geography." *Journal of Economic Geography* 3: 117–144.

198 References

Bathelt, H., and J. Glückler. 2005. "Resources in Economic Geography." *Environment and Planning A* 37: 1545–1563.

Bathelt, H., and J. Glückler. 2011. The Relational Economy: Geographies of Knowing and Learning. Oxford and New York: Oxford University Press.

Bathelt H., A. Malmberg, and P. Maskell. 2004. "Clusters and Knowledge: Local Buzz, Global Pipelines and the Process of Knowledge Creation." *Progress in Human Geography* 28: 31–56.

Batnitzky A., and L. McDowell. 2011. "Migration, Nursing, Institutional Discrimination and Emotional/Affective Labour: Ethnicity and Labour Stratification in the UK National Health Service." *Social and Cultural Geography* 12: 181–201.

Baumann, A. 2002. "Informal Labour Market Governance: The Case of British and German Media Production Industries." *Work, Employment and Society* 16 (1): 27–46.

Beer, D. 2013. "The Precarious Double Life of the Recording Engineer." *Journal for Cultural Research*. DOI: 10.1080/14797585.2013.826444.

Bennett, A., and R. A. Peterson. eds. 2004. *Music Scenes Local, Translocal, and Virtual*. Nashville: Vanderbilt University Press.

Bennett, S. 2009. "Revolution Sacriledge! Examining the Technological Divide among Record Producers in the Late 1980s." *Journal on the Art of Record Production* 4. http://arpjournal.com/.

Bennett, S. 2012a. "Revisiting the 'Double Production Industry': Advertising, Consumption and 'Technoporn' Surrounding the Music Technology Press." In Kärjä, A., L. Marshall, and J. Brusila. eds. *Music, Business and Law: Essays on Contemporary Trends in the Music Industry*. International Institute for Popular Culture: 117–145. http://iipc.utu.fi/MBL.

Bennett, S. 2012b. "Endless Analogue: Situating Vintage Technologies in the Contemporary Recording and Production Workplace." *Journal on the Art of Record Production* 7. http://arpjournal.com/.

Berk, M. 2000. "Anolog Fetishes and Digital Futures." In Shapiro, P. ed. *Modulations: A History of Electronic Music*. New York: Caipirinha: 190–201.

Blair, H. 2001. "'You're only as Good as Your Last Job': The Labour Process and Labour Market in the British Film Industry." *Work, Employment and Society* 15 (1): 149–169.

Blair, H. 2009. "Active Networking: Action, Social Structure and the Process of Networking." In McKinlay, A., and C. Smith. eds. *Creative Labour: Working in the Creative Industries*. Basingstoke: Palgrave Macmillan: 116–134.

Blair, H., S. Grey, and K. Randle. 2001. "Working in Film: Employment in a Project Based Industry." *Personnel Review* 30 (2): 170–185.

Boggs, J. S., and N. M. Rantisi. 2003 "The 'Relational Turn' in Economic Geography." *Journal of Economic Geography* 3: 109–116.

Bolton S. C. 2000. "Who Cares? Offering Emotion Work as a 'Gift' in the Nursing Labour Process." *Journal of Advanced Nursing* 32: 580–586 .

Bolton S. C. 2005. *Emotion Management in the Workplace*. Basingstoke: Palgrave Macmillan.

Borgatti, S. P., M. G. Everett, and L. C. Freeman. 2002. *UCINET for Windows: Software for Social Network Analysis*. Harvard: Analytic Technologies.

Born, G. 2005. "On Musical Mediation: Ontology, Technology and Creativity." *Twentieth-Century Music* 2 (1): 7–36.

Bourdieu, P. 1986. "The Forms of Capital." In Richardson, J. ed. *Handbook for Theory and Research for the Sociology of Education*. New York: Greenwood Press: 241–258.

Bowman, R. M. J. 1997. *Soulsville, U.S.A.: The Story of Stax Records*. New York: Schirmer Trade Books.

Bradley, L. 2001. *Bass Culture: When Reggae was King*. London: Penguin.

References 199

Brown, P. 2010. *Are We Still Rolling? Studios, Drugs and Rock 'n' Roll—One Man's Journey Recording Classic Albums*. Tape Op Books.

Bryson, J. R. 2007. "The 'Second' Global Shift: The Offshoring or Global Sourcing of Corporate Services and the Rise of Distanciated Emotional Labour." *Geografiska Annaler B* 89 (1): 31–43.

Bunnell, T. G., and N. M. Coe. 2001 "Spaces and Scales of Innovation." *Progress in Human Geography* 24: 569–589.

Callon, M., and J. Law. 1997. "After the Individual in Society: Lessons on Collectivity from Science, Technology and Society." *Canadian Journal of Sociology* 22 (2): 165–182.

Christopherson, S. 2002. "Project Work in Context: Regulatory Change and the New Geography of Media." *Environment and Planning A* 34: 2003–2015.

Cogan, J., and W. Clark. 2003. *Temples of Sound: Inside the Great Recording Studios*. San Francisco: Chronicle.

Cohen, S. 1991. *Rock Culture in Liverpool: Popular Music in the Making*. Oxford: Oxford University Press.

Cohen, S., and B. Lashua. 2010. "Pubs in the Precinct: Music Making, Retail Developments and the Characterization of Urban Space." In Leonard, M., and R. Strachan. eds. *The Beat Goes On: Liverpool, Popular Music and the Changing City*. Liverpool: Liverpool University Press: 65–83.

Cole, A. 2008. "Distant Neighbours: The New Geography of Animated Film Production in Europe." *Regional Studies* 42 (6): 891–904.

Cole, S. J. 2011. "The Prosumer and the Project Studio: The Battle for Distinction in the Field of Music Recording." *Sociology* 45 (3): 447–463.

Coleman, J. 1988. "Social Capital in the Creation of Human Capital." *American Journal of Sociology* 94 (special supplement): S95–S120.

Condry, I. 1999. "Japanese Rap Music: An Ethnography of Globalization in Popular Culture." Unpublished dissertation, Yale University.

Connell J., and C. Gibson. 2003. *Sound Tracks: Popular Music, Identity, and Place*. London: Routledge.

Cooper, C. 2004. *Sound Clash: Jamaican Dancehall Culture at Large*. New York: Palgrave Macmillan.

Coryat, K. 2008. *Guerrilla Home Recording: How to Get a Great Sound from Any Studio (No Matter How Weird or Cheap Your Gear Is)*. Milwaukee, WI: Hal Leonard.

Coulson, S. 2012. "Collaborating in a Competitive World: Musicians' Working Lives and Understandings of Entrepreneurship." *Work, Employment and Society* 26 (2): 246–261.

Crang, P. 1994. "It's Showtime: On the Workplace Geographies of Display in a Restaurant in Southeast England." *Environment and Planning D* 12: 675–704.

Critcher, C. 2000. "'Still Raving': Social Reaction to Ecstasy." *Leisure Studies* 19 (3): 145–162.

Crooks, J. 2012. "Recreating an Unreal Reality: Performance Practice, Recording, and the Jazz Rhythm Section." *Journal on the Art of Record Production* 6. http://arpjournal.com/.

Crossley, N. 2008. "Pretty Connected: The Social Network of the Early UK Punk Movement." *Theory, Culture & Society* 25 (6): 89–166.

Crossley, N. 2009. "The Man Whose Web Expanded: Network Dynamics in Manchester's Post/Punk Music Scene 1976–1980." *Poetics* 37: 24–49.

Crowdy, D., and K. Neuenfeldt. 2003. "The Technology, Aesthetic and Cultural Politics of a Collaborative, Transnational Music Recording Project: Veiga, Veiga and the Itinerant Overdubs." *Transformations* 7—New Media Technologies. http://www.transformationsjournal.org/journal/issue_07/article_06.shtml

200 References

Cummins-Russell, T.A., and N.M. Rantisi. 2012. "Networks and Place in Montreal's Independent Music Industry." *The Canadian Geographer* 56 (1): 80–97.

Cunningham, M. 1998. *Good Vibrations: A History of Record Production.* London: Sanctuary Publishing.

Currid, E. 2007a. *The Warhol Economy: How Fashion, Art, and Music Drive New York City.* Princeton, NJ: Princeton University Press.

Currid, E. 2007b. "How Art and Culture Happen in New York." *Journal of the American Planning Association* 73 (4): 454–467.

Danielsen, A. 2005. "Technological Mediation and the Musicalization of Reality on Public Enemy's Fear of a Black Planet." Paper presented at the Art of Record Production Conference, London, September 17–18.

Davenport, T., and C. Arthur. 2012. "Apple Developing New Audio File Format to Offer 'Adaptive Streaming.'" The *Guardian* online. 28 February 2012. http://www.guardian.co.uk/technology/2012/feb/28/apple-audio-file-adaptive-streaming?newsfeed = true.

De Carvalho, A.T. 2012. "The Discourse of Home Recording: Authority of 'Pros' and the Sovereignty of Big Studios." *Journal of the Art of Record Production* 7. http://arpjournal.com/.

DeFillippi, R.J., and M.B. Arthur. 1998. "Paradox in Project-Based Enterprise: The Case of Film Making." *California Management Review* 40 (2): 125–139.

Dex, S., J. Willis, R. Peterson, and E. Sheppard. 2000. "Freelance Workers and Contract Uncertainty: The Effects of Contractual Changes in the Television Industry." *Work, Employment & Society* 14 (2): 283–305.

Dicken, P. 2011. *Global Shift: Mapping the Changing Contours of the World Economy.* 6th ed. London: Sage.

Dicken, P., P.F. Kelly, K. Olds, and H.W. Yeung. 2001. "Chains and Networks, Territories and Scales: Towards a Relational Framework for Analysing the Global Economy." *Global Networks* 1 (2): 89–112.

Drake, G. 2003. "'This Place gives me Space': Place and Creativity in the Creative Industries." *Geoforum* 34 (4): 511–524.

Dudrah, R. 2007. *Bhangra.* Birmingham: Punch.

Duffy M., G. Waitt, A. Gorman-Murray, and C. Gibson. 2011. "Bodily Rhythms: Corporeal Capacities to Engage with Festival Spaces." *Emotion, Space and Society* 4 (1): 17–24.

Du Gay, P., G. Salaman, and B. Rees. 1996. "The Conduct of Management and the Management of Conduct: Contemporary Managerial Discourse and the Constitution of the 'Competent' Manager." *Journal of Management Studies* 33: 263–282.

Dunn, S. 2004. "Lands of Fire and Ice: An Exploration of Death Metal Scenes." *Public: New Localities* 29: 107—125. http://pi.library.yorku.ca/ojs/index.php/public/article/viewFile/30359/27887.

Dyer, S., L. McDowell, and A. Batnitzky. 2008. "Emotional Labour/Body Work: The Caring Labours of Migrants in the UK's National Health Service." *Geoforum* 39: 2030–2038.

Ekinsmyth, C. 1999. "Professional Workers in a Risk Society." *Transactions of the Institute of British Geographers* 24 (3): 353–366.

Ekinsmyth, C. 2002. "Project Organization, Embeddedness and Risk in Magazine Publishing." *Regional Studies* 36 (3): 229–243.

Ekman, P. 1973. "Cross Culture Studies of Facial Expressions." In Ekman, P. ed. *Darwin and Facial Expressions: A Century of Research.* New York: Academic Press: 169–233.

England, P., and G. Farkas. 1986. *Households, Employment, and Gender: A Social, Economic and Demographic View.* New York: Aldine.

References   201

Entwistle, J., and E. Wissinger. 2006. "Keeping Up Appearances: Aesthetic Labour in the Fashion Modelling Industries of London and New York." *The Sociological Review* 54 (4): 774—794.

Ettlinger, N. 2001. "A Relational Perspective in Economic Geography: Connecting Competitiveness with Diversity and Difference" *Antipode* 33: 216–227.

Ettlinger, N. 2003. "Cultural Economic Geography and a Relational and Microspace Approach to Trusts, Rationalities, Networks and Change in Collaborative Workplaces." *Journal of Economic Geography* 3 (2): 145–171.

Farmelo, A. 2013. "The Era of Hi-Res Digital Audio Is Here." *Tape Op: The Creative Music Recording Magazine* (online), 2 October 2013. http://tapeop.com/blog/2013/11/01/era-hi-res-digital-audio-upon-us/.

Faulconbridge, J. R., J. V. Beaverstock, B. Derudder, and F. Witlox. 2009. "Corporate Ecologies of Business Travel in Professional Service Firms." *European Urban and Regional Studies* 16 (3): 295–308.

Feld, S. 1981. "The Focused Organisation of Social Ties." *American Journal of Sociology* 86: 1015–1035.

Feld, S. 1982. "Social Structural Determinants of Similarity Across Associates." *American Sociological Review* 47: 797–801.

Florida, R. 2002. *The Rise of the Creative Class—and How It's Transforming Work, Leisure, Community and Everyday Life*. New York: Basic.

Florida, R., and S. Jackson. 2010. "Sonic City: The Evolving Economic Geography of the Music Industry." *Journal of Planning Education and Research* 29 (3): 310–321.

Foord, J. 1999. "Reflections on 'Hidden Art.'" *Rising East* 3 (2): 38–66.

Fraser, A., and N. Ettlinger. 2008. "Fragile Empowerment: The Dynamic Cultural Economy of British Drum and Bass Music." *Geoforum* 39 (5): 1647–1656.

Frenette, A. 2013. "Making the Intern Economy: Role and Career Challenges of the Music Industry Intern." *Work and Occupations* 40 (4): 364–397.

Friedmann, J. 1978. "The spatial organization of power in the development of urban systems." In Bourne, L.S. and J.W. Simmons. eds. *Systems of Cities*. New York: Oxford University Press: 328–40.

Friedman, J. 2001. "The Iron Cage of Creativity: An Exploration." In Liep, J. ed. *Locating Cultural Creativity*. London: Pluto Press: 46–61.

Furia, P. 1992. *The Poets of Tin Pan Alley: A History of America's Great Lyricists.* New York: Oxford University Press.

Gallan, B. 2012. "Gatekeeping Night Spaces: The Role of Booking Agents in Creating 'Local' Live Music Venues and Scenes." *Australian Geographer* 41 (1): 35–50.

Gallan, B., and C. Gibson. 2013. "Mild-Mannered Bistro by Day, Eclectic Freak-Land at Night: Memories of an Australian Music Venue." *Journal of Australian Studies* 37 (2): 174–193.

Gibson, C. 1999. "Subversive Sites: Rave Culture, Spatial Politics and the Internet in Sydney, Australia." *Area* 31 (1): 9–33.

Gibson, C. 2005. "Recording Studios: Relational Spaces of Creativity in the City." *Built Environment* 31 (3): 192–207.

Gibson, C., and S. Homan. 2004. "Urban Redevelopment, Live Music and Public Space: Cultural Performance and the Re-Making of Marrickville" *International Journal of Cultural Policy* 10 (1): 67–84.

Giddens, A. 1991. *Modernity and Self-Identity: Self and Society in the Late Modern Age*. Cambridge: Polity.

Giddens, A. 1994. "Replies and Critiques." In Beck, U., A. Giddens, and S. Lash. eds. *Reflexive Modernisation; Politics, Tradition, and Aesthetics in the Modern Social Order*. Cambridge: Polity Press.

202 References

Gill, R., and A.C. Pratt. 2008. "In the Social Factory? Immaterial Labour, Precariousness and Cultural Work." *Theory, Culture and Society* 25 (7–8): 1–30.

Gill, W. 1993. "Region, Agency and Popular Music: The Northwest Sound, 1958–1966." *The Canadian Geographer* 37 (2): 120–131.

Glover, T.D. 2003. "Regulating the Rave Scene: Exploring the Policy Alternatives of Government." *Leisure Sciences* 25 (4): 307–325.

Glückler, J. 2005. "Making Embeddedness Work: Social Practice Institutions in Foreign Consulting Markets." *Environment and Planning A* 37: 1727–1750.

Glückler, J. 2007. "Geography of Reputation: The City as Locus of Business Opportunity." *Regional Studies* 41 (7): 949–961.

Glückler, J., and T. Armbrüster. 2003. "Bridging Uncertainty in Management Consulting: The Mechanisms of Trust and Networked Reputation." *Organization Studies* 24: 269–297.

Goodwin, A. 1988. "Sample and Hold: Pop Music in the Digital Age of Reproduction." *Critical Quarterly* 30 (3): 34–49.

Goodwin, A. 1998. "Drumming and Memory: Scholarship, Technology and Music-Making." In Swiss, T., J. Sloop, and A. Herman. eds. *Mapping the Beat: Popular Music and Contemporary Theory.* Oxford: Blackwell.

Gordon I.R., and P. McCann. 2003. "Industrial Clusters: Complexes, Agglomeration and/or Social Networks?" *Urban Studies* 37: 513–532.

Goulding, C., A. Shankar, and R. Elliott. 2002. "Working Weeks, Rave Weekends: Identity Fragmentation and the Emergence of New Communities." *Consumption, Markets and Culture* 5 (4): 261–284.

Grabher, G. 2001a. "Ecologies of Creativity: The Village, the Group, and the Heterarchic Organisation of the British Advertising Industry." *Environment and Planning A* 33 (2): 351–374.

Grabher, G. 2001b. "Locating Economic Action: Projects, Networks, Localities, Institutions." *Environment and Planning A* 33 (8): 1329–1331.

Grabher, G. 2002a. "Fragile Sector, Robust Practice: Project Ecologies in New Media." *Environment and Planning A* 34: 1911–1926.

Grabher, G. 2002b. "The Project Ecology of Advertising: Task, Talents, and Teams." *Regional Studies* 36: 245–262.

Grabher, G. 2002c. "Cool Projects, Boring Institutions: Temporary Collaboration in Social Context." *Regional Studies* 36: 205–214.

Grabher, G. 2006. "Trading Routes, Bypasses, and Risky Intersections: Mapping the Travels of 'Networks' between Economic Sociology and Economic Geography." *Progress in Human Geography* 30 (2): 1–27.

Granovetter, M. 1985. "Economic Action and Social Structure: The Problem of Embeddedness." *American Journal of Sociology* 91: 481–510.

Grindstaff, L. 2002. *The Money Shot: Trash, Class, and the Making of TV Talk Shows.* Chicago: University of Chicago Press.

Guile, D. 2009. "Conceptualizing the Transition from Education to Work as Vocational Practice: Lessons from the UK's Creative and Cultural Sector." *British Educational Research Journal* 35 (5): 761–779.

Gunderson, P.A. 2004. "Danger Mouse's *Grey Album,* Mash-Ups, and the Age of Composition." *Post-Modern Culture* 15 (1): no pagination.

Halfacree, K.H., and R.M. Kitchin. 1996. "'Madchester Rave On': Placing the Fragments of Popular Music." *Area* 28 (1): 47–55.

Hanneman, R.A., and M. Riddle. 2005. *Introduction to Social Network Methods.* Riverside, CA: University of California. http://faculty.ucr.edu/~hanneman/nettext/.

Haunschild, A., and D.R. Eikhof. 2009. "Bringing Creativity to Market: Actors as Self-Employed Employees." In McKinlay, A., and C. Smith. eds. *Creative Labour: Working in the Creative Industries.* Basingstoke: Palgrave Macmillan: 156–173.

References 203

Hebdige, D. 1979. *Subculture: The Meaning of Style.* London: Routledge.

Helms, D., and T. Phleps. 2007. eds. *Sound and the City: Populäre Musik im urbanen Kontext.* Bielefeld: Transcript.

Hennion, A. 1989. "An Intermediary between Production and Consumption: The Producer of Popular Music." *Science, Technology, and Human Values* 14 (4): 400–424.

Hennion, A. 1990. "The Production of Success: An Antimusicology of the Pop Song." In Frith, S., and A. Goodwin. eds. *On Record.* London: Routledge: 154–171.

Hesmondhalgh, D. 1998. "The British Dance Music Industry: A Case Study of Independent Cultural Production." *The British Journal of Sociology* 49 (2): 234–251.

Hesmondhalgh, D. 2010. "User-Generated Content, Free-Labour and the Cultural Industries." *Ephemera* 10 (3–4): 267–284.

Hesmondhalgh, D., and S. Baker. 2008. "Creative Work and Emotional Labour in the Television Industry." *Theory, Culture and Society* 25 (7–8): 97–118.

Hesmondhalgh, D., and S. Baker. 2010. "'A Very Complicated Version of Freedom': Conditions and Experiences of Creative Labour in Three Cultural Industries." *Poetics* 38: 4–20.

Hewitt, H. 2006. *Front Desk Talk: A Study of Interaction Between Receptionist and Patients in General Practice Surgeries.* Edinburgh: University of Edinburgh.

Hochschild, A.R. 1979. "Emotion Work, Feeling Rules, and Social Structure." *The American Journal of Sociology* 85: 551–575.

Hochschild, A. R. 1983. *The Managed Heart: Commercialization of Human Feeling.* Berkeley, CA: University of California Press.

Holman Jones, S. 1999. "Women, Musics, Bodies, and Texts: The Gesture of Women's Music." *Text and Performance Quarterly* 19: 217–235.

Holt, F., and F. Lapenta. 2010. "Introduction: Autonomy and Creative Labour." *Journal for Cultural Research* 14: 223–229.

Homan, S. 2000. "Losing the Local: Sydney and the Oz Rock Tradition." *Popular Music* 19: 31–49.

Homan, S. 2002. "Cultural Industry or Social Problem? The Case of Australian Live Music." *Media International Australia incorporating Culture and Policy* 102: 88–100.

Homer, M. 2009. "Beyond the Studio: The Impact of Home Recording Technologies on Music Creation and Consumption." *Nebula* 6 (3): 85–99.

Horning, S.S. 2004. "Engineering the Performance: Recording Engineers, Tacit Knowledge and the Art of Controlling Sound." *Social Studies of Science* 34 (5): 703–731.

Horning, S.S. 2012. "The Sounds of Space: Studio as Instrument in the Era of High Fidelity." In Frith, S., and S. Zagorski-Thomas. eds. *The Art of Record Production: An Introductory Reader for a New Academic Field.* Farnham: Ashgate: 28–42.

Hoyler, M., and C. Mager. 2005. "HipHop ist im Haus: Cultural Policy, Community Centres, and the Making of Hip Hop Music in Germany." *Built Environment* 31 (3): 237–254.

Hracs, B.J., D. Jakob, and A. Hauge. 2013. "Standing Out in the Crowd: The Rise of Exclusivity-Based Strategies to Compete in the Contemporary Marketplace for Music and Fashion." *Environment and Planning A* 45: 1144–1161.

Huang, S., and B.S.A. Yeoh, 2007. "Emotional Labour and Transnational Domestic Work: the Moving Geographies of 'Maid Abuse' in Singapore." *Mobilities* 2: 195–217.

Hubbard, P. 2006. *City.* London: Routledge.

Hughes, J., and K.R. Lang. 2003. "If I Had a Song: The Culture of Digital Community Networks and its Impact on the Music Industry." *International Journal on Media Management* 5 (3): 180–189.

204 References

IFPI. 2013. *Digital Music Report 2013: Engine of a Digital World.* International Federation of the Phonographic Industry. http://www.ifpi.org/content/library/DMR2013.pdf.

Ingham, J., M. Purvis, and D.B. Clarke. 1999. "Hearing Places, Making Spaces: Sonorous Geographies, Ephemeral Rhythms, and the Blackburn Warehouse Parties." *Environment and Planning D: Society and Space* 17 (3): 283–305.

Jacobs, J. 1961. *The Death and Life of Great American Cities.* New York: Random House.

James, N. 1989. "Emotional Labour: Skill and Work in the Social Regulation of Feelings." *Sociological Review* 37 (1): 15–42.

Jarrett, M. 2012. "The Self-Effacing Producer: Absence Summons Presence." In Frith, S., and S. Zagorski-Thomas. eds. *The Art of Record Production: An Introductory Reader for a New Academic Field.* Farnham: Ashgate: 129–148.

Jazeel, T. 2005. "The World is Sound? Geography, Musicology and British-Asian Soundscapes." *Area* 37 (3): 233–241.

Jessop, B., Brenner, and M. Jones. 2008. "Theorizing Socio-Spatial Relations." *Environment and Planning D: Society and Space* 26: 389–401.

Johns, J. 2010. "Manchester's Film and Television Industry: Project Ecologies and Network Hierarchies." *Urban Studies* 47 (5): 1059–1077.

Johnson, H. 2006. *If These Halls Could Talk: A Historical Tour though San Francisco Recording Studios.* Boston, MA: Thomson Course Technology.

Jones, C. 1996. "Careers in Project Networks: The Case of the Film Industry." In Arthur, M. B., and D.M. Rousseau. eds. *The Boundaryless Career: A New Employment Principle for a New Organizational Era.* Oxford: Oxford University Press.

Jones, C. 2002. "Signalling Expertise: How Signals Shape Careers in Creative Industries." In Peiperl, M. A., M.B. Arthur, and N. Anand. eds. *Career Creativity: Explorations in the Remaking of Work.* Oxford: Oxford University Press: 209–228.

Jones, M. 2009. "Phase Space: Geography, Relational Thinking, and Beyond." *Progress in Human Geography* 33 (4): 487–506.

Katz, D. 2003. *Solid Foundation: An Oral History of Reggae.* London: Bloomsbury Publishing.

Kealy, E. 1990. "From Craft to Art: The Case of Sound Mixers and Popular Music." In Frith, S., and A. Goodwin. eds. *On Record: Rock, Pop and the Written Word.* London: Routledge: 207–220.

Kloosterman, R. C. 2005. "Come Together: An introduction to Music and the City." *Built Environment* 31 (3): 181–191.

Knoke, D., and S. Yang. 2008. *Social Network Analysis.* London: Sage.

Knowles, J., and D. Hewitt. 2012. "Performance Recordivity: Studio Music in a Live Context." *Journal of the Art of Record Production* 6. http://arpjournal.com/.

Korczynski, M. 2003. "Communities of Coping: Collective Emotional Labour in Service Work." *Organization* 10 (1): 55–79.

Korczynski, M. 2009. "The Mystery Customer: Continuing Absences in the Sociology of Service Work." *Sociology* 43: 952–967.

Kosser, M. 2006. *How Nashville Became Music City, U.S.A.: 50 Years of Music Row.* Milwaukee, WI: Hal Leonard.

Krims, A. 2007. *Music and Urban Geography.* London: Routledge.

Kruml, S. M., and D. Geddes. 2000. "Exploring the Dimensions of Emotional Labour: The Heart of Hochschild's Work." *Management Communication Quarterly* 14: 8–49.

Lam, A. 2000. "Tacit Knowledge, Organizational Learning and Societal Institutions: An Integrated Framework." *Organization Studies* 21 (3): 487–513.

Latour, B. 1992. "Where Are the Missing Masses? The Sociology of a Few Mundane Artefacts." In Bijker, W.E., and J. Law. eds. *Shaping Technology/Building Society: Studies in Sociotechnical Change.* Cambridge, MA: MIT Press: 225–259.

References 205

Latour, B. 2005. *Reassembling the Social: An Introduction to Actor-Network Theory.* Oxford: Oxford University Press.

Law, J. 1994. *Organising Modernity.* Oxford: Blackwell.

Leitner, H., and B. Miller. 2007. "Scale and the Limitations of Ontological Debate: A Commentary on Marston, Jones and Woodward." *Transactions of the Institute of British Geographers* 32: 116–125.

Leyshon, A. 2001. "Time-Space (and Digital) Compression: Software Formats, Musical Networks, and the Reorganization of the Music Industry." *Environment and Planning A* 33 (1): 49–77.

Leyshon, A. 2003. "Scary Monsters? Software Formats, Peer-to-Peer Networks, and the Spectre of the Gift." *Environment and Planning D* 21 (5): 533–558.

Leyshon, A. 2009. "The Software Slump? Digital Music, the Democratization of Technology, and the Decline of the Recording Studio Sector within the Musical Economy." *Environment and Planning A* 41: 1309–1331.

Leyshon, A., D. Matless, and G. Revill. 1995. "The Place of Music." *Transactions of the Institute of British Geographers* 20 (4): 423–433.

Leyshon, A., D. Matless, and G. Revill. eds. 1998. *The Place of Music.* New York: Guilford Press.

Leyshon, A., P. Webb, S. French, N. Thrift, and L. Crewe. 2005. "On the Reproduction of the Musical Economy after the Internet." *Media, Culture and Society* 27: 177–209.

Lively, J. K. 2002. "Client Contact and Emotional Labor: Upsetting the Balance and Evening the Field." *Work and Occupations* 29: 198–225.

Lloyd, R. D. 2006. *Neo-Bohemia: Art and Commerce in the Post-Industrial City.* New York: Routledge.

Longhurst, B. 1995. *Popular Music and Society.* Cambridge: Polity Press.

Lorenzen, M., and L. Frederiksen. 2005. "The Management of Projects and Product Experimentation: Examples from the Music Industry." *European Management Review* 2 (3): 198–211.

Lovering, J. 1998. "The Global Music Industry: Contradictions in the Commodification of the Sublime." In Leyshon, A., D. Matless, and G. Revill. eds. *The Place of Music.* New York: Guilford Press.

Luckman, S., C. Gibson, J. Willoughby-Smith, and C. Brennan-Horley. 2008. "Life in a Northern (Australian) Town: Darwin's Mercurial Music Scene." *Continuum* 22 (5): 623–637.

Lundin, R. A., and A. Söderholm. 1995. "A Theory of the Temporary Organization." *Scandinavian Journal of Management* 11: 437–455.

Major, C. 2008. "Affect Work and Infected Bodies: Biosecurity in an Age of Emerging Infectious Diseases." *Environment and Planning A* 40: 1633–1646.

Marston, S. A., J. P. Jones III, and K. Woodward. 2005. "Human Geography without Scale." *Transactions of the Institute of British Geographers* 30: 416–432.

Maskell, P. 2001. "The Firm in Economic Geography." *Economic Geography* 77 (4): 329–344.

Maskell, P., and A. Malmberg. 1999. "Localised Learning and Industrial Competitiveness." *Cambridge Journal of Economics* 23: 167–186.

Massey, D. 2004. "Geographies of Responsibility." *Geografiska Annaler B* 86(1): 5–18.

Massey, H. 2000. *Behind the Glass: Top Record Producers Tell How They Craft the Hits.* San Francisco: Backbeat Books.

Matsue, J. M. 2009. *Making Music in Japan's Underground: The Tokyo Hardcore Scene.* London: Routledge.

McCarroll, T. 2011. *Oasis: The Truth.* London: John Blake Publishing.

McCourt, T., and P. Burkart. 2003. "When Creators, Corporations and Consumers Collide: Napster and the Development of On-Line Music Distribution." *Media, Culture & Society* 25: 333–350.

206 References

McDowell, L., A. Batnitzky, and S. Dyer. 2009. "Precarious Work and Economic Migration: Emerging Immigrant Divisions of Labour in Greater London's Service Sector." *International Journal of Urban and Regional Research* 33: 3–25.

McGuigan, J. 2010. "Creative Labour, Cultural Work and Individualisation." *International Journal of Cultural Policy* 16 (3): 323–335.

McIntyre, P. 2012. "Rethinking Creativity: Record Production and the Systems Model." In Frith, S., and S. Zagorski-Thomas. eds. *The Art of Record Production: An Introductory Reader for a New Academic Field.* Farnham: Ashgate: 149–162.

McLeod, K. 2005. "MP3s are Killing Home Taping: The Rise of Internet Distribution and its Challenge to the Major Label Music Monopoly." *Popular Music and Society* 28 (4): 521–531.

McRobbie, A. 1994. *Postmodernism and Popular Culture.* London: Routledge.

McRobbie, A. 2002. "Clubs to Companies: Notes on the Decline of Political Culture in Speeded up Creative Worlds." *Cultural Studies* 16 (4): 516–531.

Meier, L. M. 2011. "Promotional Ubiquitous Musics: Recording Artists, Brands and 'Rendering Authenticity.'" *Popular Music and Society* 34: 399–415.

Miller, K. E., and B. M. Quigley. 2011. "Sensation-Seeking, Performance Genres and Substance Use Among Musicians." *Psychology of Music* 39 (3): 1–22.

Moorefield, V. 2010. *The Producer as Composer: Shaping the Sounds of Popular Music.* Cambridge, MA: MIT Press.

Morey, J. 2009. "Arctic Monkeys—The Demo vs. the Album." *Journal on the Art of Record Production* 4. http://arpjournal.com/.

Morton, F. 2005. "Performing Ethnography: Irish Traditional Music Sessions and the New Methodological Spaces." *Social and Cultural Geography* 6: 661–676.

Murdoch, J. 2006. *Post-Structuralist Geography: A Guide to Relational Space.* London: Sage.

Murdock, G. 2003. "Back to Work: Cultural Labour in Altered Times." In Beck, A. ed. *Cultural Work: Understanding the Cultural Industries.* London: Routledge.

Murphy, J. T. 2006. "Building Trust in Economic Spaces." *Progress in Human Geography* 30 (4): 427–450.

Neff, G., E. Wissenger, and S. Zukin. 2005. "Entrepreneurial Labor among Cultural Producers: 'Cool' Jobs in 'Hot' Industries." *Social Semiotics* 15: 307–334.

Negus, K. 1992. *Producing Pop: Culture and Conflict in the Popular Music Industry.* London: Edward Arnold.

Negus, K. 1999. *Music Genres and Corporate Cultures.* London: Routledge.

Negus, K., and M. Pickering. 2004. *Creativity, Communication and Cultural Value.* London: Sage.

Neilson, B., and N. Rossiter. 2005. "From Precarity to Precariousness and Back Again: Labour, Life and Unstable Networks." *Fiberculture* 5: no pagination.

Nisbett, A. 1995. *The Sound Studio.* Oxford: Focal Press.

Patterson, R. 2001. "Work Histories in Television." *Media, Culture & Society* 23: 495–520.

Pinch, T., and K. Bijsterveld. 2004. "Sound Studies: New Technologies and Music." *Social Studies of Science* 34 (5): 635–648.

Porcello, T. 2002. "Music Mediated as Live in Austin: Sound, Technology, and Recording Practice." *City and Society* 14 (1): 69–86.

Power, D., and J. Jansson. 2004. "The Emergence of a Post-Industrial Music Economy? Music and ICT Synergies in Stockholm, Sweden." *Geoforum* 35: 425–439.

Prior, N . 2012. "OK COMPUTER: Mobility, Software and the Laptop Musician." *Information, Communication and Society* 11 (7): 912–932.

Quispel, C. 2005. "Detroit, City of Cars, City of Music." *Built Environment* 31 (3): 226–236.

References 207

Raeburn, S. D., J. Hipple, W. Delaney, and K. Chesky. 2003. "Surveying Popular Musicians' Health Status Using Convenience Samples." *Medical Problems of Performing Artists* 18: 113–119.

Raffo, C., J. O'Connor, A. Lovatt, and M. Banks. 2000. "Attitudes to Formal Business Training Amongst Entrepreneurs in the Cultural Industries: Situated Business Learning through 'Doing it with Others.'" *Journal of Education and Work* 13 (2): 215–230.

Ramone, P., and C.L. Granata. 2007. *Making Records: The Scenes Behind the Music.* New York: Hyperion.

Randle, K., and N. Culkin. 2009. "Getting In and Getting On in Hollywood: Freelance Careers in an Uncertain Industry." In McKinlay, A., and C. Smith. eds. *Creative Labour: Working in the Creative Industries.* Basingstoke: Palgrave Macmillan.

Riddell, A. 2001. "Data Culture Generation: After Content, Process as Aesthetic." *Leonardo* 34 (4): 337–343.

Rimmer, M. 2007. *Digital Copyright and the Consumer Revolution.* Cheltenham: Edward Elgar.

Rogers, A. 2011. "Butterfly Takes Flight: The Translocal Circulation of Creative Practice." *Social & Cultural Geography* 12 (7): 663–683.

Rogers, R. A. 1998. "A Dialogics of Rhythm: Dance and the Performance of Cultural Conflict." *The Howard Journal of Communication* 9: 5–27.

Rogers, T. 2003. "On the Process of and Aesthetics of Sampling in Electronic Music Production." *Organised Sound* 8 (3): 313–320.

Ross, A. 2008. "The New Geography of Work: Power to the Precarious?" *Theory, Culture and Society* 25 (7–8): 31–49.

Said, E.W. 1990. "Figures, Confrontations, Transfigurations." *Race and Class* 32 (1): 1–16.

Sanjek, D. 2001. "'Don't Have to DJ No More': Sampling and the 'Autonomous' Creator." In Harrington, C.L., and D.D. Bielby. eds. *Popular Music Culture: Production and Consumption.* Malden, MA: Blackwell.

Sarup, M. 1996. *Identity, Culture and the Postmodern World.* Edinburgh: Edinburgh University Press.

Saundry, R., V. Antcliff, and M. Stuart. 2007. "'It's More Than Who You Know'— Networks and Trade Unions in the Audio-Visual Industries." *Human Resource Management Journal* 16 (4): 376–392.

Scott, A.J. 1997. "The Cultural Economy of Cities." *International Journal of Urban and Regional Research* 21 (2): 323–339.

Scott, A.J. 1999a. "The Cultural Economy: Geography and the Creative Field." *Media, Culture and Society* 21 (6): 807–817.

Scott, A.J. 1999b. "The US Recorded Music Industry: On the Relations between Organisation, Location, and Creativity in the Cultural Economy." *Environment and Planning A* 31 (11): 1965–1984.

Scott, J. 1991. *Social Network Analysis.* London: Sage.

Shapiro, H. 2003. *Waiting for the Man: The Story of Drugs and Popular Music.* London: Helter Skelter Publishing.

Sharma, U., and P. Black, 2001. "Look Good, Feel Better: Beauty Therapy as Emotional Labour." *Sociology* 34: 913–931.

Sharpe, E.K. 2005. "'Going Above and Beyond': The Emotional Labor of Adventure Guides." *Journal of Leisure Research* 37: 29–50.

Sheller, M. 2004. "Mobile Publics: Beyond the Network Perspective." *Environment and Planning D: Society and Space.* 22 (1): 39–52.

Shiga, J. 2007. "Copy-and-Persist: The Logic of Mash-Up Culture." *Critical Studies in Media Communication* 24 (2): 93–114.

Shuker, R. 1994. *Understanding Popular Music.* London: Routledge.

208 *References*

Shuker, R. 2001. *Understanding Popular Music.* 2nd ed. London: Routledge.

Shuler, S., and B. D. Sypher. 2000. "Seeking Emotional Labour: When Managing the Heart Enhances the Work Experience." *Management Communication Quarterly* 14 (1): 50–89.

Simons, S. 2004. *Studio Stories: How the Great New York Records Were Made: From Miles to Madonna, Sinatra to The Ramones.* London: Backbeat Books.

Singer, M., and G. Mirhej. 2006. "High Notes: The Role of Drugs in the Making of Jazz." *Journal of Ethnicity in Substance Abuse* 5 (4): 1–38.

Small, C. 1998. *Musicking: The Meanings of Performing and Listening.* London: Wesleyan University Press.

Smernicki, P. 2013. "Sound Quality Suffers as MP3s Take Over" *Telegraph Online,* 31 March 2013. http://www.telegraph.co.uk/technology/news/9959904/Sound-quality-suffers-as MP3s-take-over.html.

Smith, A. C., and S. Kleinman. 1989. "Managing Emotions in Medical School: Students' Contact with the Living and the Dead." *Social Psychology Quarterly* 52 (1): 56–69.

Sound on Sound. 2000. "Moby: Recording Moby's 'Why Does My Heart Feel so Bad?'" *Sound on Sound Magazine,* February 2000. http://www.soundonsound.com/sos/feb00/articles/tracks.htm.

Steinberg, R. J., and D. M. Figart. 1999. "Emotional Labour Since: The Managed Heart." *The Annals of the American Academy of Political and Social Science* 561 (8): 8–26.

Storey, J., G. Salaman, and K. Platman. 2005. "Living with Enterprise in an Enterprise Economy: Freelance and Contract Workers in the Media." *Human Relations* 58 (8): 1033–1054.

Storper, M. 1997. *The Regional World: Territorial Development in a Global Economy.* New York: Guilford Press.

Storper, M., and A. J. Venables. 2004. "Buzz: Face-to-Face Contact and the Urban Economy." *Journal of Economic Geography* 4: 351–70.

Straw, W. 1991. "Systems of Articulation, Logics of Change: Communities and Scenes in Popular Music." *Cultural Studies* 5 (3): 368–388.

Sunley, P. 2008. "Relational Economic Geography: A Partial Understanding or a New Paradigm?" *Economic Geography* 84 (1): 1–26.

Sutton, R. I. 1991. "Maintaining Norms about Expressed Emotions: The Case of Bill Collectors." *Administrative Science Quarterly* 36: 245–268.

Tankel, J. D. 1990. "The Practice of Recording Music: Remixing as Recoding." *Journal of Communication* 40 (3): 34–46.

Taylor, M. 1996. "Industrialisation, Enterprise Power, and Environmental Change: An Exploration of Concepts." *Environment and Planning A* 28: 1035–1051.

Taylor, M., and B. Asheim. 2001. "The Concept of the Firm in Economic Geography." *Economic Geography* 77 (4): 315–328.

Taylor, P. J., D.R.F. Walker, G. Catalano, and M. Hoyler. 2002. "Diversity and Power in the World City Network." *Cities* 19 (4): 231–41.

Taylor, S. 1998. "Emotional Labour and the New Workplace." In Thompson, P., and C. Warhurst. eds. *Workplaces of the Future.* London: Macmillan: 84–102.

Taylor, S., and K. Littleton. 2008. "Art Work or Money: Conflicts in the Construction of a Creative Identity." *The Sociological Review* 56: 275–292.

Taylor, S., and M. Tyler. 2000. "Emotional Labour and Sexual Difference in the Airline Industry." *Work, Employment and Society* 14 (1): 77–95.

Terranova, T. 2004. *Network Culture: Politics of the Information Age.* London: Pluto Press.

Théberge, P. 1989. "The 'Sound' of Music: Technological Rationalization and the Production of Popular Music." *New Formations* 8: 99–111.

Théberge, P. 1997. *Any Sound You Can Imagine: Making Music/Consuming Technology.* Hanover, NH: Wesleyan/University Press of New England.

References   209

Théberge, P. 2004. "The Network Studio: Historical and Technological Paths to a New Deal in Music Making." *Social Studies of Science* 34 (5): 759–781.

Théberge, P. 2012. "The End of the World as We Know It: The Changing Role of the Studio in the Internet Age." In Frith, S., and S. Zagorski-Thomas. eds. *The Art of Record Production: An Introductory Reader for a New Academic Field.* Farnham: Ashgate: 77–90.

Thoits, P. A. 1985. "Self-Labelling Processes in Mental Illness: The Role of Emotional Deviance." *The American Journal of Sociology* 9: 221–249.

Tjora, A. H. 2009. "The Groove in the Box: A Technologically Mediated Inspiration in Electronic Dance Music." *Popular Music* 28 (2): 161–177.

Todorović, M., and A. Bakir. 2005. "Inaudible Noise: Belgrade's Academy Club: Legacy, Old Locals and New Spaces." *Leisure Studies* 24 (4): 415–434.

Toop, D. 2000. *Rap Attack #3: African Rap to Global Hip Hop.* 3rd ed. London: Serpent's Tail.

Törnqvist, G. 2004. "Creativity in Time and Space." *Geografiska Annaler B* 86 (4): 227–243.

Toynbee, J. 2000. *Making Popular Music: Musicians, Creativity and Institutions.* London: Arnold.

Urry, J. 2003. "Social Networks, Travel and Talk." *British Journal of Sociology* 54 (2): 155–175.

Ursell, G. 2000. "Television Production: Issues of Exploitation, Commodification and Subjectivity in UK Television Labour Markets." *Media, Culture and Society* 22: 805–825.

Van Maanen, J. 1991. *Tales of the Field.* Chicago, IL: University of Chicago Press.

Vinodrai, T. 2006. "Reproducing Toronto's Design Ecology: Career Paths, Intermediaries, and Local Labor Markets." *Economic Geography* 82: 237–263.

Ward, G. C., and K. Burns. 2000. *Jazz: A History of America's Music.* New York: Alfred A. Knopf.

Ward, J., and R. McMurray. 2011. "The Unspoken Work of GP Receptionists." *Social Science and Medicine* 72: 1583–1587.

Warner, T. 2003. *Pop Music—Technology and Creativity: Trevor Horn and the Digital Revolution.* Aldershot: Ashgate.

Watson, A. 2008. "Global Music City: Knowledge and Geographical Proximity in London's Recorded Music Industry." *Area* 40 (1): 12–23.

Williams, A. 2007. "Divide and Conquer: Power, Role Formation, and Conflict in Recording Studio Architecture." *Journal of the Art of Record Production* 1. http://arpjournal.com.

Williams, A. 2012. "I'm Not Hearing What You're Hearing: The Conflict and Connection of Headphone Mixes and Multiple Audioscapes." In Frith, S., and S. Zagorski-Thomas. eds. *The Art of Record Production: An Introductory Reader for a New Academic Field.* Farnham: Ashgate: 113–128.

Williams, C. 2003. "Sky Service: The Demands of Emotional Labour in the Airline Industry." *Gender, Work and Organization* 10: 513–550.

Williamson, J., and M. Cloonan. 2007. "Rethinking the Music Industry." *Popular Music* 26 (2): 305–322.

Wolfe, D. A., and M. Gertler. 2004. "Clusters From the Inside and Out: Local Dynamics and Global Linkages." *Urban Studies* 41: 1071–1109.

Wood, N., M. Duffy, and S. J. Smith. 2007. "The Art of Doing (Geographies of) Music." *Environment and Planning D: Society & Space* 25 (5): 867–889.

Wood, N., and S. J. Smith. 2004. "Instrumental Routes to Emotional Geographies." *Social and Cultural Geography* 5: 533–548.

Yeung, H. W. 2003. "Practicing New Economic Geographies: A Methodological Examination." *Annals of the Association of American Geographers* 93 (2): 442–462.

210 References

Yeung, H. W. 2005a. "The Firm as Social Networks: An Organizational Perspective." *Growth and Change* 36 (3): 307–328.

Yeung, H. W. 2005b. "Rethinking Relational Economic Geography." *Transactions of the Institute of British Geographers* 30: 37–51.

Zafirau, S. 2008. "Reputation Work in Selling Film and Television: Life in the Hollywood Talent Industry." *Qualitative Sociology* 31: 99–127.

Zagorski-Thomas, S. 2012. "The US vs. the UK Sound: Meaning in Music Production in the 1970s." In Frith, S., and S. Zagorski-Thomas. eds. *The Art of Record Production: An Introductory Reader for a New Academic Field.* Farnham: Ashgate: 57–76.

Zak, A. 2001. *The Poetics of Rock: Cutting Tracks, Making Records.* London: University of California Press.

Zak, A. 2007. "Editorial." *Journal on the Art of Record Production* 1. http://arpjournal.com/.

Index

acoustics 62–82, 185–6: basic principles 63–7; echo chamber 64–5; isolation 67–9; live recording 67–73; of the mastering studio 79–81; microphone placement 74–9
Actor Network Theory 6, 38, 188
Allen, R. and Wilcken, L. 88
Atlanta, Georgia 132
Attali, J. 36
Austin, Texas 73

Banks, M. 160
Bath, Real World Studios 111
Bathelt, H. and Glückler, J. 10; et al. 89
Beer, D. 29–30
Bennett, S. 20, 72, 146, 152
Berlin 116; Hansa Ton Studios 79, 96
Bhangra 92
Birmingham 92
Blair, H. 174
blues 96
Bourdieu, P. 174
Bowman, R. M. J. 95
Bristol 127, 132
British-Asian 88
Brussels 116
bulimic working patterns 162
Burns, Scott 96, 97–8
buzz 89
Byron Bay 151

Chicago, Illinois 87, 88
Christopherson, S. 175
Cole, S. J. 190
collaboration 32–6, 94, 106–7, 110, 103–17; at distance 110, 113–15; face-to-face 115–17, 187; modes of 33; in projects

106–7; service ethic 35; social collaboration 94; technologies for 109–13; across time zones 111–12
creativity 36–45, 93; and city diversity 93; and experimentation 36–9; learning and 39–42; in mastering 44–5; and sampling 37; and technology 38–9; and time constraints 42–3
Critcher, C. 102
Crossley, N. 87, 90
Crowdy, D. and Neuenfeldt, K. 110
Cubase. *See* Digital Audio Workstations
Currid, E. 87

death metal 97, 98
DeCarvalho, A. T. 148
democratisation of music production 150–1
Detroit, Michigan 86, 87, 96
Dex, S. et al. 168
Dicken, P. et al. 7–9
Digital Audio Workstations 21–3, 135, 145–6, 149; *see also* Pro-Tools
digital music downloads 140
digital music subscription services 140
diversification of record company activities 140
Dodd, Clement Seymour 96, 97
Dublin 132

electronic music making 18–22, 37; consumer technologies 20; drum machines 18, 21; MIDI 19–22; sampling 19, 37; synthesiser 19–20
emotional labour 47–61, 180–2, 185; and building relationships 54–6; and creating studio atmosphere

212 *Index*

49–52; definition of 48; distanciated emotional labour 115, 187; and the elicitation of emotions 52–4; emotional neutrality 57; emotive trust 55; empathetic emotional labour 53; and reputation 180–2; the producer as audience 51–2; and substance abuse 58–9
employment relations 158–62; employment uncertainty 159–60, 168; entrepreneurial producers and engineers 159; producer management companies 160–1; retained staff 159, 189; supplementary income 161; *see also* freelancing
engineer, role of 27–31
Ettlinger, N. 55, 188

File Transfer Protocol 23, 109
financial rewards 163, 167–8
Florida, R. and Jackson, S. 87
Fraser, A. and Ettlinger, N. 102
free labour 164, 167; *see also* internships
freelancing 158–60, 163, 174, 189
Frenette, A. 166

Gibson, C. 4–5, 40, 41, 78, 184; Connell J. and 72, 86, 89, 92, 150, 151; Gallan and 91
Giddens, A. 55
Gill, R. and Pratt A. C. 162
Gill, W. 99
Glasgow 132
Glückler, J. 176
Goodwin, A. 26, 27
Gothenburg, Studio Fredman 96, 97–8
Grabher, G. 6, 89, 106, 177, 181
Grannoveter, M. 10
Grindstaff, L. 57
grunge 97
Gunderson, N. 42, 147

headphones 144
Hesmondhalgh, D. and Baker, S. 167
hierarchy of roles 165
high definition audio 143
hip-hop 88, 100
Hochschild, A. 47–8
Homan, S. 91
home recording 20–2, 145–53; cost of 20, 147–9; democratisation of

production 41, 150–1; guides to 145–6, 148; and the music press 20, 146; technologies for 21–2, 145–6
Horning, S. S. 25, 39–40, 62, 81
Hoyler, M. and Mager, C. 100–1
Hracs, B. et al. 150

illegal file sharing 23, 137–9; litigation 139
intellectual property rights. See illegal file sharing
internships 163–7
iPod 141
ISDN 23, 109, 111–13, 115
iTunes 122, 140, 150

Japanese hardcore 94
Jarrett, M. 52
Jazeel, T. 88
jazz 72, 92, 96, 99

Kazaa 138
Kealy, E. 28, 33
Kingston, Studio One 96, 97
Korczynski, M. 48

Leitner, H. and Miller, B. 7
Leyshon, A. 3, 18, 35, 137, 152, 158
Liverpool 86
Logic Pro. *See* Digital Audio Workstations
London 3, 88, 116, 123–33, 161; Abbey Road Studios 2, 18, 66, 96, 113; AIR Management Company 161; AIR Studios 2–3, 17, 18, 66–7, 109, 113, 158; centrality and power in urban networks 131–2; connectivity in urban networks 127–31; The Exchange Studios 126; Metropolis Studios Group 18, 124–6, 161, 190–1; Olympic Studios 3, 18; output of music albums 123–5; Sarm Studios 123
Longhurst, B. 34
Los Angeles 3, 75, 116, 123–33, 161; Bernie Grudman Mastering 125–6; Capitol Studios 2, 18, 66, 96; centrality and power in urban networks 131–2; Chalice Recording Studios 123; connectivity in urban networks 127–31; Gold Star Studios 75;

Marcusen Mastering 125; output of music albums 123–5

Manchester 86, 90, 92, *96*
Marston, S. A. et al. 7
mash-ups 138–9
mastering 24–5; 44–5; 79–81, 124–6, 145, 161; concentration of 124–7; creativity in 44–5; loudness war 45; Mastered for iTunes 142–3; stem-mastering 24, 44; vinyl mastering 24
Matsue, J. M. 94
Melbourne 124, 130, 132
Memphis, Tennessee 87, 94, 95; Stax Records 95, *96*; Sun Studios 94, *96*
Miami 132
mixing 17, 24; stem-mixing 24; *see also* recording consoles
Moorefield, V. 25, 27, 63, 71, 79, 76, 141
Motown 86, *96*
MP3 file format 135–45: and audio quality 141–5; development of 136–7; impact of 139; *see also* mash-ups
multi-tracking 13–14, 25–30; aesthetic of composition 25–8; development of 14; and the role of the recording engineer 27–30; and the role of the record producer 25–7; *see also* Digital Audio Workstations; recording consoles
Munich 116

Napster 138, 139, 140
Nashville, Tennessee 87, 124; Blackbird Recording 123; Music Row 86; RCA Studios *96*
Negus, K. and Pickering, M. 33
networking 172–80; active networking 174; social networks 172–5; *see also* social capital
NEVE. *See* recording consoles
New Orleans, Louisiana 87; J&M Studios 94
New York 3, 88, 92, 99, 116, 123–33, 161; Atlantic Studios 93; A&R Studios 3, 93, *96*; centrality and power in urban networks 131–2; Columbia Studios 93; connectivity in urban networks

127–31; Masterdisk Mastering 125; 123–5; Mira Sound Studios 93; Right Track Studios 66; Sterling Sound Mastering 124–6; Tin Pan Alley 86, 93
Norstrum, Fredrik 97, 98

Oz rock 91

Paris 116
Philadelphia, Pennsylvania, Sigma Sound Studios *96*
popular music 20–1, 72
Porcello, T. 73
Portland, Maine 124–5, 133; Gateway Mastering 125
Power, D. and Jansson, J. 106
producer, role of 25–7
projects 105–8; definition of 105; market-based projects 105; recordings as projects 106; repeated cooperation 106; 181
project studios 19
Pro-Tools 22, 110, 146
punk 90, *96*

Randle, K. and Culkin, N. 172
recording consoles 14–18; development of 16–17
reggae *96*, 97, 100
relations 5–10; across spatial scales 7–9; agent inter-relations 5–7; economic 9–10; relational turn 5
reputation 175–82; commercial success 178; and emotional labour 180–2; negative reputation 179–80; networked reputation 176; portfolios 177; public reputation 176; reputation work 175–6
Rodgers, T. 37
Rome 116
Ross, A. 168

San Francisco 3
Seattle, Washington 97
Shuker, R. 29
Singapore, Form Studios 111
Small, C. 4
social capital 174–5, 190
Social Network Analysis: flow betweeness measure 121; power-based centrality measure 120: use in city network analysis 120–1

214 *Index*

soul 95, *96*
Spector, Phil 75
SSL. *See* recording consoles
Stockholm 106, 132
Straw, W. 87
Sydney 91, 116, 124

Tampa, Florida, Morrisound Studios 97, 98
Tankel, J. D. 25–6, 37
technological determinism 36, 152
Théberge, P. 3, 13, 23, 26, 94, 109, 117, 152, 188
Tokyo 94
Törnqvist, G. 88
trust: active 55; capacity 55, 180; emotive 55, 182; swift 177

urban music scenes 85–103; definitions of 87, 89; live music venues 90–2; and recording studios 93–8
urban networks 127–33: city centrality and power rankings 131–2; city connectivity rankings 127–31; core-periphery 132–3

Visconti, Toni 79

wall of sound. *See* Spector, Phil
Warner, T. 14, 20
Williams, A. 67–9
Wollongong, New South Wales 91
Wood, N. et al. 62

Yeung, H. 8, 9, 190

Zafirau, S. 175–6
Zagorski-Thomas, S. 34
Zak, A. 26, 38, 39, 74–6, 184

Printed by PGSTL